# RESURRECTING
# LEONORA PIPER

# RESURRECTING LEONORA PIPER

*HOW SCIENCE DISCOVERED*
*THE AFTERLIFE*

BY

MICHAEL TYMN

WHITE CROW

www.whitecrowbooks.com

*On the whole, I believe that all observers, both in America and in England, who have seen enough of Mrs. Piper in both states (conscious and trance) to be able to form a judgment, will agree in affirming (1) that many of the facts given could not have been learnt even by a skilled detective; (2) that to learn others of them, although possible, would have needed an expenditure of money as well as of time which it seems impossible to suppose that Mrs. Piper could have met; and (3) that her conduct has never given any grounds whatever for supposing her capable of fraud or trickery. Few persons have been so long and so carefully observed; and she has left on all observers the impression of thorough uprightness, candor, and honesty.*

*– Frederic W. H. Myers*

# CONTENTS

# Foreword

# The Many Faces of Mrs. Piper

Paul D. Biscop, Ph.D.

I first learned a bit about Mrs. Piper in my early days as a graduate
student in cultural anthropology during the late 1970s. My senior
supervisor had been interested in the condition known as Multiple
Personality and had published some papers and a book in that area.
During his research he had come upon Mrs. Piper, as I recall, whom
he thought was relevant to his research, believing her to be an example
of Multiple Personality. I found the matter interesting, but I was too
busy to give it much more thought.

My background before studying anthropology in graduate school
was in mental health work, where I had interned in art therapy and
ran a program in an adolescent psychiatric in-patient unit. That
background tended to give me an *a priori* acceptance of the idea
that the phenomena associated with Mrs. Piper were of the Multiple
Personality type, probably manifesting more psychiatric symptoms
than spirits. My opinion has now changed radically after reading
Michael Tymn's brilliant book about Mrs. Piper and the early psychical researchers.

As a cultural anthropologist, I am aware that a prime characteristic
of human consciousness is a profound need for meaning in life, a need
for meaning that appears to be an innate development in the evolution of human consciousness. Our need to make sense out of human
life and experience, including both living and dying, may not always
be recognized consciously, but the evidence of such a need is obvious

through both the ethnographic as well as the archaeological records of cultures all over the world.

This need for meaning leads inevitably to the creation of cultural meaning systems, religions being prime examples of such meaning systems, but so also are science, economics, philosophy, and other ways of thinking that help us cope with living. Meaning systems are held collectively but are acquired individually as well as collectively. The collective system reinforces the individual system, and the individual system reinforces the collective system. But the need for meaning is filled at a high price – by fiction, deceit, falsity, truth, or any combination thereof. In other words, the need for meaning is independent of truth. As long as the system "works," or achieves its goal or appeals to sufficient numbers of people, it can be accepted with out the need for verification.

Science and social science are also meaning systems, independent of the truth or falsity of the findings of either one. They give meaning to those holding such paradigms, or frames of reference, on a professional basis. For many professionals their paradigms also give meaning to their personal lives. Generally speaking, there will be a social-psychological "fit" between aspects of the professional/personal self and the professional meaning system of the discipline or profession.

Indeed, such a fit can be seen in the ways various researchers have studied Mrs. Piper's mediumship. When personal/professional paradigms are challenged by any kind of anomalous phenomenon, the tendency will be to perceptually reframe the phenomenon to fit the paradigms in some way. That tendency may include debunking, denying, distancing or redefining the phenomenon in some discipline-appropriate way. In other words, the tendency with an anomalous phenomenon is always to try to normalize it in some way in relation to known and accepted/shared concepts of reality. If unable to do so, the matter can be denied completely.

But of course there are always exceptions to the above usual reactions. "Conversions" may occur, for example, if the phenomenon can be retrofitted to previous meaning systems that were acquired and internalized in early socialization. Somewhere in this maze of possibilities I can find myself. I am a former advertising agency writer and art director, child care counselor and practicing registered art therapist, becoming a cultural anthropologist and post secondary educator. Through all of these many changes, however, I have also been something else for the past 43 years of my life. I have been an evidential clairvoyant medium, publicly demonstrating spirit communication in Spiritualist churches, psychic societies and other venues in various parts of Canada, from Montreal to Vancouver and on Vancouver Island. I have never made my living as a medium, however, and I never will, because such is not my calling.

As a result, then, for the bulk of my professional life I have also been a practicing medium. I have been the anomalous anthropologist who did field work in the two worlds, the living world of embodied Spiritualists and others interested in such matters, as well as in the world of the deceased or discarnate, the world of the dead. As a medium my prime interest has been in producing evidential material, or material that tends to provide proof of survival of physical death. That material comes from the wealth of detail that is communicated from the spirit world about particular spirits who are communicating through the medium to the living. As an anthropologist doing fieldwork, all I needed was to accept that Spiritualists considered mediumship to prove survival as real, and therefore to me as the fieldworker, that was true. I did not have to accept such a situation as ontologically real in order to do my fieldwork. My experience as a medium, however, has always given me the certainty that such is truth. If anything, during fieldwork, I had to try and suspend that certainty, again a rather anomalous situation.

And so I was reintroduced to Mrs. Piper, to a resurrected Mrs. Piper, because now I could really see her, so to speak, through the medium of Michael Tymn's book. The drama of belief/disbelief, of paradigm threats and retreating back to safe grounds of disbelief or denial, and so forth, are all illustrated very well in the tale of Mrs. Piper. But what Tymn's book reveals most clearly, startling so at times, is the profound evidentiality of Mrs. Piper's work.

That evidentiality has been obscured in the works of research done on her, most probably because her work so challenged the cherished explanatory models and paradigms of those who so assiduously studied her. What a shame that she has been buried so long.

Associated with meaning systems, of course, is power and authority, and status comes along too. But mediumship back then, and still today, challenges power, authority and status, at least indirectly. Whether those holders of power and authority are religious, academic, scientific or social scientific, all have a powerful investment in denial of the possibility of life after death when that possibility is allied to the issue of communication with the dead. Proof of the survival of physical death is potentially the greatest disruptor of all to the holders of the *status quo* of major paradigms and definitions of reality in the world, no matter what the nature of those paradigms. In fact, proof of survival and spirit communication could potentially change the entire world for the better, and we wouldn't want that, would we?

Tymn has written a powerful book, a book of great potential, based on documentation and sources that are available in the public domain. Anyone can check his presentation and accuracy of the material. There is no fiction here. This is the real thing. Let those who have eyes to see, see, and those who have the will to understand, understand. You, the reader, have the choice to be one of those.

Nanaimo, BC, Canada, September 2012

# Preface

# Filtering Out the "Bosh"

When I first read about the mediumship of Leonora Piper some two decades ago, I wasn't very impressed. In fact, since I had read somewhere else that Mrs. Piper was the *best* medium studied by the early psychical researchers, I was a bit disappointed. Although Professor William James referred to her as the "white crow," the one who proved that all crows are not black, all I could see was gray and not an especially light shade of gray.

Like the skeptics of yesteryear *and* today, I expected more lucidity, more clearness, and more meaningful communication than what I read with the Piper research. I thought it would be much like a phone call between the "dead" and the "living," and couldn't understand why the messages were often so fragmentary, so confusing, at times so meaningless, and sometimes so wrong. As James put it, there was so much "bosh" mixed in with the seemingly meaningful material that the skeptic could easily jump to the conclusion that it was all "humbug."

A few years after that introduction to Mrs. Piper, I came upon Dr. Henry Holt's 1914 book, *On the Cosmic Relations*, one of the key references for this book. Holt offered much more detail about the Piper research, including transcripts of a number of the better sittings by esteemed researchers representing the Society for Psychical Research (SPR), than in what I had previously read. As I digested Holt's chapters on Mrs. Piper and later studied some SPR transcripts not offered in Holt's book, things became a little more clear, though there was still much "bosh," and I moved from a middle shade of gray to a somewhat lighter one, though still far from white.

It was difficult to visualize what was going on in the many sittings the researchers had with Mrs. Piper, due in part to the fact that the researchers couldn't initially decide if a "secondary personality" buried in her subconscious was telepathically tapping into the sitter's memory bank or into some cosmic reservoir, or if an actual spirit of the dead was communicating. At times, the researchers would say that Mrs. Piper did something or said something and at other times they would say that Dr. Phinuit, her "spirit control," did it or said it. There was little uniformity in the reporting.

When I read James's remarks about Mrs. Piper (or Dr. Phinuit) "fishing" for information from the sitter, I had serious doubts about her, even though James otherwise attested to her honesty and integrity. What I didn't fully grasp until my third or fourth read of the material was that the so-called fishing was taking place in the spirit world, assuming that one concedes the reality of the spirit world. That is, Phinuit and the other spirit controls, acting as mediums in the spirit world, were getting thought images from the communicating spirits which they had to interpret, and since the messages were not always clear, they were searching for interpretations to the messages. This was later made clear by Professor James Hyslop. Of course, William James, who resisted the spirit hypothesis, would have been endorsing the spirit hypothesis if he had said that the fishing was on the "other side" of the veil. Though James remained on the fence relative to the spirit hypothesis, anyone reading between the lines might suspect that he accepted it much more than he let on, but was reluctant to admit it because of the potential damage to his reputation among materialistic scientists. Nevertheless, his resistance influenced my view of it and my inability to see a "white" crow.

It wasn't until I read several books by Hyslop that the pieces began to fall in place. Although very long-winded, Hyslop explained the dynamics of Mrs. Piper's mediumship better than the earlier researchers. He succeeded James, Dr. Richard Hodgson, Professor Oliver Lodge, Frederic Myers, and the others who studied Mrs. Piper and so was able to take advantage of their research and better pull things together into a coherent picture.

However, academic writers, like Hyslop, don't always present things in a clear, concise, and to-the-point manner, as journalists are taught to do. Having been schooled as a journalist, I decided to see if I could filter out the "bosh" and explain the Piper mediumship in a way that the person not really familiar with the subject matter might better understand.

This book is not intended as a biography of Mrs. Piper, nor as a scientific treatise. It is simply an attempt to explain the dynamics of her mediumship, including the difficulties associated with it, and to offer some of the best evidence for survival of consciousness after death that came from her mediumship. To put it another way, my objective in writing the book was to separate the wheat from the chaff. It is an attempt to see Mrs. Piper as more than "humbug."

A few months before I began writing the book, I was asked to contribute to an anthology on spiritual matters. I offered to write a 5,000 word essay on ectoplasm, that mysterious substance often associated with physical mediums (which Mrs. Piper was not). Some time after I submitted my essay to the editor, he sent it back to me and asked me if I could make it a little more balanced. That is, he wanted more of the skeptical side presented, as my paper clearly made a strong case for the genuineness of ectoplasm. He referred to it as an *apologia* for ectoplasm.

The editor's request brought to mind my interview with Dr. Gary Schwartz eight or nine years earlier. Schwartz, who had done some significant research with clairvoyant type mediums at his University of Arizona laboratory, stressed that there are two sides to each story – the medium's and the skeptic's. However, when a researcher, such as himself, found evidence favoring the medium's side, the TV producers and other media people found it necessary to call in a paid "skeptic" or debunker to "balance" the issue. In effect, the TV producers saw Schwartz as having joined sides with the medium, as if he had become the medium's advocate, and therefore insisted that "balance" be restored with a paid debunker, who, in all likelihood, had done no research of his own but based his arguments on debunking theory, such as cold reading, chance guesses, etc. The contestants in the debate then became the medium and Schwartz on one side versus the debunker on the other side, when it should have been the medium vs. the debunker with Schwartz as the judge or arbitrator. Instead of the viewing audience appreciating the strong evidence supporting mediumship, the desired result was a draw or a standoff. And so it seems that this was the desired goal of the editor of the anthology.

With this need for *balance* by the media, as well as by academia, is it any wonder that no significant progress has been made in convincing the general public of the reality of mediumship and other phenomena lending themselves to the truth of life after death? Is it any wonder that the research involving Mrs. Piper's mediumship was not widely appreciated at the time and for the most part is forgotten today?

As I pointed out to the editor of the anthology, all of the esteemed researchers cited in my paper supposedly began as skeptics. They established strict controls to rule out fraud and other explanations for each phenomenon. At the conclusion of their investigations, all of the researchers discussed in my paper were certain of the reality of ectoplasm. "Balance" would have meant finding a dozen or more researchers who wrote it all off as fraud...or humbug. I know of no such researchers or references. I know of many scientific fundamentalists who had one sitting with a medium and refused to believe that it was anything but fraud and I know that there were a number of actual frauds, using cheese cloth or some other substance to simulate ectoplasm. But why bother with the one-time sitters or the actual frauds when such respected scientists as those quoted in my paper, had scores, even hundreds, of sittings with genuine mediums and were able to attest to the reality of it?

I wonder if all the research suggesting a positive correlation between lung cancer and smoking can be balanced by citing many research projects indicating no positive correlation, or even a negative correlation. Or should all that research pointing to a positive correlation be discounted because every now and then we hear of someone 100 or older who claims to have been a life-long smoker?

Clearly, there were a number of scientific men and women who observed Leonora Piper and concluded that she was a fake, but very few of them had more than one sitting with her. All of those who studied her over a period of time came to the conclusion that supernatural things were taking place with or through her. Whether they suggested spirits or some form of unconscious telepathy was the big question among those researchers who studied her extensively. Eventually, the key researchers – Hodgson, Lodge, Myers, and Hyslop – all came to believe that spirits were, in fact, communicating. James, more observer than researcher, remained on the fence, at least publicly.

If the reader is looking for "balance," he or she should put this book down and go on to another one. If I were writing a book about a Hall of Fame baseball player, I would not dwell on his strike outs. The best offensive players fail two times out of three, and it wouldn't make for a very interesting book if I devoted equal space to all of the outs the player made during his career. I would focus on the game-winning hits. And that is what I have attempted to do in this book – focus on the "hits" – but, at the same time, I have explained why there were often misses or "strike outs." Communicating from the "other side," it seems, is much more difficult than hitting a 98-mph fast ball, an extremely difficult task in itself.

Those readers unconcerned about the *modus operandi* of the medium might skip ahead and read Chapters Seven, Eight, and Nine, then, if they find those chapters interesting, go back and start from the beginning.

As I wrote this book and read the records and references a fourth, fifth, and even sixth time, I moved from a somewhat cloudy white to a very bright white. I don't know if the reader will be able to see a "white crow" in Mrs. Piper on one read only, but I feel certain that the open-minded reader will at least see beyond the bosh and recognize her as more than humbug.

Some might ask – "To what end?" The skeptics – really the pseudoskeptics – are always saying that there is no empirical evidence for life after death. The vast majority of them are unaware of such research by esteemed scientists and scholars, as in the case of Mrs. Piper, or if they have heard of it, they have dismissed it, based on hearsay, as bad science, if science at all. The skeptical literature is filled with the "bosh" material, which is enough for the person with a will to disbelieve to dismiss it as just so much bunk…or humbug. This book is intended for those with more open minds – those with a will to believe and who would like to move from blind faith to conviction.

"We should be living for today, not concerning ourselves with a distant afterlife," some are likely to react to the last sentence. However, I believe William James hit the nail on the head when he said that the luster of the present hour is always borrowed from the background of possibilities it goes with. To put it another way, we cannot effectively live in the moment without some regard, whether it be consciously or subconsciously, for what is to come. Many people succeed to some degree by escaping from reality into a world of unreality or by totaling occupying themselves with the mundane, but for the thinking person – the one who looks for some meaning in it all – the conviction that we do not die into a world of nothingness can lead to true peace of mind, especially in his or her later years.

To really live in the moment, we must "live in eternity," which involves living in the past, present, and future all at the same time. The ability to "live in eternity" comes, not from blind faith, but from conviction, or true faith. Fully understood, the phenomena of Leonora Piper can provide such conviction.

# Introduction

# Religion Impeached, Science Invoked

*Men hardly cared to look beyond*
**F. W. H. Myers**

Well before Darwinism, as it came to be called, impacted the educated world during the last four decades of the 19<sup>th</sup> Century, mainstream religion was in decline, as science and its concomitant, rationalism, took hold. Thomas Paine's book, *The Age of Reason*, published in three parts (1794, 1795, and 1807) influenced many educated people to repudiate their religious beliefs, including both God and the idea of an afterlife. For those who sat on the fence, unsure as to what to believe, Darwinism was the knock-out blow, since it was perceived as totally refuting the biblical account of creation as set forth in the *Book of Genesis*, which said that God created the world in seven days. *Falsus in uno, falso in omnibus* – false in one, then false in all – seems to have been the logical conclusion. After all, if the Bible had been inspired by God, as religious leaders proclaimed, how could an all-knowing God be so wrong? Therefore, god must not exist, and if there is no god, then there must not be an afterlife, either, was the logical assumption.

As philosopher Eugene Rose observed, much of the literature of the 19<sup>th</sup> Century had *non-serviam* as a constant theme. The objective was to overthrow God and crush all His institutions, permitting "triumphant Man to ascend His throne to rule in his own right."[1] This mindset, Rose concluded, was a result of "righteous" indignation against the injustices and tyranny of God and His earthly representatives and was based much more on passion than on the truth.

Because of the "death of God," as decreed by Friedrich Nietzsche, the latter part of the 19th Century was a time of despair and hopelessness for many. "We were all in the first flush of triumphant Darwinism, when terrene evolution had explained so much that men hardly cared to look beyond," wrote Cambridge scholar and pioneering psychical researcher Frederic W. H. Myers, in explaining why he began searching for evidence of the soul.[2]

As Myers saw it, the old-world sustenance was too unsubstantial for the modern cravings, the result being that advances in science and technology were leading to unprecedented prosperity, but, at the same time, this prosperity brought about a decline in the dignity of life. It was suddenly life without meaning. In effect, the advances in science and technology outpaced man's ability to mentally and morally adjust to them, thereby creating an emotional void. There were many who repressed the idea of Nietzsche's "nothingness" by escaping into earthly activities, but there were others who could not completely repress it or escape from it and suffered from what William James called "soul sickness."

Historian Donald J. Mrozek observed much the same thing in his study of that era. "The liveliness and energy of late nineteenth-century American culture all but necessitated that its 'search for order' would be accompanied by a search for meaning," he wrote, going on to say that "although the yearning for spiritual fulfillment remained, supernatural forces faced impeachment in a century of rapidly accumulating scientific discoveries, many of which ran counter to the traditional sources of spiritual guidance."

As materialism, or rationalism, or nihilism, or scientism, became the new philosophy, "the late nineteenth century also ached for the comfort and assurance of the religious sensibility, even as specific creeds fell and denominations dissembled," Mrozek continued. "The need for renewal – on an emotional and spiritual level perhaps even more than a physical one – may have been even stronger beneath the surface than its public expressions, in the face of challenges from science and skepticism, suggested."[3]

Man's search for meaning independent of religion seems to have its roots in an event that took place on March 31, 1848 at the small home of the John D. Fox family in Hydesville, New York, not far from Rochester. Shortly after moving into the house on December 11, 1847, the family of four, including daughters Margaret, 14, and Kate, 8, began hearing strange raps and taps, but it wasn't until March 31 that the two daughters realized that they could communicate with the "raps" by snapping their fingers. Upon learning of this, Mrs. Fox asked the "raps" to respond to questions by giving two raps for a "yes" and silence for "no." She asked if a human being was making the raps. There was no response. When she asked, "Is it a spirit?" there were two raps. Neighbors were called in and dozens of questions were put to the "spirit." It was determined that the communicating spirit had been murdered in the house about five years earlier, before the Fox family moved in.

The questioning by this primitive method went on for days and it was further determined that the communicating spirit's body had been buried beneath the house. Digging began and at a depth of five feet human hair and bones were found. It was soon realized that the Fox sisters were mediums and were thus able to bring through other spirits. Some amazing phenomena produced by their spirit controls were witnessed by a number of eminent men and women, including Horace Greeley, J. Fenimore Cooper, and William Cullen Bryant. However, the credibility of the sisters was compromised after they were turned into a sideshow act by P. T. Barnum, the showman. With audiences paying money to see them perform, they apparently turned to trickery when their powers failed them. Many years later, after being convinced by religious fundamentalists that she was being used by the devil, Margaret, who had become an alcoholic and was suffering financially, told the *New York Herald* in an interview that she had resorted to fraud. She later repudiated the confession, stating that she needed money and was paid for the interview. Thus, the Fox sisters have gone down in many of the history books as outright frauds, when, in fact, they were likely "mixed mediums" – able to produce real phenomena at times but resorting to tricks at other times. Such was also the plight of Italy's Eusapia Paladino, called by some researchers the greatest physical medium of her time. She was investigated by a dozen or more eminent scientists and scholars, all of whom were convinced that the phenomena they had observed, including spirit materializations, were genuine. Yet, they recognized that when her powers failed, she attempted to trick them. The attempted tricks did not produce any major phenomena, but it did affect her credibility. That there have been mixed mediums and outright charlatans is clear, but it is equally clear to those who have thoroughly studied the subject that there have been genuine mediums that did not resort to fraud.

In spite of limited mass communications in those days, the Hydesville story quickly spread and turned into an epidemic of spirit communication. Mediums began developing in all parts of the United States as well as in Europe as the phenomena progressed from rappings and tappings to table tilting and turning and even table levitations. The table phenomena usually involved sitters placing their hands on the table and the table lifting off the floor, although there were many observations of the table tilting, turning, or lifting independently of any hands. The spirit communicator would then respond to questions by tilts of the table. In addition to the simple "yes" and "no" method employed in the Fox case, spirits would tap out letters of the alphabet (one tap for "A," five taps for "E," etc.) or would respond with a tap when the alphabet was recited by someone present, thereby slowly spelling out words and sentences. Other mediums would go into a trance and the spirits would speak through them. The "madness" came to be called "Spiritualism."

If the spirits who communicated in the years immediately following the Hydesville event are to be believed, there was a plan behind it all – a plan that resulted from a growing loss of faith and spiritual values in an increasingly materialistic world. "It is to draw mankind together in harmony, and to convince skeptics of the immortality of the soul," was the reply given to Territory of Wisconsin Governor Nathaniel P. Tallmadge when he asked a communicating spirit claiming to be John C. Calhoun, former vice-president of the United States, about the purpose of the strange phenomena.[4]

While a number of distinguished scientists and scholars, including Alfred Russel Wallace, co-originator with Charles Darwin of the natural selection theory of evolution, observed and documented various mediumistic phenomena during those first few decades of the spiritualism "epidemic," it was not until 1882 that several of them decided that a formal organization was needed to apply scientific methodology to the research and to provide a peer review journal.

Some three years after the Society for Psychical Research (SPR) was founded in London, Leonora Piper, a young Boston, Massachusetts housewife, was "discovered" by William James, a pioneering psychologist, of Harvard University. Messages were delivered through Mrs. Piper that seemed to be coming from spirits of the dead. Soon after the discovery of Mrs. Piper, the American branch of the SPR (ASPR) was formed under the guidance of Professor James, and its primary task became the study of her mediumship, although it undertook the investigation of other mediums and paranormal phenomena, as well.

Apparently, some progress was made in restoring belief in a here-after by 1914. In reviewing a book about life after death for the April 1914 issue of the *Journal of the American Society for Psychical Research*, Professor James Hyslop, one of the researchers who studied Mrs. Piper, wrote: "The primary importance of the book is the simple fact that the subject can be discussed, when twenty-five years ago a book either af-firming or denying immortality would not have received publication, most probably. Skepticism and agnosticism have been so confident of their positions ever since Immanuel Kant and Herbert Spencer, that no man has dared venture to show himself on the affirmative side for fear of being accused of being religious or of being a fool."

A number of other reputable scientists and scholars studied Mrs. Piper for a quarter of a century. Unfortunately, because of the resis-tance of mainstream science on one end and orthodox religion on the other, the latter seeing communication with spirits as demonic, the re-search has been, for the most part, filed away in dust-covered cabinets and written off by many as outdated. Skeptics deride it as the product of hallucination and delusion and conclude that Mrs. Piper was just another charlatan, one clever enough to dupe many intelligent men and women in hundreds of observations over some 25 years. But those who carefully study the research and take the time to understand it will likely see Leonora Piper as the "white crow" that William James proclaimed her to be.

---

[1] Rose, 64

[2] Hamilton, 80

[3] Mrozek, Preface xvii-xviii

[4] Harding, 90

# -One-

# The Discovery of
# a "White Crow"

*I am baffled as to spirit return.*
**– William James**

During his final years at Harvard University, where he received his degree in medicine, William James is said to have suffered from fits of depression, what he called "soul sickness." Apparently, the "death of God" and the increasingly materialistic worldview of the times brought on by the Ages of Reason and Enlightenment and then accentuated by Darwinism seriously affected him, even to the point that he considered suicide. However, he overcame his depression to some extent in 1872 when he accepted a position to teach physiology and anatomy at Harvard.

Soon thereafter, James integrated his physiology course with psychology, and in 1876 founded the first laboratory for experimental psychology in the United States. Along with Wilhelm Wundt, John Dewey, and Sigmund Freud, James is considered one of the pioneers of modern psychology. However, after concluding that the root cause of man's behavior was to be found in philosophy, where the meaning of life was explored, he gradually moved from psychology to philosophy.

When, in 1885, James was told by his mother-in-law and sister-in-law that they sat with a medium named Leonora Piper, a Boston resident, and were given much information about deceased relatives, James, though skeptical, was curious and decided to have his own sitting with Mrs. Piper. He left his first visit with her convinced that she either had supernormal powers or was an excellent detective. After a dozen sittings in which deceased relatives and friends communicated with him through the entranced medium, James came to accept her supernatural powers, certain that much of the information that came through her could not have been researched. Writing in the July 1886 *Proceedings* of the American Society for Psychical Research, he reported:

> This lady can at will pass into a trance condition, in which she is 'controlled' by a power purporting to be the spirit of a French doctor, who serves as an intermediary between the sitter and the deceased friends. This is the ordinary type of trance-mediumship at the present day...
> ..I am persuaded by the medium's honesty, and of the genuineness of her trance; and....I now believe her to be in possession of a power as yet unexplained.[1]

Born on June 27, 1859 in Nashua, New Hampshire as Leonora Evelina Simonds, young Leonora (or Leonore, her nickname) is said to have had clairvoyant experiences as a child. She recalled that, at age 8, she was playing in the garden when she felt a sharp blow on her right ear accompanied by a "prolonged sibilant sound" that gradually resolved itself into the letter "S," which was then followed by the words, "Aunt Sara not dead, but with you still."[2] Leonora ran to her mother and told her of the experience. Two days later, Leonora's mother was informed that her sister, Sara, had died unexpectedly. She estimated the time of death to be around the time that Leonora ran into the house.

Several weeks later, Leonora informed her mother of a bright light in her bedroom with many faces in it and said that her bed wouldn't stop rocking. Except for a few more experiences of this kind, she seems to have had a normal childhood. Her father and mother were both of English ancestry, deeply religious and members of the Congregational Church, in which Leonora was baptized. Her father gave her a small Bible on her ninth birthday as a reward for having read the book from cover to cover. The fourth of six children, Leonora was fond of athletic activities during her teens and became an expert needlewoman. She was described as tall, slender, with Grecian features and masses of golden hair, carrying herself with grace and dignity. She married William Piper of Boston on October 6, 1881, at age 22, and gave birth to their first child, Alta, on May 16, 1884, and their second child, Minerva, on October 7, 1885.

Shortly after Alta's birth, Leonora was persuaded by James Piper, her father-in-law, to consult Mr. J. R. Cocke, a blind healing medium. In Alta's 1929 biography of her mother, she states than an injury in a "coasting" accident was the reason for seeing Mr. Cocke, but Leonora told Dr. Richard Hodgson, who began studying her in 1887, that she was suffering from a tumor. Whether she believed that the accident gave rise to a tumor is unclear, but whatever the reason, she took the advice and first visited the clairvoyant on June 19, 1884. Cocke claimed to be controlled by a deceased French physician whose name was pronounced *Finny*. During her first visit with Cocke, Leonora felt curious twitchings, and thought she might become completely unconscious. "On a second visit to Mr. Cocke he placed his hands on her head, and shortly after she became unconscious," Hodgson related the story as told to him. "As she was losing consciousness she was aware of a flood of light and saw strange faces, and a hand moving before her. The 'flood of light' she had experienced once before, a few months previously; it immediately preceded a swoon, caused by a sudden blow on the side of the head." [3]

After she lost consciousness during her second visit, Leonora got up from her chair, walked to a table in the center of the room, picked up a pencil and paper, wrote rapidly for a few minutes, then handed the paper to Judge Frost, a hard-headed and respected jurist, and returned to her chair, still entranced. After regaining consciousness and having no recollection of what took place, she was told by Frost that the paper contained a remarkable message from his son, who had been fatally injured in an accident some 30 years earlier. The spirit who controlled Leonora was said to have been an Indian girl named "Chlorine." Leonora had several more sittings with Cocke and each time was again controlled by Chlorine.

As researchers eventually came to understand, the "control" is a spirit entity that takes over the body of the entranced medium and speaks through her or him, or, as with Mr. Cocke, administers healing. Apparently, few spirits have the ability to take control of a medium's body, and thus the control often functions as an intermediary between the sitters and spirits who want to communicate with them, passing on messages and acting as something of a medium on the other side of the veil. It was said that the control has to put him- or herself into an altered state of consciousness on that side of the veil in order to control the medium's body. In addition to relaying messages, these controls sometimes attempt to communicate higher truths to the sitters. When

3

another spirit is able to communicate directly by controlling the medium's body, the primary control acts as something of a "gatekeeper," by maintaining order among the spirits who want to communicate and fending off low-level spirits who attempt to invade the sitting.

Word spread fast of Frost's experience and Leonora began receiving many requests for sittings. She tried sitting at home with relatives and friends with some success. In addition to Chlorine, various sprits controlled her and communicated, including Dr. Phinuit (believed to be Cocke's Finney), Mrs. Siddons, Bach, Longfellow, Commodore Vanderbilt, and Loretta Ponchini. Mrs. Siddons reportedly recited a scene from Macbeth through Leonora, while Longfellow wrote some verses and Loretta Ponchini, who said she had been an Italian girl, made some drawings. Sebastian Bach claimed to have formed her "band," and Chlorine acted as the principal control during those first few months. Phinuit came initially only to give medical advice to sitters and claimed that other matters were "too trivial" for him to bother with, but by the time Professor James began studying Leonora during the autumn of 1885, Phinuit had become her primary control for communication purposes. Leonora (hereinafter, "Mrs. Piper") recalled that she had not given sittings several months before and several months after the birth of Minerva during 1885 and when she started up again Phinuit had taken over. She described the trance condition as she experienced it:

> I feel as if something were passing over my brain, making it numb, a sensation similar to that I experienced when I was etherized, only the unpleasant odor of the ether is absent. I feel a little cold, too, not very, just a little, as if a cold breeze passed over me, and people and objects become smaller until they finally disappear, then, I know nothing more until I wake up, when the first thing I am conscious of is a bright, very very bright light, and then darkness, such darkness. My hands and my arms begin to tingle just as one's foot tingles after it has 'been asleep,' and I see, as if from a great distance, objects and people in the room; but they are very small and very black. [4]

Prominent author and publisher Dr. Henry Holt had several sittings with Mrs. Piper. He related that after being seated a minute or two, her eyeballs rolled upward, her face became slightly convulsed, and then she began talking in a rough voice not her own. He recalled the voice affecting him as if it were coming from a statue, "pouring forth at one moment some brusquerie in the rough deep tones of Phinuit; at the next, in the same voice softened to gentleness, petting a child; then, perhaps, a return to the gruff tones in some biting sarcasm to some interloping control; then perhaps issuing from the same mouth, a child's voice singing the little boat song – all going on amid the weeping relatives who join in the song." [5]

Barrett Wendell, who sat with Mrs. Piper on May 26, 1886, described her recovery from the trance states as "perhaps the most shocking sight I ever witnessed." [6] It was said to have involved convulsion-like movements that alarmed many people.

Mrs. Gibbins, Professor James's mother-in-law, heard about Mrs. Piper from her maid, Bridget, who had been informed of "the queer doings of young Mrs. Piper" by the Pipers' Irish servant, Mary. At the time, Leonora and William were living with his parents in Arlington Heights, a suburb of Boston. In addition to his 12 sittings with Mrs. Piper, James arranged for a number of friends, relatives, and associates to sit with her. Twelve of the sitters got nothing, except unknown names or trivial talk, but 15 of the sitters received meaningful information, which, James concluded, the medium could not have come upon in a normal way. James admitted, however, that he was "derelict" in keeping a record of his own sittings with Mrs. Piper, as, at the time, he was interested in satisfying only himself about her and did not recognize it as a possible contribution to psychical research.

Dr. Minot J. Savage, a Unitarian minister and one of James's friends, did keep a written record of his first sitting with Mrs. Piper early in 1886. He reported:

Immediately on becoming entranced, her control, Dr. Phinuit, said there were many spirit friends present. Among them he said was an old man, whom he described, but only in a general way. Then he said, 'He is your father, and he calls you Judson.' Attention was also called to the fact that he had a peculiar bare spot on his head, and Mrs. Piper put her hand on the corresponding place on her own head.

Now for the facts that give these two apparently simple points whatever significance they possess. My father had died during the preceding summer, aged ninety years and six months. He had never lived in Boston, and Mrs. Piper, I am quite sure, had never seen him nor been in any way interested in him. He wasn't all that bald, but when quite young had been burned; so that there was a bare spot on the right side of the top of his head, perhaps an inch wide and three inches long, running from the forehead back towards the crown. This he covered by combing his hair over it. This was the spot that Mrs. Piper indicated. Now as to the name by which he addressed me: I was given the middle name, Judson, at the request of a half-sister, my father's daughter, who died soon after I was born. Out of tenderness for her memory (as I always supposed) father always used, when I was a boy, to call me Judson, though all the rest of the family called me by my first name, Minot. In his later life father also got to calling me by my first name. No one, therefore, had called me by my second name for many years. I was therefore naturally struck and surprised by suddenly hearing one who claimed to be my father giving me once more my old boyhood name. I was not consciously thinking of either of these things; and I am convinced that Mrs. Piper couldn't have known anything about them.

During this same sitting Mrs. Piper's control also said, 'Here is somebody who says his name is John. He was your brother. No, not your own brother, your half-brother.' Then, pressing her hand on the base of her brain, she moaned, as she swayed to and fro. Then she continued, 'He says it was so hard to die way off there all alone! How he did want to see mother!' She went on to explain that he died from a fall, striking the back of his head. Her whole account of this was realistic in the extreme. My half-brother, John, the son of my mother – for both father and mother had been twice married – died several years previous to this sitting. While building a mill in Michigan he fell, striking the back of his head on a piece of timber. He was far from friends; and was a most tender lover of his mother. I was not thinking of him until told that he was present.

Many other things occurred during the sitting. But I mention only these, because, though simple, they are clear-cut and striking, and because I see no way by which Mrs. Piper could ever have known them. [7]

On a much later visit to Mrs. Piper, Savage was told that his son, who had died at age 31 three years earlier, was present. "Papa, I want you go at once to my room," Savage recalled his son communicating with a great deal of earnestness. "Look in my drawer and you will find a lot of loose papers. Among them are some which I would like you to take and destroy at once." The son had lived with a personal friend in Boston and his personal effects remained there. Savage went to his son's room and searched the drawer, gathering up all the loose papers. "There were things there which he had jotted down and trusted to the privacy of his drawer which he would not have made public for the world," Savage ended the story, commenting that he would not violate his son's privacy by disclosing the contents of the papers.[8]

In his 1911 book, *Glimpses of the Next State*, Vice-Admiral W. Usborne Moore, a retired British naval commander turned psychical researcher, told of a sitting he had with Maggie Gaule Reidinger, a New York City medium. Before sitting with Reidinger, Moore visited Minot Savage to discuss Mrs. Piper. Savage told Moore of the sitting with her in which his son communicated, and pointed to a picture of his son hanging in his office. He also gave Moore a letter of introduction to Mrs. Piper. At the sitting later that day, Reidinger mentioned Moore's visit with Savage and said that Savage's son was there at the time. "He is beside me now," Reidinger continued, "and he wishes me to tell his father that he was with him in his study this morning when you called upon him. He says: 'My father pointed to a picture, and said, "That is my son." He afterwards showed you another portrait of him. He gave you a letter, or authorized you to use his name, to assist you to obtain an interview with Mrs. Piper. Let me tell you, you will not get that appointment yet, next week, nor the week after, but you will achieve your objective before re-crossing the ocean. Will you convey the message to Dr. Savage from his son? You have written to Dr. Hodgson today."[9] Moore was very much impressed and certain that Mrs. Reidinger did not know his name. He recontacted Savage to confirm that he had not spoken to Mrs. Reidinger to inform her of his visit that night.

Savage further reported on a December 28, 1888 sitting which his brother, the Rev. W. H. Savage, also a friend of William James's, had with Mrs. Piper. Speaking through Mrs. Piper, Phinuit told him that somebody named Robert West was there and wanted to send a message to Minot. The message was in the form of an apology for something West had written about Minot "in advance." W. H. Savage did not understand the message but passed it on to Minot, who understood it and explained that West was editor of a publication called *The Advance* and had criticized his work in an editorial. During the sitting, W. H. Savage asked for a description of West. An accurate description was given along with the information that West had died of hemorrhage of the kidneys, a fact unknown to Savage but later verified.

"There was no reason for the [apology] unless it be found in simply human feeling on [West's] part that he had discovered that he had been guilty of an injustice, and wished, as far as possible, to make reparation, and this for peace of his own mind," Minot Savage recorded.[10]

When W. H. Savage sat with Mrs. Piper two weeks later, West again communicated, stating that his body was buried at Alton, Illinois. He gave the wording on his tombstone, "Fervent in spirit, serving the Lord." Savage was unaware of either of these facts, but later confirmed them as true. "Now the striking thing about this lies in the fact that my brother was not thinking of this matter and cared nothing about it," Minot Savage ended the story, feeling that this ruled out mental telepathy on the part of Mrs. Piper.

Gertrude Savage, the daughter of Minot Savage, sat with Mrs. Piper on October 23, 1888. She reported that she went under the name Margaret Brown, while also giving a false address. Mrs. Piper informed her that she had been suffering from a headache and wasn't sure if she could provide a satisfactory sitting. However, she offered to give it a try, after which they went into a darkened room, where Mrs. Piper took Gertrude's hand in her hand. Gertrude Savage, who was a stenographer, recorded:

Immediately her fingers began to twitch and then her whole body, and she groaned and ground her teeth, and constantly muttered, 'Oh, what's the matter? What *is* the matter?'

Before entering the dark room, I had taken three locks of hair, each one enclosed in an envelope, and had placed one in the front of a book, one in the back, and one in the middle. The one in the middle I knew was my mother's; it was only a few hairs, taken by stealth, for she would not give her consent to my having them. The other two I had not looked at, and had no idea to whom they belonged. They were sent me by a friend, already enclosed in the little envelopes, and I was purposely ignorant concerning them – all to make the test more complete. It was on this errand, for this friend, Mr. Fred Day, that I went to see Mrs. Piper.

On going into the trance state, Mrs. Piper's voice became guttural, harsh, and she spoke with a decided accent. Keeping my hand in hers, and pressed against her forehead, she began instantly to speak, and she talked with me incessantly for an hour. She said: 'I never talked with you before, and you are very peculiar; it is not easy for me to tell you anything about yourself personally, you are so queer. I do not know who you are. I cannot get your name. My name is Dr. Finway (sic). Can you understand me? Sometimes people cannot, because I speak with an accent.' 'Oh, yes,' I answered. 'I can understand you perfectly. I want to give you a lock of hair for you to examine.' I then gave into Mrs. Piper's hand the lock of hair from the envelope in the front of the book – not knowing myself whose it was. Immediately on receiving it, Dr. Finway exclaimed. 'Fred! Oh yes, Fred, a young man, very thin, wears glasses, little beard, great friend of yours. This Fred – I never had his hair before, but the influence does not seem new! Imogene – who's Imogene?' 'I do not know,' said I. 'Yes, Imogene, a young lady, friend of Fred's, influence very strong. Who is she?' 'I am sure I do not know. I did not know he had a friend named Imogene. I do not think he has.' 'He has! Don't contradict me!' exclaimed he. Then he resumed, 'This Fred is an only child, mother plump, a lovely lady, but she is not long for your world. This Fred is going on a long journey, across the water, within a year or two. He has already taken two long journeys, one across the water, hasn't he, now?' 'I am not sure,' said I. 'Well, he has,' replied he. 'You ask him. What I tell you I *know*...I can see it all, and I only tell you facts, and you will find that they are so.'

I then gave him the other unknown lock of hair, from the back of the book. Immediately, he exclaimed, 'Ugh! This is crazy! It makes me sick!' 'Well,' he said, 'I cannot tell you anything about this, because the influence is so mixed; it has been handled by too many people, and it was not cut off near the head, where the magnetism from the body could permeate it. I can't tell you about it.' (It proved to have been the hair of Mr. Day's aunt Mary, who died within the year, and it has passed through several people's hands, and was cut off near the end of the hair.)

Then I gave him the little lock of my mother's hair, from the center of the book. 'Ella,' he cried, 'she is stingy enough with her hair! This Ella is very sweet dispositioned, very, but she is not at all well. She has trouble with her head; she has fearful bilious headaches, and they come from the weak state of the nerves of the stomach; and her liver is, of course, disordered; you tell her that I am a physician, and that I say for her to take hot douche baths; now *remember*! She is, it seems to me, some relation to you. Wait a moment – she is your mother, I think. Yes, she

is your mother. And she has *un, deux, trios, quatre* – four children –
two girls and two boys. You have a brother who is off, away from you,
somewhere, a little west of you; he is very independent; he is a strong
influence in Ella's life. And you have a younger brother, and a sister;
her name begins with H—e--. Hellen, I think it is. But there is an old
lady here – in the spirit. She has only left the body within a month,
and she is your grandmother. You, young lady, are a flirt!' 'No,' said I,
'I am not.' 'The devil you aren't. You are!,' cried he. 'You are flirty, because you do not know; you have not made up your mind; you like
your friends in general, but no one of them in particular. I can see
the picture of some of them. There is Clifford – he is moody. And
his brother Fred is cranky, like you; he does not know his own mind.
Then there is Chester; he is out West making his fortune; and he will
make a big one, too. And who is Bert?' 'I do not know,' said I. 'Yes, you
do. He is a very good friend to you, very good, although he is not very
demonstrative in his speech.' (I then knew he meant a young friend
of mine, a Harvard man, whom I call Herbert, usually.) Then he said,
'And there is this Fred; he is a true friend to you; his last name is Day
– Fred Day; and oh! I can see books, papers, and pictures all about
him; I think he must take pictures himself for amusement.

'I suppose you think I cannot see you, but I can – you have dark eyes
and light hair. I always liked dark eyes and light hair – now, what are
you laughing at? – and you will be married. But there is no hurry, not
a bit – and in the latter part of your life, you will not live here – it will
be in some foreign country – England, I think. I can see you crossing
the water with a middle-aged lady and a young man. Your life, so far,
has been rather even, not eventful, but it will be full of action, later on.
But you are so peculiar; and this Fred is so peculiar...you tell your father that he will, within a year, realize something from some money
he invested out West, about two years ago; you tell him I said so, and
I *know*. And you tell Ella that she will be better in a few years if she
takes care of herself; she is a little over forty now, and she is often, on
the street, even, taken with dizziness, and with darkness before her
eyes. It all comes from the weak state of her nerves. And now I am
getting tired. Is there anything you want to ask me? I will tell you if I
can. I cannot seem to get your influence separate from the others –
Fred, and Ella, and all. If you will come some time without any locks
of hair, I will see how it will be then.'

Mrs. Piper then came out of the trance, with a face drawn and haggard, and with a dazed look in her eyes. 'Who are you?' she said. 'I do not know who you are, do I?' I said, 'No, but I will tell you now. I am Gertrude Savage; you have met my father, I think.' She was delighted to know me, and who I was, and asked if she had told me anything satisfactory. She was very glad when I told her she had.

Everything she told me when in trance was true as to fact: the prophecies remain to be verified. The 'Imogene' so insisted upon, was immediately verified by Mr. Day, as his old friend, Miss Imogene Gurney, whose first name I had forgotten. The lock of hair was his own – and everything she said in connection with it was true.

During the sitting Dr. Finway talked with me a little in French, but I assured him I had forgotten my French. 'Oh,' he said, and laughed. 'I suppose *je ne sais pas* is all you can say?' And one thing further: He insisted upon it that I must either play or embroider or draw, or do *something* with my fingers. 'No,' said I; 'my accomplishments are highly practical.' 'Well, I see notes of music, anyway,' said he. 'What do you do?' 'I write shorthand.' 'Why didn't you say so before? That's it. Shorthand looks like music notes. You do not print it afterwards, though; you are not a regular stenographer; you just do it for some friend, to help him, I think.'

All of which, as well as all of the whole interview, was perfectly true.[11]

It was later noted by Minot Savage that Fred Day visited England in 1889, that Clifford and Fred were friends of his daughter, that Chester's home was in Pennsylvania, and that he (Dr. Savage) had invested money out West about two years previously, but, while he still considered it a good investment, there had been no significant change of any note.

William James also arranged for a Mr. "A.Y." of Boston to sit with Mrs. Piper on June 13, 1886. A.Y. provided a written report to James, stating, in part:

At the first interview several remarkable phenomena occurred. Although I was introduced by another name, my true name was early given and some incidents of my life stated, which by no conceivable way could have been known to the medium, even if she had known who I

11

was. The persons seeking communication with me were described by name and by person, with much particularity, and the inquiries made were such as they would have made if in conscious communication with me. I was told that I was about to make a journey to a distant part of the country, which I had no intention to make, and which, indeed, had never been in my mind, but which soon afterwards it became necessary for me to make, and I did make it. One thing prominent at this interview and very unusual, so far as I know, was the concurrent descriptions of persons in life and in the other world and their relations to each other. For example: It was said to me that there was an elderly gentleman in the spirit world, who was very desirous of speaking with me, and a full description of his person and his occupation, while in this life, was given, also a like description of an elderly lady, as to her person, and what she was at the moment doing. After a moment it was said that the lady is in the flesh, and the gentleman was her husband, and in the spirit world, and that he wished me to give his love to her. A moment later I was told that I am his son-in-law, which is correct, as all of the other circumstances were. At this interview I do not remember that there was one thing incorrect, but some statements were more vague than others, and this seemed not only to be known but to be accounted for in this way, namely, that the communicators had less power with the medium than would be the case after some further experience but that there would be an increase of power with a repetition of attempts.[12]

A. Y. further reported that his second "interview" was less satisfactory as Mrs. Piper seemed less composed and somewhat anxious. Some of her own personality seemed to be coming through. However, some evidential information was communicated, including information that a friend of his was fatally ill, a fact unknown to A.Y. at the time but later verified, and the pet name by which he addressed his wife when she was living was given. A third sitting was uneventful, apparently the result of rainy weather causing unfavorable conditions for the medium.

Although William James did not record his initial sittings with Mrs. Piper, he did record several later sittings. On March 6, 1889, Alice James, his wife, and Robertson James, his brother, sat with Mrs. Piper and were informed by Phinuit that "Aunt Kate" (Kate Walsh) had died early that morning and that a letter or telegram saying she was gone would be received later that day. It was known to the two sitters that Aunt Kate had been seriously ill, but neither was aware that she had died. After leaving Mrs. Piper's home, Robertson James reported the sitting to Professor James and Dr. Richard Hodgson. "On reaching home an hour later I found a telegram as follows," William James recorded: – 'Aunt Kate passed away a few minutes after midnight. – E. R. Walsh.'" [13]

Alice James recorded her version: "It may be worth while to add that early at this sitting I inquired, 'How is Aunt Kate?' The reply was, 'She is poorly.' This reply disappointed me, from its baldness. Nothing more was said about Aunt Kate till towards the close of the sitting, when I again said, 'Can you tell me nothing more about Aunt Kate?' The medium suddenly threw back her head and said in a startled way, 'Why Aunt Kate's here. All around me I hear voices saying, "Aunt Kate has come."' Then followed the announcement that she had died very early that morning, and on being pressed to give the time, shortly after two was named." [14]

Six months later, Aunt Kate communicated from the other side. James wrote: "The 'Kate Walsh' freak is very interesting...In September, sitting with me and my wife, Mrs. Piper was suddenly 'controlled' by her spirit, who spoke directly (i.e., without the assistance of Phinuit) with much impressiveness of manner, and great similarity of temperament to herself. Platitudes. She said Henry Wyckoff had experienced a change and that Albert was coming over soon; nothing definite about either. Queer business!" [15] In a subsequent report James wrote that he knew nothing of the health conditions of Henry and Albert at the time of the sitting, but that he later found the comments to be factual.

In another sitting, James was told by Phinuit that the spirit of a boy named Robert F. was the companion of his deceased child, Hermann, who had died as an infant in 1885. The F.'s were cousins of his wife and were living in a distant city. On his return home, James told his wife of the reading and asked for particulars on the baby lost by her cousin, as he did not recall the name, sex, and age of the child mentioned by Phinuit. Much to his surprise, his wife corrected him and confirmed Phinuit's version.

According to James, Phinuit would often introduce other spirits and at times would give long lectures about things he (James) was certain were well beyond Mrs. Piper's intellect. He wrote:

> The most remarkable thing about the Phinuit personality seems to me the extraordinary tenacity and minuteness of his memory. The

medium has been visited by many hundreds of sitters, half of them, perhaps, being strangers who have come but once. To each Phinuit gives an hour full of disconnected fragments of talk about persons living, dead, or imaginary, and events past, future, or unreal. What normal waking memory could keep this chaotic mass of stuff together? Yet Phinuit does so…So far as I can discover, Mrs. Piper's waking memory is not remarkable, and the whole constitution of her trance-memory is something which I am at a loss to understand.[16]

Perhaps out of concern for his reputation in the scientific community, James continued to struggle, at least outwardly, in accepting the spirit hypothesis. However, in the end, he appeared to see it as more probable than other explanations, such as telepathy of a limited or more cosmic scope. "One who takes part in a good sitting has usually a far livelier sense, both of the reality and of the importance of the communication, than one who merely reads the records," he offered. "I am able, while still holding to all the lower principles of interpretation, to imagine the process as more complex, and to share the feelings with which Hodgson came at last to regard it after his many years of familiarity, the feeling which Professor (James) Hyslop shares, and which most of those who have good sittings are promptly inspired with [i.e., the spirit hypothesis]."[17]

And while James remained perched on the fence relative to the spirit hypothesis, he had no difficulty professing his faith. He concluded *The Varieties of Religious Experience* by stating: "I *can*, of course, put myself into the sectarian scientist's attitude, and imagine vividly that the world of sensations and of scientific laws and objects may be all. But whenever I do this, I hear that inward monitor of which W. K. Clifford once wrote, whispering the word 'bosh!' Humbug is humbug, even though it bear the scientific name, and the total expression of human experience, as I view it objectively, invincibly urges me beyond the narrow 'scientific' bounds."[18]

In 1909, the year before his death, James, who called Leonora Piper his "white crow," the one who proved that all crows are not black, wrote:

I am baffled, as to spirit return, and as to many other special problems. I am also baffled as to what to think of this or that particular story, for the sources of error in any one observation are seldom fully knowable. But weak sticks make strong faggots; and when the stories fall into consistent sorts that point each in a definite direction, one gets a sense of being in a presence of genuinely natural type of phenomena. As to there being such real natural types of phenomena ignored by orthodox science, I am not baffled at all, for I am fully convinced of it...I personally am as yet neither a convinced believer in parasitic demons, nor a spiritist, nor a scientist, but still remain a psychical researcher waiting for more facts before concluding.[19]

But James admitted that he was willfully taking the point of view of the so-called 'rigorously scientific' disbeliever, and making an *ad hominem* plea, stating that tactically, it is better to believe too little than too much.

---

[1] Holt, 400

[2] Piper, 12

[3] Hodgson 46

[4] Piper, 67

[5] Holt, 381-382

[6] Hodgson, 97

[7] _____, 100-101

[8] Savage 107

[9] Moore, 28

[10] Holt, 415

[11] Hodgson, 100-103

[12] _____, 96

[13] Holt, 411

[14] _____, 412

[15] _____, 413

[16] _____, 455-456 (Pr. SPR, VI, 651f.)

[17] _____, 708

[18] James (1961), 401

[19] Murphy, 322-323

# -Two-

# A Debunker is Converted

*I had but one object, to discover fraud and trickery.*
— **Richard Hodgson**

E ncouraged by Professor William Barrett, a British physicist who was a cofounder of the Society for Psychical Research in London (SPR) in 1882, Professor William James was instrumental in forming the American branch of the SPR (ASPR) in late 1884. The first meeting of the ASPR was held on December 18, 1884 in Boston, although it did not become an official organization until January 8, 1885. As with the SPR in London, much of the early focus of the ASPR was on thought-transference, or telepathy, as Frederic W. H. Myers, one of the founders of the SPR, named it. It was believed by many scientific men of the time that mediumship could be explained by thought-transference. That is, the medium was reading the mind of the sitter. However, the telepathy hypothesis, though seemingly ruling out spirits as communicating through mediums, was nevertheless opposed to the mechanistic universe that many scientists had come to accept, since it indicated extra-sensory perception of some kind. Thus, many scientists and scholars rejected telepathy with the same vehemence that they rejected spirits of the dead. Most of the early members of the SPR and ASPR were open-minded in this respect and saw telepathy as an acceptable explanation, one that did not necessarily suggest a step backwards to the superstitions of religion.

Because of his academic duties, James was unable to devote much time to the work of the ASPR. Thus, Dr. Richard Hodgson, a hard-core skeptic, was imported from the SPR in England during 1887 to serve as executive secretary of the ASPR and its chief investigator. The invitation to Hodgson was prompted by Mr. R. Pearsall Smith of Philadelphia, one of the original officers of the ASPR. Smith was a disbeliever in mediumship and his intent was to debunk all mediums, as he believed that his grieving brother had been led astray by a charlatan.

Hodgson is thought to have been the first full-time, paid psychical researcher. Born in Melbourne, Australia and raised a Methodist, he earned his bachelor's, master's, and doctorate (in law) degrees at the University of Melbourne before moving to England, and entering the University of Cambridge as a scholar of St. John's College, studying moral sciences. He apparently chose St. John's because William Wordsworth, whose works he admired, had attended the school.

After taking honors in 1881, Hodgson began teaching poetry and philosophy at University Extension. In 1884, he accepted a position at Cambridge as lecturer on the philosophy of Herbert Spencer. However, according to Alex Baird, Hodgson's biographer, Hodgson "imbibed enough of an idealistic philosophy to eliminate the materialistic tendencies of Spenser." Baird said that Hodgson was too strong an individualist to follow any philosopher completely, as "unconsciously he was searching for the Source and Secret of All Life." [1]

While attending Cambridge, Hodgson joined an organization called the Cambridge Society for Psychical Research, which was started in 1879 and was a forerunner of the SPR. When the SPR was formed in 1882, Hodgson became one of its first members. He took an active part in the Society, exposing several fraudulent mediums. While lecturing on Spencer at Cambridge, he was asked by the SPR to travel to India to investigate the Theosophical Society and its leaders, including Madame H. P. Blavatsky. After more than four months in India, Hodgson concluded that Blavatsky was a charlatan. A bitter controversy resulted from this, the Theosophists claiming that Hodgson did not understand the physical phenomena resulting from Blavatsky's mediumship and was too hasty and harsh in his judgment. Upon returning to England, Hodgson investigated several other physical mediums and issued a report that "nearly all the professional mediums are a gang of vulgar tricksters who are more or less in league with one another." [2]

Hodgson had heard about Mrs. Piper before he left London and was confident that he would unmask her. "I was compelled to assume in the first instance, that Mrs. Piper was fraudulent and obtained her information previously by ordinary means, such as inquiries by confederates, etc.," he wrote. "Not only was this assumption as to Mrs. Piper's fraud necessary, but it was also needful to suppose that she worked herself into a hyperaesthetic state during which she obtained much further information given in various ways by the sitter, consciously or unconsciously, by speech gesture, and other muscular action." [3]

Hodgson had his first sitting with Mrs. Piper on May 4, 1887, careful not to reveal his name or purpose for being in the country. After Mrs. Piper went into the trance state, Dr. Phinuit took over her body. With his reactions in brackets, Hodgson recorded the sitting:

> Mother living, father dead, little brother dead. [True] Father and mother described correctly, though not with much detail. In connection with the enumeration of the members of our family, Phinuit tried to get a name beginning with "R," but failed. [A little sister of mine, named Rebecca, died when I was very young, I think less than eighteen months old.] Four of you living besides mother.' [True]

> Phinuit mentioned the name 'Fred.' I said that it might be my cousin. 'He says you went to school together. He goes on jumping-frogs, and laughs. He says he used to get the better of you. He had convulsive movements before his death, struggles. He went off in a sort of spasm. You were not there.' [My cousin Fred far excelled any other person that I have seen in the games of leap-frog, fly the garter, etc. He took very long flying jumps, and whenever he played the game was lined by crowds of school-mates to watch him. He injured his spine in a gymnasium in Melbourne, Australia in 1871, and was carried to the hospital, where he lingered for a fortnight, with occasional spasmodic convulsions, in one of which he died.] [4]

Phinuit then changed the subject but returned to "Fred" in Hodgson's fourth sitting with Mrs. Piper, Hodgson recording:

> The chief new matter was: (a) That I was not there when he swung on the trapeze and fell and injured his spine, finally dying in a convulsion. [At my first sitting the accident was not described, only the death, at which I was rightly said not to have been present. At this sitting the accident was described, at which also I was rightly said not to have been present.] (b) That he wanted to remind me of Harris at school,

who was a very able man, etc. [I believe it was also stated that Fred and myself talked together about Harris, and that Harris had a high opinion of Fred's ability. This was all true. Harris was a schoolmaster who taught Fred and myself (Melbourne, Australia), about 1868 or 1869. I saw Harris, I think, a short time after my cousin's death (in 1871), and he expressed his regrets, etc. I do not recall having seen or heard anything of Harris since. (c) That his father was my mother's brother. [True][5]

After talking about Fred in that first sitting, Phinuit began describing a lady who was very close to Hodgson. He said that she "died slowly" and Hodgson was not with her. He could not get her name, but said it ended with a "sie," which Hodgson confirmed as true. For privacy reasons, Hodgson did not want to name the woman in his report and referred to her only as "Q." Hodgson's biographer Alex Baird revealed that her name was Jessie, the one and only love affair of his youth. Their relationship ended in 1875 because her parents objected to Hodgson's increasing reluctance to accept the tenets of the Methodist faith.

Phinuit mentioned two rings, but Hodgson could not recall any rings. At his second sitting with Mrs. Piper, Phinuit again brought up "Q" and said that she was a great friend of his sister's and that he (Hodgson) heard about her death from his sister. In a sixth sitting, Phinuit returned to "Q" and said that her left eye *is* brown and on the right eye there is a spot of a light color in the iris, the spot being straggly and of a bluish cast. He said it was a birthmark. Hodgson recalled the eye blemish, but thought it was gray rather than blue. He asked Phinuit how he knew about the eye. Phinuit replied that "Q" was standing close to him and showing him her right eye, so that he could see it plainly.

There was also a reference to a book of poems. Hodgson remembered lending "Q" Tennyson's *The Princess* and her having returned it. He recalled writing her name on one of the fly leaves.

There was much more in the way of evidential information that came through, although there were various bits of information that made no sense to Hodgson or that he was unsure of. Nevertheless, he was very much impressed and his whole attitude about mediums began to change after those first few sittings. He would devote a good part of the last 18 years of his life studying Mrs. Piper on behalf of the ASPR, arranging for various people to sit with her and usually sitting in to monitor and record them.

Apparently influenced by the opinion of Professor James, Hodgson considered telepathy as a possible explanation. As he initially saw it, Dr. Phinuit was a secondary personality buried in Mrs. Piper's subconscious, and this secondary personality had the ability to read the minds of the sitters, even to tap into minds not present at the sitting. Hodgson was not prepared to buy into the spiritistic hypothesis, as it was clearly opposed to scientific progress.

But after those initial sittings Hodgson wondered how telepathy, if it existed, could explain things he didn't know. For example, in one sitting Phinuit informed Hodgson that his sister in Australia would soon be giving birth to a fourth child, a boy. This proved to be true, but Hodgson was not even aware at the time that his sister was expecting.

Hodgson also wondered why Phinuit couldn't get Jessie's name, since he clearly was focused on her name when he asked Phinuit on several occasions to see if he could get it. "Vivid conscious thinking of a circumstance does not seem, indeed, to help Phinuit in any way, but rather the contrary," he recorded.[6] Moreover, he noted that most of the things mentioned by Phinuit were not on his conscious mind at the time.

As for the possibility that Mrs. Piper researched the individual beforehand, as some skeptics suggested, Hodgson did not see how that was possible, especially when the sitter went anonymously, as he did in his first visit with her. And what source could provide her with information about Fred and Jessie? But to completely rule out such fraud, he arranged for a detective agency to report on her daily activities for a period of time. The detectives found no foul play on her part.

Sometime around the beginning of 1888, Hodgson put Mrs. Piper under contract to the Society and began arranging anonymous sittings by various people with her. She would give an average three sittings a week for his research and he would often sit in and observe while taking notes. One of the most evidential sittings was that of Mr. J. Rogers Rich, an artist, who offered a detailed account of 11 sittings he had between September 5, 1888 and July 17, 1889. Rich reported that he was at first reluctant to sit with Mrs. Piper because he disliked the whole idea of mediumship, but he did make the appointment and upon meeting her was immediately disarmed by her simple and sympathetic manner. He further reported:

> I was at once struck with the peculiar light, or inward look, in her eyes. Her voice was full and agreeable, but in every way a 'feminine' voice,

and there was an entire absence of any masculinity in her manner, which I had been expecting to find under the circumstances.

With little trouble she went into the trance – a state which was entirely new to my experience – and after a moment's silence, which followed her rather violent movements, I was startled by the remarkable change in her voice – an exclamation, a sort of grunt of satisfaction, as if the person had reached his destination and gave vent to his pleasure thereat by this sound, uttered in an unmistakably male voice, but rather husky. I was at once addressed in French with, 'Bonjour, Monsieur, comment vous portez vous?' To which I gave answer in the same language, with which I happen to be perfectly familiar. My answer was responded to with sort of inquiring grunt, much like the French. 'Hein?' and then the conversation continued in English, with rarely a French word, and more rarely a French expression coming into it. Nearly all my interviews were begun in the same manner. I had given no means of identification, and simply awaited results. At the time I made my first visit to Mrs. Piper I was quite unwell with nervous troubles, for which I had been under treatment by a noted specialist. The first thing told me was of a 'great light behind me, a good sign.' Then suddenly all my ills were very clearly and distinctly explained and so thoroughly that I felt certain that Mrs. Piper herself would have hesitated to use such plain language! Prescriptions were given to me for the purchase of herbs, and the manner of preparing them, which I was to do myself.... My profession, painting, was described, and my particular talents and mannerisms in design were mentioned. I was surrounded with pictures – 'Oh! Pictures everywhere!' At this interview my mother was clearly described! She was beside me, dressed as in her portrait (painted a year or two before her death), and wearing a certain cameo pin, the portrait of my father. Two living aunts, who were very dear to me, my brother and his wife 'Nellie' were well described, and in such a way as to have made it impossible for Mrs. Piper to have so minutely informed herself about them.[7]

At his second sitting a month later, Rich was told by Phinuit that he would soon hear from an old friend, Lennox. "You call him Frank," Phinuit said. Rich asked if Frank was still in California. Phinuit said that he was not, but had "gone across the water to Al – Aul – Aula – how you call that?" Rich suggested "Australia," which seemed to puzzle

Phinuit, who hesitated and said, "Yes, Australia." In fact, Rich later found that Frank had gone to Alaska, not Australia.

Phinuit then told Rich that his deceased niece was frequently in his surroundings and that she was then at his side. Rich further recorded:

> Up to this time I had not heard my name mentioned so I asked of it from my niece. The 'Doctor' was again puzzled and said, 'What a funny name – wait, I cannot go so fast!' Then my entire name was correctly spelled out but entirely with the French alphabet, each separate letter being clearly pronounced in that language. My niece had been born, lived most of her short life, and died in France. Then the attempt to pronounce my name was amusing – finally calling me 'Thames Rowghearce Reach.' The 'Doctor' never called me after that anything but 'Reach.'[8]

In his third sitting, Rich heard from a deceased friend. "Hullo, here's Newell!" Phinuit said, referring to Rich's friend who had died some months before. Rich asked him to repeat the name and Phinuit repeated it with a strong foreign accent. Then, there was a moment in which Rich heard a "mingling of voices," as if in a dispute, followed by silence and heavy breathing by Mrs. Piper. "All at once I was astonished to hear, in an entirely different tone and in the purest English accent, "Well, of all persons under the sun, Rogers Rich, what brought you here? I'm glad to see you, old fellow? How is X and Y and Z, and all the boys at the club?"

Apparently, Newell did not require the assistance of Phinuit and was able to "control" Mrs. Piper on his own. Newell reminded Rich that he followed him in college by some years and that all of his acquaintances were younger than Rich. Rich then noticed an odd movement by Mrs. Piper. She appeared to be twirling an imaginary moustache, something which Newell frequently did when alive.

In his seventh sitting, Rich informed Phinuit that the medicine he had prescribed for him was not working well. Phinuit told him that his cook had not used the proper proportions, as he had not properly instructed her. On inquiry, Rich found that to be a fact, as his cook had understood him to say a quart instead of a pint, and confessed to having forgotten the proportions and allowing the mixture to "boil down."

In his ninth sitting, Rich asked Phinuit if he could again talk with Newell. Rich then recorded:

The 'Doctor' said, 'I'll send for him,' and kept on talking with me for a while. Then he said, 'Here's Newell, and he wants to talk with you "Reach," so I'll go about my business whilst you are talking with him, and will come back again later.' Then followed a confusion of words, but I clearly heard the voice of the 'Doctor' saying: 'Here, Newell, you come by the hands while I go out by the feet,' which apparently being accomplished in the proper manner, my name was called clearly as 'Rogers, old fellow!' without a sign of accent, and the same questions put as to how were the 'fellows at the club.' My hand was cordially shaken, and I remarked the same movement of twisting the moustache, which was kept up by Mrs. Piper during the interview. Newell spoke of a 'pastel' I was drawing as a wedding present, and described the pleasure he had in watching me do it. He told me of certain private family affairs which I knew to be correct. Finally he bade me goodbye. Before going he spoke to me of his 'present life,' and told me that he was writing a poem; that he was now pursuing his literary studies with the greatest pleasure, &c, &c. 'But,' he said, 'was I not sick, and did I not suffer before I left you all? Why, the leaving of the material body, Rogers, is terrible. It is like tearing limb from limb; but once free, how happy one is.' When Newell left me, there was the usual disturbance in the medium's condition and then the resumption of the familiar voice, accent, and mannerisms of Dr. Phinuit.[9]

At one of the sittings, Phinuit told Rich that a child was constantly beside him and in his surroundings. The child was, Phinuit told him, attracted to Rich and had much influence over him. "It is a blood relation, a sister," Phinuit communicated. Rich told him that he had no sister, to which Phinuit explained that she had died at birth some years before he was born. On questioning an aunt, Rich learned that such had been the case, though he had never been informed of it by his parents.

At the request of William James, Hodgson arranged for a person identified in his report only as "C.W.F., M.D." to sit with Mrs. Piper during 1889. CWF began by testing Dr. Phinuit, asking him what medical men were prominent in Paris in his time. Phinuit responded with the names "Bouvier" and "Dupuytren." Bouvier died in 1827, Dupuytren in 1835. Dr. CWF later admitted that he knew about Dupuytren but knew nothing about Bouvier and had four other physicians in mind, thus leading him to question the telepathy hypothesis. However, he asked Phinuit if he was reading his mind. "I get nothing from your mind," Phinuit replied. "I can't read your mind any more than I can see through a stone wall."

Phinuit then gave the names of CWF's three deceased sisters and his brother, George. CWF asked Phinuit to have George identify some incident in his life known only to the two of them. Phinuit mentioned the loss of their luggage in Europe. CWF recalled that a train went off without them, taking with it their coats and luggage.

CWF was told by Phinuit that his friend "William" was there, but he could not get the last name. Later, as Mrs. Piper was coming out of the trance, the word "Pabodie" was spoken with great force, and Mrs. Piper reacted with a start, saying that somebody had spoken right in her ear and wondered if CWF had done so. William Pabodie was the name of a friend who had committed suicide in 1870.

Phinuit told CWF that Robert and Clara were very grateful for CWF having taken care of their son, Georgie, CWF's nephew. CWF thought it would be interesting to have Georgie sit with Mrs. Piper but didn't want Mrs. Piper to know of any connection between them, so he had a third person arrange for Georgie's sitting. After Mrs. Piper went into trance, Georgie, a professor at M.I.T., was given the names of his father and mother. When Georgie asked how his uncle (CWF) was, Phinuit responded, "Oh, C.W., he has (correctly named an affliction)." Phinuit also said that his uncle plays the violin, a factual statement. However, Georgie told CWF that he was not impressed and refused to believe in spirits.

At his next sitting with Mrs. Piper, CWF was spontaneously told by Phinuit that his nephew Georgie had been there. CWF replied that Georgie is skeptical about Phinuit being a spirit. "No matter how smart George is, he will have to learn that there is another life," Phinuit said, adding that "many people think I am the medium; that is all bosh."

CWF asked Phinuit if he could identify the ghost he saw in his house some years earlier. "That was your sister Clara," Phinuit told him. CWF confirmed that it appeared to be his sister, whose name was Clarissa but later changed to Clara. CWF asked Phinuit how he knew such things and Phinuit told him that he gets it from CWF's "astral light."

Overall, Dr. CWF was very impressed with his three sittings. "All have been interesting, and rather force me to believe that Dr. P. is not a fictitious personage," he wrote in a report to Professor James. He added that Dr. Phinuit "had partially forgotten his French, so far as speaking it goes, yet I am convinced that he understands all I say in that language, and that Mrs. P[iper] does not, from my tests of her capacity, and she impresses me as being a truly honest woman." [10]

Ella Wilson, referred to by Hodgson as a "most excellent and discriminating witness," had 45 sittings with Mrs. Piper between November 12,

1886 and June 19, 1889. She provided Hodgson with a detailed report of her sittings, some of the highlights abridged below:

> In forty-one of [the 45 sittings] the control was taken, for at least a part of an hour, by a personal friend whose subjects of conversation, forms of expression, and ways of looking at things were distinctly unlike either Mrs. Piper's or Dr. Phinuit's. The clearly-marked personality of that friend, whom I will call T., is to me the most convincing proof of Mrs. P's supernatural power, but it is a proof impossible to present to anyone else. Messages, in some instances characteristic, were received from other friends, but no long-sustained conversations were held save with T. and Dr. Phinuit. T., who was, while living, a Congregational minister, talked of religious subjects (of which Phinuit disclaimed either interest or knowledge), of professional matters, of our large circle of mutual acquaintances, and of many private affairs known only to himself and me.

> T. was a Western man, and the localism of using *like* as a conjunction clung to him, despite my frequent correction, all his life. At my sitting on December 16<sup>th</sup>, 1886, he remarked: 'If you see it like I do.' Forgetful for the instant of changed conditions, I promptly repeated, '*As* I do.' 'Ah,' came the response, 'that sounds natural. That sounds like old times.'

> March 1<sup>st</sup>, 1888, he requested, 'Throw off this rug,' referring to a loose fur-lined cloak which I wore. I noted the word as a singular designation for such a garment, and weeks after recalled that he had once, while living, spoken of it in the same way as I threw it over him on the lounge...

> March 2<sup>nd</sup>, 1887, came this: 'I never knew you had a little sister here. She tells me she has been here a long time, ever since she was a little toddling baby.' Certainly not I, nor Mrs. P., who has children of her own, would speak of a four months old child as a '*toddling* baby.' It is more thinkable of a man who like T., never knew anything of young children...

> I quote two tests of partial clairvoyance. March 2<sup>nd</sup> 1887, I was asked by my mother to inquire the whereabouts of two silver cups, heirlooms, which she had misplaced. Said Dr. P.: 'They are in your house,

in a room higher up than your sleeping room, in what looks to me like the back part of the house, but very likely I am turned around. You'll find there a large chest filled with clothing, and at the very bottom of the chest are the cups, Annie [my mother's name] placed them there and will remember it.' Returning home I went to a room on the third floor at the front of the house, but remotest from the stairway, found the chest (of which I knew) and the contents (of which I was ignorant) both as described, but no silver. Reporting the message to my mother I learned that she had at one time kept the cups in that chest, but more recently had removed them...[11]

The second test involved a request by Ella's sister, "L." to ask Dr. Phinuit the whereabouts of her missing card-plate. Ella took her sister's calling card with her and placed it in Mrs. Piper's hand, asking for the whereabouts of the plate from which it was engraved. Phinuit told her that it could be found in a box with a brush and bottle and that the box was in a drawer under something that looks like a cupboard or closet. As it turned out, Ella and her sister went to the place indicated by Phinuit and found her stencil-plate, not her card-plate.

On one occasion, Ella's father and mother sat with Mrs. Piper. When Ella next sat with Mrs. Piper, T. told her that a little while after they left, her mother informed her father that it did not really seem like T. T. added that it was said on the piazza. Ella knew nothing of this statement by her mother but confirmed it upon returning home.

T. was not the only discarnate able to control Mrs. Piper and communicate without the assistance of Phinuit. Miss "A.M.R." reported to Hodgson that her friend "H." was able to take control of Mrs. Piper. "It seems to be quite a different personality," she related to Hodgson, "although there is something in the voice or manner of speaking that is like Dr. P. The voice, however, is not nearly so loud. When I asked him once why this was, he told me that Dr. P. was right by him and that he could not stay a moment without his help. In a great many little ways he is quite like what my friend used to be when living, so much so that I am afraid it would take a great deal of explanation to make me believe that his identical self had not something to do with it, wholly apart from the medium's powers or from anything that may be in my own mind concerning him."[12]

AMR added that H. did not always know how to spell his name correctly. He told her that the longer he is away the more he forgets about things in this life, though he does not forget his friends. He also told her that the lameness he had in his physical life was no longer with him but that he had to come back that way so that she could recognize him. The lameness had earlier been reported by Phinuit in describing H. and was before he learned how to take control himself.

Lilian Whiting sat with Mrs. Piper on January 4, 1889 and asked her (or Dr. Phinuit) to describe her rooms at the Brunswick. "One thing described was a photograph of the novelist, Edgar Fawcett," Whiting recorded. "What does that man do?" I inquired. "He writes books," was the reply. In my room are several pictures of Miss Kate Field. This was noted by the medium as "so many pictures of one lady – oh, a great many!" Whiting then asked Phinuit to describe the lady. "She appears before the public in some way," was the response. "Yes, I see! She lectures. She has a very strong intellect – a brilliant mind. One of these pictures I do not like. It is not good of her. You should put it away. Turn the back to the wall." Whiting agreed that the largest picture she had of her did her an injustice.[13]

In a sitting on October 31, 1889, Doctor C. L. was reminded of a near-drowning accident which he had as a seven-year-old boy. "The trance person (Phinuit) and I spoke French two or three times during the sitting," he told Hodgson. "He did not seem to be desirous of talking it a long time. He would very soon translate my answer into English, and then go on in English." Dr. C. L. added that he asked Phinuit if he could describe the gentlemen he had dined with the previous evening, and Phinuit gave a "surprisingly accurate" description of them. He further told him how many people lived at his home, including his sister Marie, whom he correctly named. And he accurately diagnosed Dr. C. L.'s stomach problem.[14]

Miss A. A. B., who sat with Mrs. Piper during February 1888, was told that someone named Mary was there (with Phinuit) and wanted to speak to her. AAB. could not think who it could be, until Phinuit told her it was the sister of Lizzie, AAB's friend. AAB then recalled that Lizzie had a sister who had died of consumption before she met Lizzie. "Without the explanation I should never have thought of her," AAB reported, adding that she asked if an aunt for whom she was named was present. Phinuit replied that she could not come because she had "grown too far away from this world." AAB asked Phinuit if they then forget this world. "All that is material is forgotten as of no consequence," Phinuit answered. "It is all spiritual growth, and all spiritual growth here will help you there."[15]

But not all sittings were evidential and some sitters left Mrs. Piper convinced that she was a charlatan. There were times when she could not achieve the trance state and other times when she struggled to bring forth information, or the spirits struggled to use her organism to communicate. Moreover, statements were made by Phinuit that were clearly not true, others which clearly suggested telepathy rather than spirits. For example, AAB asked about some lost china and was told by Phinuit that it was taken by a man who had been in the employ of the family for a long time. Several months later, however, the china was found in a place that had been overlooked in the search. As the servant had been considered a suspect by AAB and her family, it was theorized that Mrs. Piper had read AAB's mind. (Of course, it could have been that the servant had a guilty conscience and decided to return the china to a place where he thought the family might not have looked.)

Dr. O. F. Wodsworth sat with Mrs. Piper on June 15, 1888 and deemed the sitting a failure, "though one or two incidents suggested to me that the 'conditions' of success were present had Phinuit received any assurance at the beginning that he was not confused." [16] Wodsworth added that more than twenty statements and names were offered, almost all of which were wrong.

Dr. Samuel A. Hopkins reported to Hodgson that there was nothing remarkable to report and said that most of his sitting during 1888, except for one bit of communication, was "rubbish." That one exception involved a message for Lily from V-A-U-G-H-N (spelled out by Phinuit). Phinuit added that Vaughn had been there only a short time and that he is a little lame. Hopkins knew who Lily and Vaughn were, but was not aware of any lameness on the part of Vaughn. He found out later that Vaughn had been lame before passing. "The other statements of Mrs. Piper were either wrong or entirely negative," Hopkins claimed. [17]

John F. Brown sat with Mrs. Piper during June and October 1888 and was convinced that Mrs. Piper was a fraud. "In regard to Mrs. Piper, I have the secret of her power," Brown reported to Hodgson. "That is, I have a good deal of confidence that such is the case, and am anxious to have my theory tested in such a manner as to be either proved true or shown to be false. I think she proceeds by guesswork, in which she is materially assisted by the conversation of the sitters, this conversation being to a considerable extent guided and controlled by herself. So far as pure guesswork goes, I do not think she shows any great skill, that there are others who can do this much more scientifically and successfully, and that her skill lies chiefly in getting the help of the sitter, who points out the way she is to travel in a manner analogous to that in which Bishop's subjects lead him to the hidden articles." [18]

Like Brown, other sitters mentioned that Mrs. Piper seemed to be "fishing" for answers from the sitters, but Hodgson and other researchers came to understand that it was Dr. Phinuit who was fishing for interpretations to what he was seeing or hearing from spirits who were attempting to telepathically relay messages through him. Clearly, some spirits, if that is what they were, could communicate more effectively than others.

While the successful sittings seemed to far outweigh the unsuccessful ones, Hodgson was not about to make any hasty declarations in favor of spirits and survival. Indications are that he was privately leaning heavily in the direction of spirits and survival after a year or two of studying Mrs. Piper. Certainly, he was convinced that she was not a fraud, as he initially thought, but there was still the question of telepathy and the hypothesis that Phinuit was a "secondary personality" buried in Mrs. Piper's subconscious. In effect, the belief was that the secondary personality was doing the mind reading and Mrs. Piper's primary personality was unaware of what was going on. And while there were many facts related by Phinuit that were unknown to the sitters, thus seemingly ruling out simple telepathy, James, Hodgson, and other SPR members considered the possibility that there was some form of advanced telepathy, which they called teloteropathy, the ability to tap into minds anywhere in the world. When information unknown to any person anywhere came through mediums, the "Cosmic Soul" theory (more theory than hypothesis) was advanced. This theory suggested what today might be called a cosmic computer, which minds could tap into and withdraw information. Teloteropathy and the Cosmic Soul were later combined and referred to as *Superpsi* or Super ESP.

With Professor James and other men of science closely scrutinizing his research, Hodgson showed proper skepticism as he continued his study of Mrs. Piper. It would have been professional suicide to declare a belief in spirits.

---

[1] Baird, 4

[2] _____, 26

[3] Hodgson, 6

[4] _____, 60

[5] _____, 64

[6] _____, 10

[7] _____, 127

[8] _____, 128

[9] _____, 130

[10] _____, 98-100

[11] _____, 29-32

[12] _____, 113

[13] _____, 124

[14] _____, 125

[15] _____, 114-115

[16] _____, 84

[17] _____, 68

[18] _____, 89

# -Three-

# Mrs. Piper Goes to England

*My eyes began to open to the fact that there really is a spiritual world.*
**– Sir Oliver Lodge**

At the urging of Dr. Richard Hodgson, leaders of the Society for Psychical Research (SPR) in London decided to invite Leonora Piper to England to be further observed and tested. Mrs. Piper accepted the offer on the condition that her daughters, Alta and Minerva, accompany her. She arrived in Liverpool on November 19, 1889 and was met by Professor Oliver Lodge (later Sir Oliver Lodge), a renowned physicist and electricity pioneer.

Like so many other scientists caught up in the wake of Darwinism, Lodge had become a materialist, not believing in anything spiritual. "It did not seem to me possible that a man could survive the death of the body," Lodge wrote in his 1929 autobiography. "I did not think that we could ever know the truth about things of that kind, and was content with whatever destiny lay in store for us, without either inquisitiveness or rebellion. I felt that our knowledge would not make any difference, and that we had better leave questions of that kind to settle themselves in due course." [1]

However, Lodge remained open-minded on the subject and was intrigued by the idea that one person could read another's mind, something he had observed around 1883 in a stage performer called Irving Bishop. He joined the SPR shortly after witnessing Bishop's performance. "The

verification of the fact of telepathy, indicating obscurely a kind of dis-
location between mind and body, was undoubtedly impressive, so that
it began to seem probable, especially under [Frederic] Myers's tuition,
that the two – mind and body – were not inseparably connected, as I
had been led by my previous studies under Clifford, Tyndall, and Hux-
ley to believe they were," Lodge explained his change of mind. "I began
to feel that there was a possibility of the survival of personality." [2]

Between the time Mrs. Piper and her daughters arrived in England and
her departure for New York on February 5, 1890, Lodge had 83 sittings
with her, nearly all in his own home. Special precautions were taken to
hide photo albums and anything else that might give clues to Mrs. Piper
about the family history. His formal report of May 1890 began:

> At the request of Mr. Myers I undertook a share in the investigation
> of a case of apparent clairvoyance. It is the case of a lady who appears
> to go off into a trance when she pleases to will it under favourable
> surroundings, and in that trance to talk volubly, with a manner and
> voice quite different from her ordinary manner and voice, on details
> concerning which she has had no information given her.
>
> In this abnormal state her speech has reference mainly to people's rela-
> tives and friends, living or deceased, about whom she is able to hold a
> conversation, and with whom she appears more or less familiar.
>
> By introducing anonymous strangers, and by catechizing her myself
> in various ways, I have satisfied myself that much of the information
> she possesses in the trance state is not acquired by ordinary com-
> monplace methods, but that she has some unusual means of acquir-
> ing information. The facts on which she discourses are usually within
> the knowledge of some person present, though they are often entirely
> out of his conscious thought at the time. Occasionally facts have been
> narrated which have only been verified afterwards, and which are in
> good faith asserted never to have been known; meaning thereby that
> they have left no trace on the conscious memory of any person pres-
> ent or in the neighbourhood, and that it is highly improbable that they
> were ever known to such person.
>
> She is also in the trance state able to diagnose diseases, and to speci-
> fy the owners or late owners of portable property, under the circum-
> stances which preclude the application of ordinary methods.

In the midst of this lucidity a number of mistaken and confused statements are frequently made, having little or no apparent meaning or application.

Concerning the particular means by which she acquires the different kind of information, there is no sufficient evidence to make it safe to draw any conclusion. I can only say with certainty that it is by none of the ordinary methods known to Physical Science.[3]

Lodge added that he believed Mrs. Piper's assertion that she retains no knowledge of what took place during the trance state, and that she seemed anxious to have scientists explain her phenomenon to her, since she did not understand it herself. She fully understood the precautions taken to study her in a scientific manner.

Lodge invited Dr. Gerald Rendall, principal of University College, Liverpool, to attend one of the early sittings, introducing him to Mrs. Piper as "Mr. Roberts." After she was entranced, Mrs. Piper (or Dr. Phinuit) correctly gave the names of Rendall's brothers along with specific details about them. Rendall handed her a locket and received communications and reminiscences from the deceased friend to whom it had belonged. Although there were some apparently incorrect statements made, Rendall was satisfied that the correct statements were far beyond chance guessing.

Another guest at a sitting was Professor E. C. K. Gonner, a lecturer on economics at the same university. Lodge introduced him as "Mr. McCunn," who happened to be another colleague with whom he might, if fraud was a factor, be confused. That is, if Mrs. Piper had somehow been able to do research on his colleagues before traveling to England, which seemed highly improbable and would have been extremely difficult, this deception was aimed at uncovering that possibility. However, Phinuit correctly gave information relating to Gonner. Among other things, Phinuit described how Gonner's Uncle William was killed "with a hole in his head, like a shot hole, yet not a shot, more like a blow."[4] The fact was that Uncle William had been killed when a stone struck him in the head during a Yorkshire election riot.

Still another guest, on December 23, 1889, was "Dr. C.," introduced to Mrs. Piper as Dr. Jones. Lodge offered the following abstract of the statements made by Phinuit:

You have a little lame girl, lame in the thigh, aged 13; either second or third. She's a little daisy. I do like her. Dark eyes, the gentlest of the lot; good deal of talent for music. She will be a brilliant woman; don't forget it. She has more sympathy, more mind, more – quite a little daisy. She's got a mark, a curious little mark, when you look closely over her eye, a scar through forehead over left eye. The boy's erratic; a little thing, but a little devil. Pretty good when you know him. He'll make an architect likely. Let him go to school. His mother's too nervous. It will do him good. You have a boy and two girls and a baby, four in the body. It's the little lame one I care for. There are two mothers connected with you, one named Mary. Your aunt passed out with cancer. You have indigestion, and take hot water for it. You have had a bad experience. You nearly slipped out once on the water.

In fact, one of Dr. C.'s daughters was named Daisy. Although not lame, she was deaf and dumb. Whether the mother was "too nervous" was debatable. The slipping accident took place on a yacht the previous summer. Among the false assertions not included in the abstract were the name Fanny, who was unknown to Dr. C., and the comment that someone named Fred had light hair, a brownish moustache, and a prominent nose. Also, Phinuit told Dr. C. that his thesis was about lungs, which Dr. C. denied. All other statements were factual.

Dr. C. returned later that day with his wife for another sitting. One of Lodge's servants made the mistake of announcing them by name, but Phinuit did not mention the name. Lodge again offered an abstract of the communication from Phinuit with his comments in brackets.

How's little Daisy? She will get over her cold. But there's something the matter with her head. There's somebody around you lame and somebody hard of hearing. That little girl has got music in her. This lady is fidgety. There are four of you, four going to stop with you, one gone out of the body. One got irons on his foot. Mrs. Allen, in her surroundings is the one with iron on leg. [Allen was the maiden name of the mother of the lame one.] There's about 400 of that kind of a crank. Trustworthy, but cranky. She will fly off and get married, she will. Thinks she knows everything, she does. [This is the nurse-girl, Kitty, about whom they seem to have a joke that she is a walking compendium of information.] (An envelope with letters written inside, N-H-P-O-Q, was here handed in, and Phinuit wrote down B-J-R-O-I-S, not in the best of tempers.)

36

A second cousin of your mother's drinks. The little dark-eyed one is Daisy. I like her. She can't hear very well. The lame one is a sister's child [A cousin's child, the one *née* Allen, really.] The one that's deaf in her head is the one that's got the music in her. That's Daisy, and she going to have the paints I told you of. [Fond of painting.] She's growing up to be a beautiful woman. She ought to have a paper ear. [An artificial drum had been contemplated.] You have an Aunt Eliza. There are three Maries, Mary the mother, Mary the mother, Mary the mother. [Grandmother, aunt, and granddaughter.] Three brothers and two sisters your lady had. Three in the body. There were eleven in your family, two passed out small. [Only know of nine.] Fred is going to pass out suddenly. He married a cousin. He writes. He has shining things. *Lorgnettes.* He is away. He's got a catchy trouble with heart and kidneys, and will pass out suddenly. [Not the least likely. I have inquired and find that the 'Fred' supposed to be intended is still alive in 1909. O.J.L] [5]

The errors included naming Mrs. C.'s mother as Elizabeth and saying that her father is lame. Phinuit also named Katie as one of their children, when she was the family nurse. There were another half-dozen statements which were false. Lodge noted that the most striking part of the sitting was the prominence given to Dr. C.'s favourite little daughter, Daisy, a very intelligent child of a very sweet disposition, but quite deaf. While Phinuit erroneously described her as lame, he corrected this at the second sitting. He also moved from giving her name as a mere description to correctly giving it as her name. It was correct that she was suffering from a cold at the time. However, Phinuit was wrong in his predictions regarding Daisy, as she died of influenza six months later. "A list of particulars like this makes for very dull reading," Lodge wrote, "but evidentially it is as good as can be. No possible normal means can be suggested by which these things were obtained, nor was there any fishing or guidance by the sitter. The only normal explanation is that they were hit upon by chance, but that is perfectly absurd, as any one will realize who will go through these incidents and try to apply them to himself or any friend known to him. As a matter of fact they do not apply, and cannot apply in their entirety, to anybody but the person for whom they were intended." [6]

But Lodge further noted that Dr. C. was not so impressed and remained skeptical about the whole thing. He later wrote to Lodge: "The trance state seemed natural; but had more voluntary movement than I had ever seen in an epileptic attack. The entire change in Mrs. Piper's manner and behaviour is unlike an intentional effort, and it is possible she herself believes that the conditions mean something outside of herself. With regard to the result, the misses seem to balance the hits, and the 'reading' is not so impressive as the 'sitting.' After reading over your notes I think they consist of a certain amount of thought-reading and large amount of skilful guessing."[7]

Lodge wrote that he definitely did not agree with the hasty statement that "the misses balance the hits," commenting that the hits well outnumbered the misses and went far beyond skilful guessing.

On December 21, Lodge was testing Phinuit, handing him (Mrs. Piper's hand controlled by Phinuit) various objects related to deceased individuals to divine. After Lodge gave him a photo of a deceased colleague and Phinuit accurately provided information about the colleague, Lodge handed him a letter written by Edmund Gurney, who along with Frederic Myers and Professors William Barrett and Henry Sidgwick founded the SPR in 1882. Gurney had died a year earlier, in 1888. Lodge recalled that Gurney used to sit in on his lectures on mechanics and physics and struck up a friendship with him, sometimes discussing psychic matters over lunch.

With the letter in Mrs. Piper's hand, Phinuit said he could not read it word for word, but he could tell him that it had something to do with books. Then, Phinuit seemed to leave and a new personality took "control" of Mrs. Piper's organism. It was Edmund Gurney. Lodge noted that the personality represented the Edmund Gurney he knew.

"I am here, I ethereally exist," Gurney told Lodge directly, i.e., without Phinuit facilitating, in an obviously confused manner. "I wrote to you about some books for the Society (referencing the letter in Mrs. Piper's hand). I have seen a little woman that's a medium, a true medium. I have written to Myers using her hand. I did do it, I, Edmund Gurney, I."

Lodge asked Gurney if Mrs. Piper was a medium. "Yes, she's a medium," Gurney responded. "Very few you will get like Dr. Phinuit. He is not all one would wish, but he is all right. You are Lodge. I know you. Lodge we shall beat them yet. There is no death, only a shadow and then Light. Experiment and observations are indispensable. We have to use some method like this to communicate....

"Yes, God is in Nature, all Nature is God. We are a reflection of God. Don't give up a good thing. The world will know, and our Society will know, that there is no death. I didn't know. I would have given anything to have had you come and speak to me, if you had passed away first, as I am speaking to you now."

Lodge asked Gurney if it was good on his side of the veil. "Yes, it is good," Gurney answered him. "– the only good thing. Life in the material world is beautiful. Marriage is beautiful, but this is far better." Lodge asked if there is marriage on his side. "No, no, Swedenborg was all wrong," Gurney replied. "Jesus Christ was right; he knew. He was a reflection of God."[8]

Four days later, Lodge was again sitting with Mrs. Piper and Phinuit was talking when he seemed to leave. However, Lodge heard Phinuit giving *sotto voce* (whispered) instructions to someone. It was Gurney again. Gurney then took control and spoke directly to Lodge. "It's the only way Lodge; in one sense it's bad, but in another it's good. It is her work. If I take possession of the medium's body, and she goes out, then I can use her organism to tell the world important truths. There is an infinite power above us. Lodge, believe it fully, infinite over all, most marvelous."

Gurney told Lodge that it is easy to identify a medium from his side as they appear like a ball of light. Lodge, on the other hand, appeared to him as dark and as material as possible. "They are like transparent windows to see through," Gurney continued, referring to mediums. "Lodge, it's a puzzle. It's a puzzle to us here in a way, though we understand it better than you. I work at it hard. I do. I'd give anything I possess to find out. I don't care for material things now, our interest is much greater. I am studying hard how to communicate; it's not easy. But it is only a matter of a short time before I shall be able to tell the world all sorts of things through one medium or another."

Gurney asked who the other person was sitting there and Lodge told him it was his (Lodge's) brother, who was taking notes. Lodge then asked Gurney how it is that they see things, (such as when holding a letter). "I don't know, there is something about articles worn by spirits which retains their personality and a spirit controlling a medium is sensitive to such. In nine cases out of ten they will recognize their things; it doesn't come from your mind."

The sitting continued with Gurney asking about his good friend, Frederic Myers, then telling Lodge about his initial experience after dying. "Lodge, when I passed out at first I didn't know who I was, nor where I was. I hunted about for my friends and for my body. Soon however my sisters welcomed me. Three of them, all drowned. If I see Myers I will talk to him. No spirit in the spirit world is more anxious to let friends know than I was." Apparently, as evidence that it was actually him, Gurney gave the name of his wife, Kate, and his sister,

Ellen. Lodge then asked Gurney to tell him more about Phinuit. Gurney responded:

> Dr. Phinuit is a peculiar type of man; he goes about continually and is thrown in with everybody. He is eccentric and quaint but good hearted. I wouldn't do the things he does for anything. He lowers himself sometimes; it's a great pity. He has very curious ideas about things and people; he receives a great deal about people from themselves. And he gets expressions and phrases that one doesn't care for, vulgar phrases he picks up by meeting uncanny people through the medium. These things tickle him and he goes about repeating them. He said to me the other day, 'Mr. Gurney what do you think a gentleman said to me the other day: he said, 'put that in your pipe and smoke it, Doctor.' He picks up this sort of thing and it tickles him. He has to interview a great number of people and has no easy berth of it. A high type of man couldn't do the work he does. But he is a good-hearted old fellow. Good-bye Lodge. Here's the Doctor coming. [9]

When Phinuit took control back from Gurney, he asked Lodge if Gurney had been there and talked with him. Lodge replied that he had. At a sitting on February 3, 1890, Phinuit again gave way to Gurney. Lodge noted a significant change in voice, one that seemed to be more educated (in the ability to communicate) than in the earlier sittings. "It is wonderfully difficult to communicate," Gurney said. "All the time I've been here I have only found two mediums besides this one. More people might be mediums, but many won't when they can." Lodge asked Gurney what it is that constitutes a good medium. "Not too much spirituality and not too much animalism, not the highest people and not the lowest," Gurney replied. "Sympathetic and not too self-conscious, able to let their minds be given up to another – that sort of person – easily influenced. Many could, but their pride and a sense of self comes in and spoils it." [10]

After some additional dialogue between the two, Gurney said that Phinuit would soon return. "He's a good old man," he repeated some of his earlier description of Phinuit. "He has a hard place. I wouldn't do the work he does for anything. Seeing all manner of people and hunting up their friends, and often he has hard work to persuade them that they are really wanted." Lodge asked if Phinuit is reliable. "Not perfectly," Gurney continued. "He is not a bit infallible. He mixes things terribly sometimes. He does his best; he's a good old man but he does get confused, and when he can't hear distinctly he fills it up himself. He does invent things occasionally, he certainly does. Sometimes he has very hard work."

Lodge then asked about Phinuit's medical prescriptions. "Oh, he's a shrewd doctor," Gurney assured him. "He knows his business thoroughly. He can see into people and is very keen on their complaints. Yes, he is good in that way, very good."

When Lodge asked about Phinuit's ability to see into the future, and if Gurney could see ahead, Gurney said that he hadn't "gone into that," but that Phinuit "can see a little sometimes" and that Phinuit could do many things that he could not do as he had studied them a good deal.[11]

Gurney then told Lodge that he must go, after which the medium appeared to sleep for a few moments before awakening in the Phinuit personality. Here again, Lodge reported that the dramatic character of the speaking was more impressive than the things said. "The naturalness of the change in manner and memory was very pronounced," Lodge explained. "A reader may think that this is due to the perfection of conscious acting, while a sitter of any experience will hardly think that. The fluctuation of memory is certainly not artificial; it is a genuine change of personality – whatever that may be...unmistakably analogous to multiple personality, whether that be ever due to control by actual possession or not...."[12]

When Lodge asked Phinuit why Gurney could take control of Mrs. Piper but others had to relay messages through Phinuit, Phinuit explained that it was too difficult, but Gurney's experience in psychical research helped him better understand the method. "He comes and turns me out sometimes," Phinuit told Lodge. "It would be a very narrow place into which Mr. Gurney couldn't get."[13]

At a sitting on December 24, 1889, only Lodge and a shorthand reporter named Briscoe were present at the beginning of the trance, but Mary Lodge, Lodge's wife, later joined them. Phinuit was initially confused, thinking that Lodge was Dr. C., the prior sitter. After Phinuit realized it was Lodge, Lodge handed the entranced medium an old gold watch that had belonged to his deceased Uncle Jerry and which had been sent to him by his Uncle Robert, Jerry's twin brother, that very morning. Lodge asked Phinuit if he could tell him anything about the watch. Phinuit immediately said it had belonged to one of Lodge's uncles. Shortly thereafter, Phinuit said, as if impersonating Uncle Jerry, "This is my watch, and Robert is my brother, and I am here. Uncle Jerry, my watch."[14]

Lodge considered telepathy as an explanation for this and asked Phinuit if Uncle Jerry could recall some trivial details about his (Jerry's) boyhood – something unknown to him (Oliver) but known to his Uncle Robert. Uncle Jerry then recalled episodes of swimming a creek together and running a risk of drowning, killing a cat in Smith's field, the possession of a small rifle and of a long peculiar skin, like a snakeskin, which he thought was now in the possession of Robert.

Lodge checked with his Uncle Robert to determine if he recalled such boyhood incidents. Robert confirmed all but the killing of the cat, but he admitted that his memory was failing him. However, another brother, Frank, clearly recalled the cat-killing incident in Smith's field in Barking, Essex, where they lived and played.

At another sitting that same day, with Mr. and Mrs. Isaac Thompson, neighbors of the Lodges', present, and Alfred Lodge, Oliver's brother, Phinuit began by greeting Lodge, addressing him for some unexplained reason as "Captain." The stenographer recorded:

**Phinuit:** "Hulloa, Captain, I've been talking to your friends. Had a long talk with Uncle Jerry. He remembers you now, as a boy with Aunt Anne, but you were kind of small. [Lodge confirmed that this is how Uncle Jerry would have remembered him.] He knew you but he didn't know me very well; wondered what the devil I wanted trying to talk to him and how I got here. Yes, he remembers his watch – it's in possession of Robert. He used to call him Bob. [Mrs. Piper/Phinuit then took watch in hand.] Ha! Well this watch came from Russia – yes, Uncle Jerry said so. [Lodge doubted this.] Who are these people over there?"

**Lodge:** "Mr. & Mrs. Thompson."

**Phinuit:** "Oh! Why that's the gentleman to whom his father sends his love and said something about Ted. Didn't you tell him?"

**Lodge:** "Yes, I did, but wasn't sure you meant him."

**Phinuit:** "Of course I did. They're a couple, they are. One wants to do something and the other doesn't. [It was confirmed that Mr. & Mrs. Thompson had different views on a current problem.] I say, Captain, your friends have a lot to tell you, they're just clamoring to get at you. Why the devil don't you give them a chance?"

**Lodge:** "Well, next time."

**Phinuit:** "There's Marion—Agnes Ha, ha. I got it that time – Adnes-Agnes."

**Mr. Thompson:** "Agnes, all right." [Watch was again placed in Mrs. Piper's hand. It was a repeater and happened to go off.]

**Phinuit:** "Hullo, I didn't do that. Jerry did that, to remind you of him. Here, take it away – it goes springing off—it's alive."

**Mrs. Thompson:** "What can we do for Theodora's headaches?"

**Phinuit:** "Nerves of stomach out of order. Have you got anything of hers to give me?"

**Lodge:** [To Mr. Thompson] "Go and get a lock of her hair."

**Phinuit:** "It was Uncle Jerry, the one that had the fall. I'll bring you some more news of him. Give me back his nine-shooter [referring to the watch on the table.] (Isaac Thompson returned with a lock of Theodora's hair, at which time Phinuit ordered Lodge and his brother out of the room.) I don't care to talk diseases before everybody. [Phinuit then suggested some old-fashioned herb remedies for Theodora.] Confound it, I saw your influence before anyone else here [spoken to Mr. Thompson]. Didn't the Captain tell you? You lost your purse, and if you had told me I could have found it...Mighty mean trick about the purse! Lord! Done as quick as a fly. [Thompson recalled losing his purse 30 years earlier, a very serious matter at the time.] Who is the lady [who] wears a cap in the spirit? She don't (sic) part her hair in the middle – she sends her love to you." [addressing Mrs. Thompson.]

**Mrs. Thompson:** "Perhaps it is my mother."

**Phinuit:** "Well, I see more than a dozen ladies, but she wears a lace cap. There was some throat trouble in your mother [Mrs. Piper grasping her throat.] (Mrs. Thompson confirmed that her mother always wore a lace cap with ribbons to hide a lump on her throat; also she parted her hair on the side.) The mother of one of you is in the body. I think it is the gentleman's. She is an angel—she is a good woman—has

43

some trouble with ankle – left one – it catches her. She will be with you for some time." [Mr. Thompson confirmed that his mother, aged 81, was still alive and was suffering from rheumatic pains in her left ankle at the time.] [15]

The following day, Christmas, Lodge and his brother, Alfred, sat with Mrs. Piper. After she became entranced, Phinuit told the two men that their mother, father, Aunt Anne, and Uncle Jerry were all concerned about their (Oliver and Alfred's) sister. However, Phinuit referred to her as Ellen, when her name was actually Eleanor. Lodge confirmed that his sister was having physical problems and was certain that Mrs. Piper did not know of Eleanor or her problems. However, he asked Phinuit to try and get her correct name from his departed relatives. Phinuit asked for a pencil and wrote the name "Nellie," commenting that it was Aunt Anne who wrote it. Lodge noted that Nellie was Eleanor's nickname.

In a later sitting that day, Phinuit told Lodge that he met Mrs. Piper's spirit going out as he was taking over her body, and he noted that she was crying. He asked Lodge if he knew why she was crying and Lodge surmised that she had been separated from her children for a few days and had been feeling rather low.

Phinuit then said that their mother's influence was there and very strong. The entranced Mrs. Piper took Oliver's hand and felt the ring he had put on his hand just before the sitting, correctly identifying the ring as having belonged to Aunt Anne. Aunt Anne then took control of Mrs. Piper and said, "And Olly dear, that's one of the last things I ever gave you. It was one of the last things I said to you in the body when I gave it to you for Mary. I said, 'For her, through you.'" Lodge confirmed this as accurate, recalling that the ring was Aunt Anne's most valuable trinket. "Keep it in memory of me, for I am not dead," Aunt Anne continued. "Each spirit is not so dim that it cannot recollect its belongings to the body. They attract us if there has been anything special about them. I tell you, my boy, I can see it just as plain as if I were in the body..." [16]

The following day, with Mary Lodge, Oliver's wife, present, Phinuit accurately diagnosed her illness and prescribed a mixture of wild carrot infusion and laudanum lotions for her, giving detailed instructions. He further recommended Uvae Ursi, which he described as a wild cranberry. For her third son, after accurately describing his ailment, Phinuit recommended Huxum's tincture of cinchona, 2 ounces,

French lialyzed iron, and 4 ounces of druggists' simple syrup with a few drops of lemon juice, milk, lime water, and eggs.

Phinuit then talked about a painting of Mary's deceased brother. Mary asked who painted the picture. Phinuit asked her to wait a bit while he asked her brother. He came back with the fact that Mary had painted it, another correct statement. Phinuit then announced that Mary's Aunt Izzie (Isabella) was there, "beautiful as ever and as pure as snow." Isabella then took control of Mrs. Piper's body and said:

> I tell you dear thing, to be as brave as I was – always do the best you can; do what your conscience tells you. Take that advice from Isabella. Oh, what larks we had! Oh! (Laughing all over.) Do you remember Clara? [Mrs. Piper laughing again and jigging about in her chair.] I'll sing for you. Why, Mary dear, who ever thought to see you again like this, and Oliver, too? Oh, such fun! What shall I do for you now I'm here? [Mary Lodge asked her to sing one of her songs.] Shall I? You used to sing and play some yourself. Your papa and I have more fun that you could shake a stick at. Mary, how fat you are! Where are your crimps? [Mrs. Piper feeling Mary's hair] You used to crimp it. [noted by Lodge as true]. Getting lazy, eh? Well, this is fun to see you again. Oh, I do feel so happy. [17]

At that point, Phinuit returned, chuckling, commenting that he had never seen such a merry girl as Isabella. Lodge called this sitting an "extraordinary episode" and very realistic as Aunt Izzy came through just as they had remembered her. Aunt Izzy returned at the next sitting, Phinuit announcing her and then stepping aside as she further communicated:

> Shall I sing to you? What would you like? You have not been well lately. Are you glad to hear of Aunt Izzie? I could almost come back and die over again to see you. You tell Mary (Mary Lodge's mother, also named Mary) that her sister Isabel still lives; tell her she has done nobly; tell her William and I are together. That lazy gardener. [18]

Lodge noted that this was also very evidential in that his mother-in-law had been recently widowed and her gardener had been very troublesome. Many other evidential facts were offered, including Phinuit accurately describing how Mary Lodge's father had died by falling down the hold of a ship, while also accurately reporting on the death of her stepfather.

"I took every precaution that I could think of, and on the whole the result of the Piper enquiry was conclusive," Lodge wrote, adding that he was "thoroughly convinced, not only of human survival, but of the power to communicate under certain conditions, with those left behind on the earth."[19]

But Dr. Walter Leaf, another member of the SPR who had a number of sittings with Mrs. Piper, was not so impressed. He noted that Phinuit showed a "complete ignorance of French" and often seemed to be "fishing" for answers (apparently not considering that Phinuit was fishing for interpretations). He also felt that a certain amount of muscle reading was taking place "On the whole, then," Leaf concluded, "the effect which a careful study of all the reports of the English sittings has left in my mind is this: That Dr. Phinuit is only a name for Mrs. Piper's secondary personality, assuming the name and acting the part with the aptitude and consistency which is shown by secondary personalities in other known cases."[20]

In effect, Leaf saw this secondary personality as reading the minds of the sitters and otherwise tapping into some cosmic soul for information that was not known to the sitters, a view consistent with Professor James's public stance at the time. Leaf offered no opinion as to Mrs. Piper's other controls or how many secondary personalities a person might have. Responding to Leaf, Lodge wrote: "Is thought-transference from the sitter, of however free and unconscious a kind, a complete and sufficient mode of accounting for the facts? Mr. Leaf definitely takes the position that...it is sufficient, and, considering the large amount of labor he has spent on the documents, his opinion is entitled to very great weight. For myself, I am not so convinced, but I cordially admit the difficulty of any disproof of his position..."[21]

Frederick Myers, who made all the arrangements for Mrs. Piper to visit England, had a number of sittings with her and, as the story goes, received much in the way of communications from a former love interest, Annie Marshall, who died in 1876, but because of the very personal nature of the messages and the fact that Myers was then married, it was never made public. It was said that his wife destroyed the transcripts of the sittings.

Summing up Mrs. Piper's visit to England, Myers reported, in part:

We took great pains to avoid giving information in talk; and a more complete security is to be found in the fact that we were ourselves ignorant of many of the facts given as to our friends' relations, etc. As regards my own affairs, I have not thought it worth while to cite *in extenso* such statements as might possibly have been got up beforehand; since Mrs. Piper of course knew that I should be one of the sitters. Such facts as that I once had an aunt, 'Cordelia Marshall, more commonly called Corrie,' might have been learnt – though I do not think that they were learnt – from printed or other sources. But I do not think that any larger proportion of such accessible facts was given to me than to an average sitter, previously unknown; nor were there any of those subtler points which could so easily have been made by dint of scrutiny of my books or papers. On the other hand, in my case, as in the case of several other sitters, there were messages purporting to come from a friend who had been dead many years, and mentioning circumstances which I believe that it would have been quite impossible for Mrs. Piper to have discovered.

I am also acquainted with some of the facts given to other sitters, and suppressed as too intimate, or as involving secrets not the property of the sitter alone. I may say that, so far as my own personal conviction goes, the utterances of one or two of these facts is even more conclusive of supernormal knowledge than the correct statement of dozens of names of relations, etc., which the sitter had no personal motive for concealing.

On the whole, I believe that all observers, both in America and in England, who have seen enough of Mrs. Piper in both states to be able to form a judgment, will agree in affirming (1) that many of the facts given could not have been learned even by skilled detectives; (2) that to learn others of them, although possible, would have needed an expenditure of money as well as of time which it seems impossible to suppose that Mrs. Piper could have met; and (3) that her conduct has never given any ground whatever for supposing her capable of fraud or trickery. Few persons have been so long and so carefully observed; and she has left on all observers the impression of thorough uprightness, candor, and honesty. [22]

Returning to the U.S. from England during February, Mrs. Piper did not resume sittings until December that year as the trip had exhausted her. She was especially stressed and strained by the secrecy aspect, as she was unable to really socialize with any of her hosts or their families. However, Alta Piper later recalled that her mother was never too busy or too tired to listen to and sympathize with her and Minerva, offering wise counsel, and teaching them that prayer was the greatest force for good in life. She never failed to hear their good-night prayers and say "God bless you darlings," before leaving the girls to their nurse's care.

[1] Lodge (1932) 345

[2] _____, 346

[3] Lodge (1909), 204-205

[4] _____, 216

[5] _____, 217-219

[6] _____, 219

[7] _____, 220

[8] Holt, 432

[9] _____, 433-434

[10] _____, 435

[11] _____, 436

[12] _____, 437

[13] _____, 437

[14] Lodge, (1909), 228

[15] Holt, 439-440

[16] _____, 441-442

[17] _____, 444-445

[18] _____, 445

[19] Lodge (1932), 279

[20] Holt, 451

[21] _____, 455

[22] Myers, 384-385

# -Four-

# Confusion &
# Mixed Opinions

*Neither the religious nor the scientific[person] can longer
afford to ignore the facts presented here, to pass them by.*
 – **Frederic W. H. Myers**

By the time Leonora Piper completed her English sittings in February 1890, fraud had been completely ruled out by all who had closely observed her a number of times, and it was clear to them that there was something *supernormal* going on. The issue was whether it was spirits or Mrs. Piper's alter ego – a secondary personality buried in her subconscious – which, unbeknownst to her primary personality, was telepathically picking up the information from sitters or even from people not present (called teloteropathy), or even from some cosmic reservoir or "universal mind." As earlier states, the latter explanation still defied the mechanistic laws of accepted science and seemed to many even more fantastic than the spirit/survival hypothesis, but it was more acceptable to many educated men, including Doctors James, Hodgson, and Leaf, as it did not revert to the "silly superstitions" of organized religion, especially spirits of the dead or ghosts. Lodge and Myers were more inclined to accept the spirit/survival explanation, but were not prepared to go public with their views until some years later.

Reading between the lines of the various reports, one might conclude that none of the researchers was willing to publicly oppose the views of Professor James, or at least to go beyond what James had hypothesized.

Such dissent might very well have involved alienation or professional suicide. And yet, James's theories of the various Piper phenomena often seemed shallow and evasive. Writing in the November 1919 issue of the ASPR Journal, Dr. James Hyslop, who had been a professor of logic and ethics at Columbia University before becoming a full-time psychical researcher, wrote:

> [James's] interest in psychic research was partly determined by his scientific tendencies, which required him to take into account all the facts, and his difficulties with the spiritistic hypothesis were determined by the extent of his allegiance to scientific hypotheses which he had rejected without realizing that he had done so. When it came to that one doctrine and the application of his view to it, he halted with more respect than the logic of his pragmatism required...

> The fact is that he never clearly understood the problem of psychic research. This is clearly proved by his anomalous and paradoxical position in the Ingersoll lecture on the immortality of the Soul, delivered at Harvard University. He had very little to do with the Society's work, tho the public thought he had much to do with it, and after he had rejected the spiritual body doctrine of Swedenborg it was hard to make him see just what the tendencies of psychic research were. He returned to what he ought to have regarded as wallowing in the mire of Hegelianism when he felt a leaning toward the cosmic reservoir theory. But this aside, the main point is that he could never boldly decide between the respectable philosophy of pantheism or monism and the logical tendencies of his pluralism which should have taken him with less evidence into spiritism than would be required to convert the materialist.[1]

Of course, there were those who were convinced that Mrs. Piper was a charlatan. As noted in Chapter Two, Dr. O. F. Wodsworth considered his sitting a failure. Dr. Samuel A. Hopkins called it all "rubbish," and John F. Brown concluded that it was just good guesswork on Mrs. Piper's part. In England, a Professor Macalister claimed that her trance condition was an act and that the whole thing was an "imposture," and a very poor one. [2]

Well before Mrs. Piper's mediumship was discovered, Spiritualists recognized that harmony was a very essential part of a good sitting and that negativity somehow defeated phenomena. Séances often began with singing and prayers in order to establish harmony and a rapport with the "spirits." Once he came to believe in spirits, Richard Hodgson likened it to a post-accident scene, seeing the communicating spirit, often bewildered and confused by the change in vibrations, much the same as the dazed accident victim, who needs sympathy and consolation more than a cross-examination as to how the accident happened. When suddenly faced with dozens of factual questions, he is unable to focus or clear his mind.

A number of Spiritualists reported waiting an hour or longer for conditions to be harmonious enough for the spirits to get through, and there were times when the "spirits" were able to communicate enough to instruct them that a certain person in the room was obstructing communication. There were also times when the "spirits" asked the sitters to change positions in the room as some kind of flow or balance in polarity was necessary for them to effectively communicate. As Dr. R. Craig Hogan, a modern-day researcher, understands it, we on the earth plane must raise our vibrations while the discarnates must lower theirs to find just the right channel or "sweet spot" at which we and they can meet. "They spend years trying to find that channel and refine the connection," Hogan explains. "Raising our vibration requires a harmonious, loving, spiritual atmosphere. However, the energy on the Earth plane today is very dense and negative. Those living on other planes of life describe coming into the Earth plane's vibration as like trying to penetrate a deep, dark fog because of the conflict, hatred, greed, and violence in the world today."[3]

Such negativity and lack of harmony might explain Mrs. Piper's failures. While skeptics and debunkers find such an explanation self-serving and even humorous, scoffing at the whole idea, some of those studying Mrs. Piper recognized that the attitude of the sitters had a bearing on the quality of the phenomena. Henry Holt, an SPR member, author, and publisher who sat with Mrs. Piper, put it this way:

> People in general, including sitters, fall into two classes: those of the intuitive, humanistic, and sympathetic make-up, and those of the calculating scientific, skeptical make-up – 'Platonists and Aristotelians.' The first group, I need hardly say, includes the poets and most of those generally called philosophers – Socrates, Plato, and Goethe. The second group includes Aristotle, Bacon, and Spencer, all of whom the 'high priori' philosophers hardly admit to be philosophers at all.

Now the first group seems to include the dreamers and the mediums. Socrates with his inner voice and his hours of sleepless unconsciousness, was in all probability a medium; and Plato and Goethe were both great dreamers; while regarding Aristotle, Bacon, and Spencer I cannot recall at the moment any assertion of remarkable dreams.

Now it is noticeable through the reports that scientific men, especially those devoted to the inorganic sciences, get very little out of the sittings, and are disposed to vote them all humbug. Sir Oliver Lodge is a marked exception. Sir William Crookes and Sir William Barrett have devoted themselves mainly to the telekinetic phenomena.

I am as far as possible from intimating that either class is superior to the other. It would be interesting to debate whether we owe more to Shakespeare or to Spencer, although I should hardly take Shakespeare for the mediumistic type of man, but rather (if you and God will forgive me), for the medium-mystic, and he is always in *medio tutissimus.*

Assuming the generalizations in the preceding paragraphs to be well founded, we might risk a much more uncertain one – that as truth is generally indicated first to the intuitive type of mind – Kant with the nebular hypothesis and Goethe with the relations of the vertebrae to the skeleton and the leaves to the plant – so the free appearance of the phenomena of mediumship to the intuitive type of person, and the scant appearance to the scientific type, have a certain correspondence with Nature's general ways, and so far raise a presumption that the phenomena are normal and deserve study...It is not surprising, then, to be told that Professor Macalister's sitting was "unsatisfactory," and it is an amusingly incorrect one throughout.[4]

Some researchers, including even William James, were turned off by the triviality of most of the messages, apparently assuming that all spirits were advanced enough to communicate meaningful messages. James wrote:

The *prima facie* theory, which is that of a spirit-control, is hard to reconcile with the extreme triviality of most of the communications. What real spirit, at least able to revisit his wife on this earth, but would find something better to say than that she had changed the place of his photograph? And yet that is the sort of remark to which the spirits introduced by the mysterious Phinuit are apt to confine themselves. I must admit, however, that Phinuit has other moods. He has several times, when my wife and myself were sitting together with him, suddenly started off on long lectures to us about our inward defects and outward shortcomings, which were very earnest, as well as subtle morally and psychologically, and impressive in a high degree. These discourses, though given in Phinuit's own person, were very different in style from his more usual talk, and probably superior to anything that the medium could produce in the same line in her natural state.[5]

If James was aware of the profound messages which had come through other mediums during the 35 years before he came upon Mrs. Piper, he did not mention them or even allude to them. Books by Judge John Edmonds, Professor Robert Hare, Allan Kardec, and William Stainton Moses had offered a whole new philosophy of life and death allegedly based on the teachings of advanced or elevated spirits.

In their 1853 book, *Spiritualism*, Edmonds, Chief Justice of the New York State Supreme Court, and George T. Dexter, a New York physician, set forth the teachings of Emanuel Swedenborg and Francis Bacon as communicated through Dr. Dexter's trance mediumship. Swedenborg and Bacon eloquently explained the nature of reality and the meaning of life in a manner that appeals to reason. "It is not for the purpose of showing to the world that spirits can confer with man, or that God's law obtains in spirit-connection as well as physical, but it is for the purpose of showing you the truths of your spirit-life, after the spirit has left the body, that we leave our high estate and the blissful life of the spheres, and come to teach you," Swedenborg communicated..[6]

Edmonds, who began his investigation of mediums with the intent of debunking them, concluded that there was a high order of intelligence involved – "an intelligence outside of, and beyond, mere mortal agency; for there was no other hypothesis which I could devise or hear of, that could at all explain that, whose reality is established by the testimony of tens of thousands, and can easily be ascertained by any one who will take the trouble to inquire."[7]

When Edmonds asked what the manifestations were all about, the answer came: "It is the result of human progress, it is in execution, not a suspension of nature's laws, and it is not now for the first time manifesting itself, but in all ages of the world has at times been displayed."[8] He was further informed that the manifestations began a dozen or so years before the "Rochester Knockings" in 1848, but from fear of ridicule or from ignorance they went unrecognized.

Edmonds was also informed by Swedenborg and Bacon that his knowledge of nature was too imperfect to permit him to understand the phenomena and was referred to Karl Von Reichenbach's *Dynamics of Magnetism* for a better grasp of the subject. There, Edmonds learned that Von Reichenbach had discovered an unknown power in nature, which he called Od, or Odic Force, describing it as "an exceeding subtle fluid, existing with magnetism and electricity, found in fire and heat, and produced in the human body by the chemical action of respiration and digestion and decomposition, and issuing from the body in the shape of a pale flame, with sparks, and smoke, and material in its nature, though so much sublimated as to be visible only to persons of a peculiar vision." [9] (Von Reichenbach's od was apparently what was later referred to as teleplasm and ectoplasm.)

Dr. Dexter also began as a skeptic and sat with a number of mediums before he discovered his own mediumistic ability. He continued to sit with and observe other mediums and wrote:

> I have listened to the most elevated thoughts couched in language far beyond [the medium's] comprehension, describing facts in science, and circumstances in the daily life of the spirit after death, which were corroborated fact by fact, idea by idea, by other mediums with whom she was entirely unacquainted, uttered by a little girl scarce nine years old. The same medium I have heard repeat verse after verse, impromptu, of poetry, glowing with inspiration and sparkling with profound thought and sentiment, and yet this child never wrote a line of poetry before in her life...I have heard an illiterate mechanic repeat Greek, Latin, Hebrew, and Chaldaic, and describe the customs and habits of men living on the earth thousands of years ago. I have been present when a medium answered many questions in the Italian language, of which she was ignorant, and also uttered several sentences in the same language, and then gave the name of an Italian gentleman of whom she had never heard, but who was when living the friend of one of the party of the circle." [10]

At one of the séances, Edmonds asked the communicating spirit, Lord Bacon, what it was all about. Bacon replied through the entranced Dexter:

What, indeed, is the object of this new revelation? It is certain that a mere belief in the upside-down tipping of a table can be of no vital benefit to any individual or to his race. Tables may be moved and raps may be heard, but these evidences of a power not materially existing in this world can satisfy no thinking man if there were not something beyond all this worthy of being understood. Now, what is this? It is that man has not been taught his true relation even to the life he now enjoys, or his connection with that other state of existence beyond the grave. Educated after the fashion of some one sect, men imbibe certain notions characterizing that sect, which are not absolute revelations from God, or even predicated on his laws, but are the positive creations of mind materially influenced, and thus do not in the least exemplify the design of our existence or the purpose of death. If the laws of God had not been instituted for a purpose as important as his character is omnipotent, there probably would have been some different manifestation of life than that which now gives significancy to the whole material creation. But death was just as much an object following life, as was the gift or establishment of life itself. Therefore, death was to be understood, or, at least, should be, for one great idea belonging to death has scarcely been apprehended, or, in fact, appreciated. Death is the continuance-life; it is life without the restraints imposed upon it by the limits of a single planet. Now, though it is important that the designs of life should be investigated and understood, it certainly is of as much importance that that life in its continuance should be perfectly appreciated, for the one is of short duration, and the other is for eternity. This, then, is the object of spirit-communication, and it behooves all believers to understand what they believe, that when satisfied themselves they may be able to satisfy others.[11]

Hare, a professor emeritus of chemistry at the University of Pennsylvania, scoffed at the whole idea of mediumship before he began investigating the "popular madness" in 1853. Over a period of some 14 months, he sat with "22 or 23" different mediums and became a convert to Spiritualism. His 1855 book, *Experimental Investigation of the Spirit Manifestations,* detailed his investigation and his newfound philosophy, one that held that there were degrees of gradation between the lowest degrees of vice, ignorance, and folly and those of virtue, learning, and wisdom [in the afterlife realms]. One's initial place in the afterlife environment, he was told, was based on a sort of "moral specific gravity." Moreover, he was informed that spirits cannot effectively approach a medium who is much above or much below their particular level.

When Hare asked about the purpose of the mediumship epidemic, he was informed that it was "a deliberate effort on the part of the inhabitants of the higher spheres to break through the partition which has interfered with the attainment, by mortals, of a correct idea of their destiny after death." [12] To carry out this intention, he was told, a delegation of advanced spirits had been appointed. He was further informed that lower spirits were allowed to take part in the undertaking because they were better able to make mechanical movements and loud rappings than those on the higher realms.

Hare was told that the spirits encountered much difficulty in communicating. "As there are no words in the human language in which spiritual ideas may be embodied so as to convey their literal and exact signification, we are obliged oftimes to have recourse to the use of analogisms and metaphorical modes of expression," his deceased father informed him. "In our communication with you we have to comply with the peculiar structure and rules of your language; but the genius of our language is such that we can impart more ideas to each other in a single word than you can possibly convey in a hundred." [13]

While Edmonds and Hare were investigating mediumship in the United States, Kardec, a French educator, was conducting investigations in his own country. Among the superior spirits purportedly communicating with Kardec were John the Evangelist, St. Augustine, St. Vincent De Paul, St. Louis, "The Spirit of Truth," Socrates, Plato, Fénélon, Franklin, and Swedenborg. They answered questions on every conceivable subject, including God, pantheism, universal space, biblical accounts of creation, reincarnation, relationships beyond the grave, possession, the fate of children beyond the grave, spirit influence, war, capital punishment, slavery, dreams, free will, suicide, and fear of death, to name just some. As an example, on the subject of spirit possession, Kardec asked if a spirit can temporarily assume the physical envelope of a living person. "A spirit does not enter into a body as you enter into a house," was the reply. "He assimilates himself to an incarnate spirit who has the same defects and the same qualities as himself, in order that they may act conjointly, but it is always the incarnate spirit who acts at his pleasure on the matter with which he is clothed." [14] The communicating spirit further explained that the will-power of an upright man can attract the cooperation of good spirits, which will help him resist the mischievous spirit.

Kardec's questions were numerous, 1,019 of them detailed in question and answer form in his 1857 book and more to be asked later. When he asked if spirits ever take part in our occupations and pleasures, the reply came: "Commonplace spirits, as you call them, do so. They are incessantly about you, and take, in all you do, a part which is sometimes a very active one, according to their nature; and it is necessary that they should do so, in order to push men on in the different walks of life, and to excite or moderate their passions." [15]

And up in England, beginning in 1872, Moses, an Anglican priest and college educator who was initially opposed to mediumship, began receiving messages from a band of spirits under the direction of one calling himself Imperator. "I, myself, Imperator Servus Dei, am the chief of a band of forty-nine spirits, the presiding and controlling spirit, under whose guidance and direction the others work," the words came through Moses at one of the early sittings. "I come from the seventh sphere to work out the will of the Almighty; and, when my work is complete, I shall return to those spheres of bliss from which none returns again to earth. But this will not be till the medium's work on earth is finished, and his mission on earth exchanged for a wider one in the spheres." [16]

Imperator added that spirits named Rector and Doctor were his immediate assistants, while Swedenborg was one of the 49. He had come, Imperator said, to explain the spirit world, how it is controlled, and the way in which information is conveyed to humans. "Man must judge according to the light of reason that is in him." Imperator voiced through Moses. "That is the ultimate standard, and the progressive soul will receive what the ignorant or prejudiced will reject. God's truth is forced on none." [17]

Initially, the messages came through Moses by trance-speaking and were recorded by several friends who had formed a mediumship circle. On March 30, 1873, the spirit messages started coming through Moses's hand by means of automatic writing rather than by trance-speaking. This method was adopted, Moses was informed, for convenience purposes and so that he could preserve a connected body of teaching. Those teachings were compiled in two books, *Spirit Teachings*, published by Moses in 1883, and *More Spirit Teachings*, collected and published after his death in 1892.

At one sitting, Imperator communicated:

We have frequently said that God reveals Himself as man can bear it. It must need be so. He is revealed through a human medium, and can only be made known in such measure as the medium can receive the communication. It is impossible that knowledge of God should outstrip man's capacity. Were we now to tell you – if we could – of our more perfect theology it would seem to you strange and unintelligible. We shall, by slow degrees, instill into your mind so much of truth as you can receive, and then you shall see your present errors. But that is not yet. Indeed, since the conception which each frames for himself is to him his God, it cannot be that revelation can be in advance of capacity. It is in the nature of things impossible.[18]

Moses was informed that Swedenborg and Benjamin Franklin, working together on the spirit side of the veil, figured out how to communicate with the earth realm by means of raps, the initial method of getting messages through. Imperator communicated that there were barriers to communication, stating:

The busy world is ever averse from the things of spirit life. Men become so absorbed in the material, that which they can see and grasp, and hoard up, and they forget that there is a future and spirit life. They become so earthly that they are impervious to our influence; so material that we cannot come near them; so full of earthly interests that there is no room for that which shall endure when they have passed away. More than this, the constant preoccupation leaves no time for contemplation, and the spirit is wasted for lack of sustenance. The spiritual state is weak; the body is worn and weary with weight of work and anxious care, and the spirit is well-nigh inaccessible. The whole air, moreover, is heavy with conflicting passions, with heart-burnings, and jealousies, and contentions, and all that is inimical to us.[19]

Compared with the teachings recorded by Edmonds, Hare, Kardec, and Moses, the communications coming through Mrs. Piper were indeed "trivial," as James labeled them. On the other hand, James also noted that Dr. Phinuit often lectured on serious subjects, but apparently nobody bothered to record Phinuit's words in those lectures. James, Hodgson, and the other researchers were looking for evidential communication, not the unverifiable "truths" recorded by Edmonds and the others. Perhaps, those advanced spirits who saw fit to provide enlightenment decided that, after 35 years, they had given as much "light" as they could and decided to withdraw or turn it over to lower level spirits, as Dr. Phinuit seems to have been, to provide more evidential communication.

Some of the difficulties of spirit communication were communicated to Sir William Crookes, one of England's most esteemed scientist, when Crookes investigated the mediumship of Daniel Dunglas Home during the early 1870s. At a sitting on June 28, 1871, Home went into a trance state and a voice began speaking through him. One of Crookes's guests asked who was speaking. "It is not one spirit in particular," the reply came. "It is a general influence. It requires two or three spirits to get complete control over Dan. The conditions are not very good tonight." The communicating spirits were then asked to explain what the conditions should be. "That is a matter in which we cannot help you much," the spirits responded. "There are comparatively few spirits who are able to communicate at all with you. They are constantly working and experimenting to try and render the communication easier. They practice on some of you when you are asleep and in that way your dreams are influenced. Sometimes they think they have found out some of the conditions which will lead to success, and the next time something occurs which shows them that they know scarcely anything about it." Crookes noted that voices were sometimes heard in which one invisible being seemed to be instructing another invisible being on how to effect a levitation with Home.

The communicating spirits went on to say that it was like trying to get a wayward child to do what one wishes, but they continue to experiment. They added that some spirits cannot do anything because even though they have the desire they don't have the knowledge. "There are two standing here now who would like to communicate, but it would be quite impossible for them to make the slightest manifestation to you. They will be obliged to get others to tell what they wish to say. You, William, should not have had that electric light. It hurt Dan's head, and we were obliged to entrance him to calm him...It was too dazzling for Dan."[20]

There apparently was much in the way of profoundness that came through the entranced Home, but very little of it was recorded. One that was recorded, however, was this:

You do not know the difficulties that have to be overcome in communicating with you. Supposing now we want to make manifestations, four spirits would perhaps take possession of the four corners of the room, and would begin, as it were, to throw across to each other, and weave together their harmonizing influence, so as to get everything equalized and prepared for the adoption of whatever they want to do. One spirit will remain in the midst who will manage and direct all that is to be said – of course, if one of the other spirits wishes to communicate he would let him do so, they are not selfish, but one must have the direction of the manifestations to ensure unity of purpose. That is why it is so bad to wish for the presence of any particular spirit; that spirit might come, and the others not being selfish would admit him into the circle, and he not being in harmony with the others, would destroy the whole thing.[21]

And this:

Spiritual truth must come; truth is a lighthouse, a beacon, a speck, a point, leading onward to realms of love. We have no power, we can do so little that we often wonder that we are able to do anything for you. Language is too imperfect, we cannot convey to you our meaning; you cannot understand; our state is so different from your material state, that it is with great difficulty that we can work upon it to make our presence known; not that it is painful to us – no, no, it is a labour of love. But still it is an actual labour to us. The earth is still so imperfect – so underdeveloped – that we have much difficulty in dealing with material objects.[22]

It was James who arranged for Hyslop to have his first sitting with Mrs. Piper, in 1892. Hyslop was so impressed that he later resigned from his teaching position to become a full time psychical researcher. Perhaps more than any other researcher before him, Hyslop came to understand the dynamics of spirit communication. He pointed out that if the communicator realized that he had his identity to prove, he would necessarily limit himself to trivial recollections, assuming that he could control his state of consciousness at the time of communication, something apparently very difficult for spirits to do.

Adding to the confusion in the Piper observations was the fact that Phinuit told Hodgson that his full name while in the flesh was Jean Phinuit Sclivellee but that he was known as Doctor Phinuit. He said he had died at the age 70 "about" 1860. He gave his wife's name as Marie Latimer. However, he later told Professor Lodge that his name had been John Phinuit Schelevelle and his wife's name was Mary. He told both Hodgson and Lodge that he was born in Marseilles "about" 1790 and studied medicine at "Metz." (Metz was French until 1870, when it was ceded to Germany.) He informed Lodge that he died of leprosy. An attempt to find some documented evidence of Phinuit's existence was unsuccessful, although modern references give no indication as the extent of the investigation. It is known that many public records were destroyed in the civil uprisings following the Franco-Prussian War of 1870.

As Hyslop later explained, the information can be distorted or colored as it is filtered through the medium's mind. Since Jean/John and Marie/Mary have the same meaning, the confusion there might simply have been a matter of different filtering, and the spelling of the name and other information might have been distorted in the filtering process. Hyslop further explained that the process of getting communication in the trance state is the pictographic or 'mental picture' method, at least for certain specific incidents and names and thus it is subject to different interpretations. He wrote: :

> We do not know in detail all that goes on, but we can conceive that a mental picture in the mind of a communicator is transmitted, perhaps telepathically, to the psychic (medium) or to the control; even though we do not know how this occurs, we can understand why the message takes the form that it does in the mind of the psychic and why the whole process assumes the form of a description of visual, or a report of auditory images. The whole mass of facts is thus systematized as a single process, whose specific form of transmission is determined by the sense through which it is expressed. It is apparent that the pictographic process introduces into the communication various sources of mistake and confusion, and thus explains much that the ordinary man with his view of the messages cannot understand. Mental pictures have to be interpreted, either by the control or by the subconscious of the psychic, probably by both.[23]

While James had difficulty accepting the "fishing" for information by Phinuit, Hodgson and Hyslop seem to have understood it better. "I feel pretty sure that much of Phinuit's 'fishing' was due to the confusions of the more or less comatose communicators whose minds had let loose, so to speak, a crowd of earthly memories," Hodgson offered.[24] Of course, James would have had to endorse the spirit hypothesis to believe Hodgson's theory. Hyslop later explained it this way:

Fishing and guessing do take place, and yet the phenomena are still genuine. The fishing and guessing are on the other side. That is, the psychic is not fishing and guessing to try the sitter's response, but to try that of the communicator who labors under difficulties analogous to our communication over a telephone or whenever there are obstacles to communication with each other in normal life. Either the psychic or the control does not receive the messages or impressions clearly and has to guess at what they mean until the communicator assents to the right name or impression.[25]

In a 1918 book, Hyslop dealt with the secondary personality theory:

We have to reckon with what is always called the control, or the 'guide,' as it is sometimes called. We must remember also that the guide and control may be different personalities. They are not always, if ever, the same personality. It depends on circumstances. If you regard this control as a secondary personality state of the medium, you have all the complications of secondary personality in the case, serving as medium besides the automatic machinery of the living organism in the suspense of the control of the normal consciousness over it. But if you assume that the control is a spirit, as is more evidently the case for all who have intelligently investigated the problem, you have another mind beside that of the medium with which to deal in the problem. There is not only the third mind which we have called the medium (the "sitter" and the "communicating spirit" being the first two), but the fourth one complicating all its influences with those already complicated enough to make us wonder that we get any message at all from the dead.[26]

But before Hyslop gave his view on the whole idea of secondary personalities, Alfred Russel Wallace, co-originator with Charles Darwin of the natural selection theory of evolution, was one of the researchers who spoke out against the secondary personality hypothesis. He wrote:

But is this so-called explanation any real explanation, or anything more than a juggle of words which creates more difficulties than it solves? ...we have to suppose that this recondite but worser half of ourselves, while possessing some knowledge we have not, does not know that it is part of us, or, if it knows, is a persistent liar, for in most cases it adopts a distinct name, and persists in speaking of us, its better half, in the third person.[27]

Wallace added that he could not conceive how this second-self was developed in us under the law of survival of the fittest, a concept he suggested to Darwin before Darwin went public in 1858 with their parallel theories of evolution.

Researcher Minot Savage, whom we met in Chapter One, said much the same thing, mentioning that the only telepathy of which there is any real evidence is much more simple and between two people.

> How does it happen that this subconscious self is such an unconscionable, persistent, consistent, and abnormal liar about itself? Why does it not now and then by some sort of accident tell the truth? Has there ever been a case on record in which this subconscious self, which is so wise, so wonderful; which is able to travel the earth over in pursuit of facts and select the particular one which is needed; which can build up no end of distinct and consistent personalities, and put into their lips words and expressions and statements of fact and memories which shall come very near to establishing their identity with people who used to live here, – is there, I say, a case on record where this subconscious self has owned up to being a subconscious self? [28]

Savage went on to ask what the motive of all the lying could possibly be and to wonder why this secondary self makes so many mistakes. He concluded that the secondary-self idea is simply a theory designed to escape the acceptance of another theory.

There was strong evidence at the time suggesting the reality of both telepathy and teloteropathy, but none of that evidence involved will, intention, emotion, personality, and dialogue as expressed through Mrs. Piper. As Hereward Carrington, an SPR researcher, saw it, we would have to assume that the subconscious mind of the entranced medium could somehow reach into the brain of the sitter, or a person thousands of miles away, find the right engrams, like grooves cut in a phonograph record, interpret them and perceive them to be certain specific "memories," and then be prepared to carry on a dialogue relating to them. "The very formulation of such a conception renders it so preposterous as to rule it out from serious consideration," Carrington offered around 1910.[29]

Nevertheless, in 1890, some five years after James and the SPR began studying Mrs. Piper, the secondary personality combined with telepathy, teloteropathy, and the cosmic reservoir seems to have been the favored and predominant explanation. It simply was too difficult or too embarrassing for any educated person to admit to a belief in spirits or "ghosts."

---

[1] Hyslop (J 1919), 561-563

[2] Holt, 452

[3] Hogan

[4] Holt, 454

[5] _____, 456

[6] Edmonds, 353

[7] Hardinge, 98

[8] Edmonds, 39

[9] _____, 40

[10] _____, 87

[11] _____, 374

[12] Hare, 85

[13] _____, 96

[14] Kardec, 229

[15] _____, 256

[16] Moses

[17] Moses (Meilach.com)

[18] Moses 94

[19] _____, 39

[20] Medhurst, 190

[21] _____, 102-103.

[22] _____, 54

[23] Hyslop (1919), 117

[24] Holt, 523

[25] Hyslop (1925), 34

[26] Hyslop (1918), 213

[27] Wallace

[28] Savage, 163

[29] Carrington, 140-141

# -Five-

# Dr. Phinuit
# Steps Aside

*I am not dead. Don't think me dead.*
**– the discarnate George Pellew**

In concluding his discussion of Dr. Phinuit in the June 1892 *Proceedings* of the Society for Psychical Research, Dr. Richard Hodgson stated:

The hypothesis which for a long time seemed to me the most satisfactory is that of an auto-hypnotic trance in which a secondary personality of Mrs. Piper either erroneously believes itself to be, or consciously and falsely pretends to be, the 'spirit' of a deceased human being, Phinuit or Sclivelle, and further fictitiously represents various other personalities according to the latent idea of some of the sitters. Several facts which I have mentioned – especially concerning the name 'Dr. Fin-nē' as that of Mr. Cocke's 'control,' witnessed by Mrs. Piper before her trance began, the adoption of this name by Mrs. Piper's trance personality, its corruption into Phinnuit, later into Phinuit, and the subsequent apparent prevarications to explain these facts away – seem to point strongly towards this view. My confidence, however, in this explanation has been considerably shaken by further familiarity with the Phinuit personality and other allied 'manifestations' of Mrs. Piper's trance state, and I have no certain conviction that any single theory which has been put forward is really the correct one. I do not know of any precise parallel to the phenomena which we are discussing among any of the recorded types of hypnotic trance where the action of other than embodied human intelligences is a plainly superfluous hypothesis.[1]

Hodgson's confidence in his views was "shaken" after the accidental death of George Pellew, a 32-year-old member of the ASPR, during February 1892. Before his accident, which involved falling down a flight of stairs, Pellew, a Harvard graduate with a law degree and the author of two historical books as well as an editorial writer for the *New York Sun*, had told Hodgson that he could not conceive of an afterlife but that if he died before Hodgson and found himself "still existing" he would attempt to let Hodgson know.

On March 22, a little over a month after Pellew's death, Hodgson brought Pellew's friend John Hart for a sitting with Mrs. Piper. Early in the sitting, Dr. Phinuit, announced that "George" was there. Phinuit then gave Pellew's full name and the names of several close friends, including Hart's name. To give assurance that it was actually himself communicating through Phinuit, Pellew told Hart that the pair of studs he was wearing were once his and were given to Hart by his (Pellew's) parents, which Hart confirmed as true. Pellew then mentioned some mutual friends, Jim and Mary Howard, and asked Hart if he could get them to attend a sitting. He also brought up a discussion he had had with Katharine, the Howard's 15-year-old daughter, about God, space, and eternity. As neither Hart nor Hodgson, who was also in attendance and taking notes, was aware of any such discussion with Katharine, this information, later verified as fact, clearly fell outside the scope of simple telepathy.

Hodgson recorded that many personal references were made by Pellew, including one to a book he had not yet finished before his death, and that Hart was impressed, mentioning that various words of greetings and speech mannerisms were very characteristic of Pellew, even though the messages were relayed through Phinuit. For privacy reasons, Hodgson called him George "Pelham" in the research records, or otherwise referred to him simply as "G.P."

Some three weeks later, Jim and Mary Howard had a sitting with Mrs. Piper. They were somewhat reluctant to participate in such "occult activity," but Hart's account of what took place at his sitting made them curious. Hodgson did not tell Mrs. Piper their names or give her any clue as to their connection with G.P. Yet, G.P. communicated. However, rather than Phinuit speaking through Mrs. Piper and relaying messages from G.P., G.P. took over Mrs. Piper's body and spoke directly to his friends:

**G.P.:** "Jim is that you? Speak to me quick. I am not dead. Don't think me dead. I'm awfully glad to see you. Can't you see me? Don't you hear me? Give my love to my father and tell him I want to see him. I am happy here, and more so since I can communicate with you. I pity those people who can't speak…"

**Jim Howard:** "What do you do George, where you are?"

**G.P.:** "I am scarcely able to do anything yet; I am just awakened to the reality of life after death. It was like darkness. I could not distinguish anything at first. Darkest hours just before dawn, you know that, Jim. I was puzzled, confused. Shall have an occupation soon. Now I can see you, my friends. I can hear you speak. Your voice, Jim, I can distinguish with your accent and articulation, but it sounds like a big bass drum. Mine would sound to you like the faintest whisper."

**Jim Howard:** "Our conversation, then, is something like telephoning?"

**G.P.:** "Yes."

**Jim Howard:** "By long distance telephone?"

**G.P.:** (Laughs)

**Jim Howard:** "Were you not surprised to find yourself living?"

**G.P.:** "Greatly surprised. I did not believe in a future life. It was beyond my reasoning powers. Now it is as clear to me as daylight. We have an astral fac-simile of the material body. Jim, what are you writing now?"

**Jim Howard:** "Nothing of any importance."

**G. P.:** "Why don't you write about this?"

**Jim Howard:** "I should like to, but the expression of my opinions would be nothing. I must have facts."

**G.P.:** "These I will give you and to Hodgson if he is still interested in these things."

**Jim Howard:** "Will people know about this possibility of communication?"

**G.P.:** "They are sure to in the end. It is only a question of time when people in the material body will know all about it, and everyone will be able to communicate...I want all the fellows to know about me... What is Rogers writing?"

**Jim Howard:** "A novel."

**G.P.:** "No, not that. Is he not writing something about me?"

**Jim Howard:** "Yes, he is preparing a memorial of you."

**G. P.:** "That is nice; it is pleasant to be remembered. It is very kind of him. He was always kind to me when I was alive. Martha Rogers [Rogers's deceased daughter] is here. I have talked with her several times. She reflects too much on her last illness, on being fed with a tube. We tell her she ought to forget it, and she has done so in good measure, but she was ill a long time. She is a dear little creature when you know her, but she is hard to know. She is a beautiful little soul. She sends her love to her father...Berwick, how is he? Give him my love. He is a good fellow; he is what I always thought him in life, trustworthy and honorable. How is Orenberg? He has some of my letters. Give him my warmest love. He was always very fond of me, though he understood me least of all my friends. We fellows who are eccentric are always misunderstood in life. I used to have fits of depression. I have none now. I am happy now. I want my father to know about this. We used to talk about spiritual things, but he will be hard to convince. My mother will be easier..."[2]

At a later sitting, the Howards brought their daughter, Katharine. G. P. came through and asked Katharine about her violin lessons, commenting (apparently jesting) that her playing was "horrible." Not realizing the humor in it, Mary Howard spoke up to defend her daughter's music, but G.P. then explained that he mentioned it because that is what he used to do when in the flesh. It was intended as verification of his identity.

When Mrs. Piper was coming out of the trance, she told Hodgson that she felt very queer and did not know what was wrong with her. She then went back into the trance state, when Phinuit took over and shouted, complaining that G.P. forgot to signal to him that he was leaving. Phinuit then began speaking French with Katharine, who had lived in France and knew the language well. Hodgson and Howard were much impressed with the conversation that took place between Phinuit and Katharine. It certainly conflicted with reports by Professors James and Leaf that Phinuit knew little French.

As G.P. gradually learned to "manage the light," he usurped much of Phinuit's authority as a control and began mediating for other spirits. Phinuit complained to Hodgson of G. P. being too domineering. "I never saw the like of that fellow George," Phinuit grumbled to Hodgson and Professor William Newbold at a sitting on June 25, 1894. "There's another here trying to say something but he gave no chance at all. When he gets hold he keeps hold I tell you, Hodgson." [3]

As G.P. took command and subordinated Phinuit to an assistant's role, Mrs. Piper began changing from a trance-voice medium to a trance-writing medium. Now, she sat at a table and rested her head on a pillow on the table, her face toward the left. Writing material was arranged on the right side, usually 100 blank sheets and four or five soft-lead pencils. After she went into the trance state, the experimenter had to arrange the paper and place the pencil in her hand so that she could conveniently write, and he had to quickly remove each sheet of paper after it was filled.

G.P. apparently coached other spirits on how to use Mrs. Piper's hand and stood by to assist them. One sitter, identified only as "Mrs. M." by Hodgson, stated that the G.P. method of communication was even more convincing than the Phinuit method. "...perhaps the most convincing thing is the accumulation of little touches of personality which make the sittings so real to me, but which it would be impossible to reproduce in print," she wrote to Hodgson. "Peculiarities of expression in the writing and of manner in that wonderfully dramatic hand of Mrs. Piper's. Anyone who has had a good sitting with Mrs. Piper will know exactly what I mean. One feels the hand is alive with a distinct personality very different from Phinuit. The behavior of the hand when it is controlled by my husband or my brother is as distinct and as characteristic of the two men as anything of the kind could possibly be." [4]

Mrs. M. added that there was a big difference in the quality of the sittings. At some sittings, nearly everything had meaning to her, and on other days it was pretty much meaningless. She concluded that the poor sittings were on days when either she or Mrs. Piper was not feeling particularly well.

Jim and Mary Howard returned on December 19, 1892. By that time most of the communication was by writing. Mary Howard handed G.P. a letter from his father and asked him if he could read it. G.P. said it did not sound like his father would talk to him when he was in the body, but that his father does believe that he still exists and is no longer in pain. Mary Howard confirmed for Hodgson that this was the key message in the letter, which apparently was still in the envelope. G.P. continued:

> That brings me nearer to my father; now give him my tenderest love and tell him that I am very near him, and see him almost every day, if I could go by days, but I can't judge of that, because I have no idea of time; that is one thing I have lost, Hodgson…You of all others are the one that I want to be absolutely certain of my identity…Hodgson, I mean, and Jim, I want you both to feel I am no secondary personality of the medium's…Now, about my theory of spirit life independent of the material substance. I live, think, see, hear, know, and feel just as clearly as when I was in the material life, but it is not so easy to explain it to you as you would naturally suppose, especially when the thoughts have to be expressed through substance materially…Nevertheless, I am bound to do just all I can for you to prove to you that I (George [Pellew]) do absolutely exist, independent of the material body which I inhabited…You see as I was explaining to you about thought, and had not strength materially nor time to finish, I will go on to that again and in a little more detail, which will explain to you (as well as anything) how and what I am now, i.e., as a spiritual Ego. Thought is, as I said before, in no wise dependent upon body, but must necessarily, as you see, depend upon the body of another person or Ego in the material to express one's thought fully after the annihilation of one's own material body…In consequence of this you see that there must necessarily be more or less confliction between one's spiritual Ego or mind, and the material mind or Ego of the one which you are

obliged to use to explain these difficult problems to you, my friend in the material...."[5]

Hodgson asked G.P. what becomes of Mrs. Piper during the trance. G.P. responded that she "passes out" as the "etherical" does when a person sleeps. Hodgson asked if there is conflict because her brain substance is saturated with her tendencies of thought. "No, not that, but the solid substance called brain, it is difficult to control it, simply because it is material," G.P. answered. "...her mind leaves the brain empty, as it were, and I myself or other spiritual mind or thought takes the empty brain, and there is where and when the conflict arises."[6]

Jim Howard returned alone for a sitting three days later and asked G.P. to tell him something that only the two of them knew. In fact, G.P. told Howard something so private and personal that Howard did not want it made part of the record, but he told Hodgson that he was perfectly satisfied with the information. G.P. continued:

> Jim, I am dull in this sphere about some things, but you will forgive me, won't you?...but like as when in the body sometimes we can't always recall everything in a moment, can we, Jim, dear old fellow?...God bless you, Jim, and many thanks. You often gave me courage when I used to get depressed. You know how you especially used to fire at me sometimes, but I understood it all, did I not, old fellow?...and I used to get tremendously down at the heel sometimes, but I am all right now, and, Jim, you can never know how much I love you and how I delight in coming back and telling you all this...When I found I actually lived again, I jumped for joy, and my first thought was to find you and Mary. And thank the Infinite here I am, old fellow, living and well...[7]

At another sitting, when the Howards were not present, Hodgson asked G.P. if he could visit the Howard's home and report back by the end of the sitting what they were doing. Toward the end of the sitting, G.P. interrupted Phinuit to give his report. He found only Mrs. Howard at home and reported on her writing letters to his (G.P.'s) mother as well as somebody named Tyson. He also saw her handling a book that he (G.P.) had written and wondering if he (G.P.) was around at the time. Several other routine tasks were reported. When Hodgson checked with Mary Howard to see if the report was accurate, she confirmed that it was accurate, except that it all happened on the previous day, not the day of the sitting. Hodgson didn't know what to make of that, but he surmised that the agent (Mary Howard) in such an experiment had to be thinking of the subject (G.P.) for it to be successful. G.P., who had an obscure perception of the physical world, including time, had somehow tapped into her subliminal consciousness for the most recent activities in which he was emotionally on her mind.

As a further test of telepathy, Mary Howard brought three pictures to a sitting and asked G.P. to identify them. G.P. correctly identified the first picture as the Howard's summer home. He correctly identified a second picture as a country place where they had stayed, recalling a little brick henhouse which was not in the picture. Mary Howard confirmed the accuracy of this report and then showed a third picture, which G.P. could not identify. In fact, G.P. had never seen it. Had Mrs. Piper been reading Howard's mind, she should have been able to identify it, unless, of course, she could also read Mary Howard's mind relative to the test, and her subconscious was aware and devious enough to know that it was more important to show ignorance than it was to identify the location in the picture.

In spite of the successes, there were still failures, along with antagonism. Professor J. M. Pierce sat with Mrs. Piper on April 28, 1892 and received nothing of value. Dr. and Mrs. L. E. H. of New York sat with her on May 6 and received some evidential communication from deceased loved ones, but felt that it could all be explained by mind-reading. Professor N. S. Shaler had a sitting on May 25 and received some evidential communication but concluded that even though Mrs. Piper appeared to be an honest person he believed that there was some kind of deceit involved. As for Phinuit, Shaler opined that he had a first-rate French accent but that he is a "preposterous scoundrel." Dr. S. Weir Mitchell found nothing of value in his sitting with Piper and said he would have labeled her a "stupid fraud" if Professor James had not made positive statements about her.

But not all professional men were so negative or disbelieving. Professor Herbert Nichols wrote the following to William James:

> Just before coming away I had a wonderful sitting with Mrs. Piper. As you know, I have been a Laodicean toward her heretofore. But that she is no fraud, and that she is the greatest marvel I have ever met I am now wholly convinced. Think my interview more wonderful than any I have ever heard reported on her before.

Mamma and I one Christmas exchanged rings. Each had engraved in his gift the first word of his favorite proverb. The ring given me I lost many years ago. When Mamma died a year ago, the ring I had given her was, at her request, taken from her finger and sent to me. Now I asked Mrs. Piper 'What was written in Mamma's ring?' and as I asked the question I held the ring in my hand and had in mind *only that* ring. But I had hardly got the words from my mouth [when] she slapped down on the paper the word in the *other ring*.[8]

At a sitting on February 15, 1894, G.P. explained the difficulty he and others on his side of the veil had in communicating:

Remember we share and always shall have our friends in the dream life, i.e., your life so to speak, which will attract us forever and ever, and so long as we have any friends *sleeping* in the material world – you to us are more like as we understand sleep, you look shut up as one in prison, and inorder for us to get into communication with you, we have to enter into your sphere, as one like yourself asleep. This is just why we make mistakes as you call them, or get confused and muddled, so to put it, Hodgson. Your thoughts do grasp mine. Well now you have just what I have been wanting to come and make clear to you, Hodgson, old fellow. Yes, you see I am more awake than asleep; yet I cannot come just as I am in reality, independent of the medium's light.[9]

Hodgson commented that G.P. came through much better than others. G.P. responded by explaining that he was a little nearer and not less intelligent that some others. Several decades later, a similar message concerning the difficulties in communication came through to Lady (Dr.) Florence Barrett in a sitting with Gladys Osborne Leonard, referred to as the "British Mrs. Piper," at a sitting on November 5, 1929. Her husband, Sir William Barrett, a physicist and one of the founders of the SPR in 1882, had died in 1925. He communicated:

When I come into the conditions of a sitting I then know that I can only carry with me – contain in me – a small portion of my consciousness. The easiest things to lay hold of are what we may call ideas; a detached word, a proper name, has no link with a train of thought except in the detached sense; that is far more difficult than any other feat of memory or association of ideas. If you go to a medium that is new to us, I can make myself known by giving you through that medium an impression of my character and personality, my work on earth, and so forth. Those can all be suggested by thought, impressions, ideas; but if I want to say, 'I am Will,' I find that much more difficult than giving you a long, comprehensive study of my personality. "I am Will' sounds so simple, but you understand that in this case the word "Will" becomes a detached word. If I wanted to express an idea of my scientific interests I could do it in twenty different ways. I should probably begin by showing books, then giving impressions of the nature of the book and so on, till I had built up a character impression of myself, but "I am Will' presents difficulties.[10]

At a June 17, 1895 sitting, Newbold, who conducted a number of sittings with Mrs. Piper during Hodgson's absence, asked G.P. the difference between the writing and talking. G.P. responded that the difference was not apparent to him. "I only know I am writing by having been told so by Hodgson," G.P. wrote through Piper's hand. When Newbold asked G.P. what Phinuit was doing while he was controlling Mrs. Piper, G.P. said that Phinuit was "talking to John H. and a little million others, at the same time helping me hold them back and keep them from interrupting me."[11]

There were times when Phinuit would be talking through Mrs. Piper as G.P. used her hand to write. Hodgson noted that at one sitting, Phinuit was listening to the stenographic report of a previous interview, commenting upon it, and at the same time G.P. was writing freely and rapidly on other subjects while holding a conversation with another person. This went on for some 20 minutes. Hodgson reported:

> The only one that appeared to be distracted was the sitter who was talking with the 'hand,' who was remonstrated with by the 'hand' for not paying sufficient attention to it. I have never failed to get this double action when desired if Phinuit was present and the hand was being used by another 'control.' In all cases when the 'hand' is writing independently of Phinuit, the sense of hearing for the 'hand control' appears to be in the hand, whereas Phinuit apparently always hears through the ordinary channel.[12]

Hodgson wondered if the left hand might also write and if both hands would write at the same time as Phinuit also spoke. On February 24, 1894, Edmund Gurney (See Chapter Three) communicated and said that there is no reason why various spiritual minds cannot express their minds at the same time through the same organism. Hodgson told Gurney that he would like to arrange an experiment with Gurney using one hand and G.P. the other, but he was not prepared to conduct the experiment at that time. Hodgson further reported:

At my next sitting, February 26, 1894, when I was unprepared and was alone, an attempt, only very partially successful, was made to write independently with both hands at the very beginning of the sitting. On March 18, 1895, another attempt, much more successful was made, when I was accompanied for the purpose by Miss Edmunds. Her 'deceased sister' wrote with one hand, and G. P. with the other, while Phinuit was talking – all simultaneously on different subjects. Very little, however, was written with the left hand. The difficulty appeared to be chiefly in the deficiencies of the left hand as a writing machine.

After having endeavoured as best I could to follow the writing of thousands of pages with scores of different writers, after having put many inquiries to the communicators themselves, and after having analyzed numerous spontaneously occurring incidents of all kinds, I have no sort of doubt whatever but that the consciousness producing the writing – whatever that consciousness be, whether Mrs. Piper's secondary personality or the real communicators as alleged – is *not conscious of writing*, and that the thoughts that pass through 'his' mind tend to be reproduced in writing by some part of the writing mechanism of Mrs. Piper's organism. This writing mechanism is far from perfect, and it frequently produces words that cannot be read. This entails a repetition of the word and checks the thought of the communicator, already reduced to the necessity of thinking his words at the slow rate of writing, and of excluding other thoughts that he does not wish written, in a state when he has already been steeped into a state of partial sleep by coming into relation with an organism not his own, for the purpose of manifesting in the physical world.[13]

Phinuit and G.P. collaborated in sittings for several years, Phinuit controlling the voice and G.P. the hand. There appeared to be a complete independence between the two. The sense of hearing for the "hand" consciousness was in the hand, and it was necessary for the sitter to talk to the hand. One of the problems with the hand, Hodgson pointed out, was that intruding spirits would take control of the hand and write something that had no meaning for the sitter. As the "intruders" struggled to control the hand, incoherent fragments were often produced and were mixed in with replies given to the sitter by the intended communicator. There were times when the hand was "seized" and went through convulsive vagaries as Phinuit continued to talk, giving no indication of the disturbance in the hand. Hodgson explained the process as he came to understand it:

> We all have bodies composed of 'luminiferous ether' enclosed in our flesh and blood bodies. The relation of Mrs. Piper's ethereal body to the ethereal world, in which the 'communicators' claim to dwell, is such that a special store of peculiar energy is accumulated in connection with her organism, and this appears to be as a 'light.' Mrs. Piper's ethereal body is removed by them, and her ordinary body appears as a shell filled with this 'light.' Several 'communicators' may be in contact with this 'light' at the same time. There are two chief 'masses' of it in her case, one in connection with the head, the other in connection with the right arm and hand. Latterly, that in connection with the hand has been 'brighter' than that in connection with the head. If the 'communicator' gets into contact with the 'light' and thinks his thoughts, they tend to be reproduced by movement in Mrs. Piper's organism. Very few can produce vocal effects, even when in contact with this 'light' of the head, but practically all can produce writing movements when in contact with the 'light' of the hand. Upon the amount and brightness of this 'light,' *caeteris paribus*, the communications depend. When Mrs. Piper is in ill-health the 'light' is feebler, and the communications tend to be less coherent. It also gets used up during a sitting, and when it gets dim there is a tendency to incoherence even in otherwise clear communicators. In all cases, coming into contact with this 'light' tends to produce bewilderment, and if the contact is continued too long, or the 'light' becomes very dim, the consciousness of the communicator tends to lapse completely.

> Then floods of excited emotion at the presence of incarnate friends, dominant ideas that disturbed him when he was incarnate himself, the desire to render advice and assistance to other living friends and relatives, etc., all crowd upon his mind; the sitter begins to ask questions about matters having no relation to what he is thinking about, he gets more and more bewildered, more and more *comatose*, loses his 'grasp' of the 'light,' and drifts away perhaps to return several times and go through a similar experience.[14]

As more and more communication came by way of the hand, either directly or assisted by G.P., Phinuit's job became that of "gatekeeper," holding back "earthbound spirits" who were attempting to use the "light." Sometime in 1895, the quality of the messages began to deteriorate and there were indications that more and more earthbound spirits were able to get through the "gate" and control Mrs. Piper. Deceased writers Sir Walter Scott and George Eliot supposedly communicated directly through Piper's hand, but the nature of the communication suggested impostors.

G. P. and Phinuit gradually gave way to "Rector" of the Imperator band, a group of purportedly advanced spirits which had earlier controlled the Rev. William Stainton Moses, an Anglican priest (See Chapter Four). Rector told Hodgson that Piper's organism was weakening and needed a rest. Phinuit made his last appearance on January 26, 1896. On March 19, 1897, Rector communicated:

We have removed the former leading control to a much higher plane, and he has passed on from the earthly condition to a higher sphere altogether. We have prayed and earnestly worked for his salvation, and although he has been ofttimes misjudged, he was not of the highest. We have allowed a spirit sent to show him a much higher and nobler life than he had known before. It is not wise to allow lower minds to receive communications from a spirit when first controlling, who brings all such into the conditions of the earth, earthy. [15]

Five days later, Rector had this to say:

We propose to substitute instead of the rough, inharmonious and uncultivated dialect a softer melody...Instead of permitting such messengers as some who have hitherto brought messages using such dialect as we have described, we propose to keep all such in a state of penitence and servitude. We propose to render our services to all such and prepare them for the higher and better life rather than to permit them to return to thee or to other minds of exalted sciences... We are referring chiefly to the earthbound spirit Dr. Schliville...He was not exactly of this earth, earthy but bound here by the attractions of earthly minds...Say to thy medium the following: Take exercise in the open fields which God the Most High hath prepared for such. Cast out all unpleasant thoughts. Ask Him to give help and it will be given. Say to her the pure in heart shall see God...Let not the trials of life burden the soul. Ask Him to assist thee and throw thyself in all confidence upon Him. Friend, light, strength, happiness and all good will, if these instructions are obeyed, follow; otherwise may God have Mercy upon the soul.[16]

Several days later, Rector repeated that "Schliville" (Phinuit) had been taken to a higher and better life. Hodgson then gave a message for Rector to deliver to Phinuit. Rector said that the message of kindness would be delivered to him personally. He added that there was no intentional evil in him, but he lingered so long near the earth realm that he was misled.

Hodgson asked G.P. about Imperator, Rector, and the whole Imperator band of spirits. G.P. told him that Imperator was very high and much farther from the earth than anyone else who had communicated. He said that he was much nearer the sight of God. When Hodgson complained that Imperator was sometimes difficult to understand, G.P. explained that he was too high to effectively use the machine (Mrs. Piper), that it was easier for those lower to control Mrs. Piper. Although not entirely clear from the communications, Rector appears to have been at a somewhat lower level than Imperator and thus was more effective in getting through. Apparently, Rector had difficulty as well and thus had to use G.P., who was at even a lower vibration, to effectively communicate.

When Imperator and his band of 49 were communicating through the mediumship of William Stainton Moses 10 to 25 years earlier, Moses continually asked for their earthly identifications. Imperator initially refused, informing Moses that revealing their earthly names would result in casting additional doubt on the validity of the messages. However, Imperator later revealed their names, advising Moses that they should not be mentioned in the book he would write. It was not until after Moses's death that the identities were made public by A. W. Trethewy in a book, *The Controls of Stainton Moses*. Imperator was said to be Malachias, the Old Testament prophet. Rector was Hippolytus, an early Catholic Church bishop. Imperator took directions from Preceptor, who was Elijah. Preceptor, in turn, communed directly with Jesus.

On June 8, 1897, G.P. warned Hodgson not to accept anything further as coming from him, apparently suggesting that it might be an earthbound spirit posing as him. He added that he might not have the pleasure of seeing Hodgson for a long time. Rector cautioned Hodgson not to rely too much on G.P. as he was "too far away," i.e., at too high a vibration to be effective. "His spirit is pure, his mind sincere, his whole life here is one of honor and one to be respected by us all," Rector wrote through Mrs. Piper's hand. "Yet, we would speak the truth and say his work in your field is done." [17] Nevertheless, G.P. apparently continued as an assistant to Rector for a number of years, at least until 1904.

Rector was described by William James as sounding like "an aged and, when he is speaking instead of writing, like a somewhat hollow-voice clergyman, a little weary of his experience of the world, endlessly patient and sympathetic, and desiring to put all his tenderness and wisdom at your service while you are there. Critical and fastidious sitters have recognized his wisdom and confess their debt to him as a moral adviser." [18] And while James admitted that Mrs. Piper's waking capacity for being a spiritual adviser did not approach Rector's, he concluded that Rector and the whole Imperator group were "dream creations" of Mrs. Piper, probably having no existence except when she is in trance. He did not explain how this "dream creation" can be so much more intelligent than Mrs. Piper, nor did he attempt to reconcile the "dream creation" with the G.P. personality, who was known to have existed in the flesh, and who functioned in much the same way as Rector, though not so much as a spiritual advisor.

The emergence of George Pellew as a control for Mrs. Piper moved many of the researchers, including Hodgson, Lodge, and Myers away from the secondary personality hypothesis to a belief in actual spirits. There was simply too much evidence that Pellew survived and was communicating. Hodgson explained:

> [In my previous report] I urged that there were almost insuperable objections to the supposition that such 'deceased' persons were in direct communication with Phinuit, at least in anything like the fullness of personality...[however] I am now fully convinced that there has been such actual communication through Mrs. Piper's trance, but that the communication has been subject to certain unavoidable limitations... With the advent of the G.P. intelligence, the development of the automatic writing, and the use of the hand by scores of other alleged communicators, the problem has assumed a very different aspect. The dramatic form has become an integral part of the phenomenon. With the handwriting and the voice speaking at the same time on different subjects and with different persons, with the hand writing on behalf of different communicators using the hand at the sitting, as well as at different sittings, it is difficult to resist the impression that there are

here actually concerned various different and distinct and individually coherent streams of consciousness.[19]

Although he did not publish them because they were too personal, Hodgson is said to have received direct communication from Jessie ("Q"), his former love interest who had earlier passed on messages through Phinuit (See Chapter Two). After Hodgson's death in 1905, Professor Newbold, who worked closely with Hodgson, suggested that the messages from Jessie probably influenced Hodgson even more than the G.P. communication. Hodgson went on to say that to the person unfamiliar with a series of these sittings, the secondary personality hypothesis may still seem plausible, but:

> I do not, however, think it at all likely that he would continue to think it plausible after witnessing and studying the numerous coherent groups of memories connected with the different person, the characteristic emotional tendencies distinguishing such different persons, the excessive complication of the acting required, and the absence of any apparent bond of union for the associated thoughts and feelings indicative of each individuality, save some persistent basis of that individuality itself.[20]

In effect, there was too much individuality, too much purpose and persistence, expressed by G.P. to attribute it to telepathy of a limited or expanded nature. It was one thing for a medium to tap into another mind or cosmic reservoir for information, quite another for that other mind or reservoir to come back with the fullness of a personality rather than just fragmentary bits of information.

Moreover, Hodgson noted that out of 150 sitters over a period of time, 30 were known to Pellew when he was alive. In each case, Pellew greeted them by name. The non-recognition of the other 120 was contrary to the telepathic, teloteropathic, and cosmic soul theories. That is, if Pellew were reading minds or searching in some cosmic computer, he would have known the names of all of them. "Grant all the telepathy (bare information) you please – from the sitter and from incarnate intelligences the world over," Henry Holt offered on this subject. "Deny, if you please, any telepathy whatever from discarnate intelligences, you have still got to account for the give-and-take and general dramatic character of the controls. How do you propose to? By the medium's secondary personalities? Then are you ready to allow that she has a thousand?"[21]

After Hodgson died of a heart attack in 1905, he, too, began taking control of Mrs. Piper and communicating with Professors Newbold and James (See Chapter Nine)

---

[1] Hodgson, 57-58

[2] Holt, 468-469

[3] _____, 590

[4] _____, 516-517

[5] _____, 477

[6] _____, 477

[7] _____, 476

[8] _____, 495

[9] _____, 520

[10] Barrett (1937), 105

[11] _____, 590

[12] _____, 462

[13] Lodge (1909), 251-252

[14] _____, 247

[15] Holt, 584

[16] _____, 584

[17] _____, 591

[18] _____, 528

[19] _____, 519-520

[20] _____, 519-520

[21] _____, 406

Leonora Piper

Alice Flemming

Augustus P. Martin

F. W. H. Myers

James Hyslop

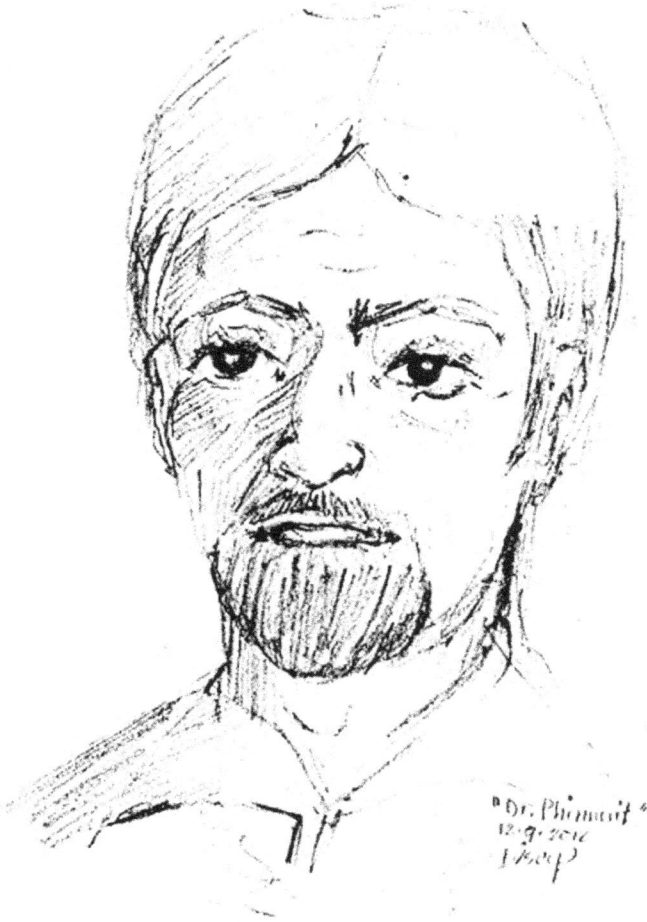

An artist's conception of Dr. Phinuit.

Richard Hodgson

Sir Oliver Lodge

William James

# -Six-

# Mounting Evidence for Spirit Return

*I make bold to say that there are conditions under which a spiritistic theory is easier to believe than the telepathic.*
**– James H. Hyslop**

Although there is little to suggest that Professor William James was influenced to adopt the spirit hypothesis by the emergence of the George Pellew (G.P.) personality, Dr. Richard Hodgson was now clearly in the spirit camp. He wrote:

This recognition of friends appears to me to be of great importance evidentially, not only because it indicates some supernormal knowledge, but because, when all the circumstances are taken into consideration, they seem to point in G.P.'s case to an independent intelligence drawing upon its own recollections…At the outset of the communications from G.P., he was particularly anxious – I describe it as it seemed *prima facie to be* – to see the Howards and his father and mother for the purpose of clearing up some private matters…On April 29<sup>th</sup> came the explanation from G.P. about the difficulties involved in the act of communicating, and I believe that I emphasized the importance of his always recognizing any friend of his who happened to attend a sitting, no matter what other communications he might wish to make. From that time onward he has never failed to announce himself to, and to recognize, with the appropriate emotional and intellectual relations, the sitters who were known to G.P. living, and to give their names in one form or another, with one exception. This exception, however, seems to me to be as noteworthy as if the recognition had been complete.[1]

The exception involved a Miss Warner, who sat with Mrs. Piper on January 7, 1897. G.P. sensed that he had met her when he was alive, but was not certain. "I long to place all of my friends, and could do so before I had been gone so long," G.P. apologetically communicated to Miss Warner. "You see, I am farther away…I do not recall your face. You must have changed."[2] At that point, Hodgson gave her name and observed excitement in Mrs. Piper's hand. G.P asked if she was the daughter of his friend, to which Miss Warner replied in the affirmative. G.P requested that she ask her mother if she remembered the long talks they used to have. Miss Warner said she was certain her mother does remember them.

As Hodgson saw it, the very non-recognition of Miss Warner was an argument for the spirit hypothesis, since if Mrs. Piper's secondary personality was reading minds she would have picked up the name. Hodgson continued:

> The continual manifestation of this personality – so different from Phinuit or their communicators – with its own reservoir of memories, with its swift appreciation of any reference to friends of G.P., with its 'give and take' in little incidental conversations of the actual presence of the G.P. personality, which it would be quite impossible to impart by any more enumeration of veritable statements. It will hardly, however, be regarded as surprising that the most impressive manifestations are at the same time the most subtle and the least communicable.[3]

On March 5, 1897, G.P. dialogued with Hodgson, telling him about his first experiences on the other side:

> **G.P.:** "Do you remember me well?...I had a sad life in many ways, yet in others I was happy, yet I have never known what real happiness was until I came here…I was an unbeliever, in fact almost an agnostic when I left my body, but when I awoke and found myself alive in another form superior in quality, that is, my body was less gross and heavy, with no pangs of remorse, no struggling to hold on to the material body, I found it had all been a dream....."

**Hodgson:** "That was your first experience?"

**G. P.:** "...The moment I had been removed from my body I found at once I had been thoroughly mistaken in my conjectures. I looked back upon my whole life in one instant. Every thought, word, or action which I had ever experienced passed through my mind like a wonderful panorama as it were before my vision. You cannot begin to imagine anything as real and extraordinary as this first awakening. You must not think, my friend, from anything you may have heard or known of my life that I was not a thinker. Should you think this, you would be mistaking me altogether."

**Hodgson:** "I have always had the most profound admiration, not merely for your psychological work in fiction, but for your clear philosophical insight and originality."

**G. P.:** "Thanks to you my friend...A few days I had a feeling of remorse, but it did not last long. When this passed away I began to feel happier than I had ever been through the whole course of my earthly existence...I immediately sang songs of love, realizing that I was a part of love itself. I cannot tarry much longer with you, my friend, but if you would have me say more of my life here, call for me in spirit, that is, in thought...My life while in my body is filled with love to... No woman on your planet to-day ever expressed more. Love is spirit; love is everything; where love is not, there nothing is...I may not be visible, that is in body, but I am determined to blow the bugle so long as I can reach a friend."[4]

Hodgson made a number of observations relative to Mrs. Piper's mediumship. In addition to discounting the 'fishing' argument, as earlier pointed out, Hodgson noted that G.P. could communicate more effectively with his father and close friends than with his more casual friends. This also conflicted with the secondary personality hypothesis, since Mrs. Piper's secondary personality would seemingly not distinguish between the close friends and the casual ones.

Moreover, Hodgson concluded that there was no evidence to suggest that the bond of continuity in the case of the most successful communicators depended for its existence upon the minds of living persons. He could see no discernible relationship between the mixture of truth and error and the consciousness of the sitters. "[They] suggest the action of another intelligence groping confusedly among its own remembrances," he explained. "And as further light appears in this confused groping, the bonds of association appear more and more to be traceable to no other assignable personality than that of the deceased."[5]

Hodgson agreed that the evidence came far short of what one might expect from real friends who once lived with us, but concluded that the ability to communicate clearly varied among spirits. Many were unable to communicate at all; some got through just bits and pieces; few were able to communicate without the assistance of Dr. Phinuit, but more got though directly once G.P. took control and moved to automatic writing; a few communicated directly but were for the most part incoherent, while even fewer communicated directly and were coherent. Hodgson opined that the ability to communicate clearly may be as rare as the gifts that make for a great artist, a great mathematician, or a great philosopher.

Perhaps a better analogy would have been the ability to meditate, especially since it was said that the spirit communicator has to lower his or her vibrations and achieve some altered state of consciousness on that side. Clearly, there are those who are very good at meditating, some who are fair, and many who cannot quiet their minds enough to meditate at all.

Referring to the confusion, Hodgson cited the case in which a "Mrs. Mitchell" was asked to repeat words which Hodgson and the sitter, her husband, had difficulty in deciphering. "No, I can't, it is too much work and too weakening, and I cannot repeat," she wrote through Mrs. Piper's hand, going on to explain that she could not figure out how her husband could hear her and that his thoughts do not reach her when she is speaking to him.[6]

It further became clear to Hodgson that the "newly dead" found it more difficult to communicate than those who had crossed over some time ago. He attributed this to the shock and wrench of death and noted that some were able to communicate effectively within days while others took months.

Hodgson also noted that between G.P.'s first appearance in early 1892 and the time of his report in 1897, "the same persistent personality has manifested itself, and what change has been discernible is a change not of any process of disintegration, but rather of integration and evolution."[7]

Between 1891 and 1895, Dr. William Romaine Newbold, a professor of philosophy and Latin at the University of Pennsylvania, had 26

sittings with Mrs. Piper. In his first sitting, his Aunt Sally communicated, but G.P. struggled to understand whether she was his aunt or
his grandmother. Newbold understood G.P.'s dilemma perfectly, explaining that his paternal grandfather's second wife had a sister whom
his (Newbold's) father married many years after his father's death, that
woman being Newbold's mother. Thus, Aunt Sally was both his aunt
and his step-grandmother. Newbold wrote:

> Individual scraps of information may be ascribed with some show of
> plausibility to a telepathic or clairvoyant origin, the arrangement of
> the scraps into mosaics of thought, which, however defaced, still of-
> ten irresistibly suggest the habits, tastes, and memories of some friend
> deceased – for this I know of no telepathic or clairvoyant analogy. For
> example, the demand made by 'Aunt Sally' that I should identify myself
> by expounding the significance of 'two marriages in this case, mother
> and aunt grandma also,' admits of no satisfactory telepathic explana-
> tion. The fact was known to me and might have been got telepathically.
> But why is the dream personality of the only communicator who died
> in my childhood the only one who seeks to identify me? [8]

In one sitting, while Newbold observed G.P. writing as Phinuit
was talking, he heard Phinuit say that he shouldn't be in such a hurry.
Newbold thought Phinuit was talking to him and replied that he was
in no hurry. Phinuit said he wasn't talking to Newbold but rather to a
young man in spirit who was in a great hurry to begin communicating. Hodgson was also there, recording the session. When the young
man referred to by Phinuit communicated, he seemed confused as
Mrs. Piper's hand felt Hodgson's head. The young man then said that
he did not know Hodgson. Since Mrs. Piper certainly knew Hodgson,
this was not consistent with the secondary personality hypothesis, unless it is claimed that Mrs. Piper was play-acting.

At a sitting on June 19, 1895, Newbold asked G.P. if it was possible
to have William Stainton Moses (the medium previously controlled
by the Imperator band), who had died in 1892, communicate. A short
time later, Phinuit began talking to Newbold (Billie). The session was
recorded:

**Phinuit:** "George (G.P.) is shaking his fingers at me. He sent me after
that gentleman (Moses). I found him in another part of our world."

**Newbold:** "Far away?"

**Phinuit:** "It would be a long way to you Billie but not so far to me. George had difficulty in having him come but they had a long talk and George made it all right with him. He didn't understand what we wished of him."

**Newbold:** "Who is he?"

**Phinuit:** "I don't know his name. George called me and sent me after him – you understand Billie – [he] said: 'You go and find him for me, doctor.'"

**Newbold:** "How did you know whom he wanted?"

**Phinuit:** "He said, 'I want you to find a friend of mine who used to be a medium in the body,' used the light, you know. Oh, he has a great deal of light, more than anybody."

**Newbold:** "Do spirits have light too?"

**Phinuit:** "What d'you mean Billie? Spirits are all light."

**Newbold:** "I mean does a person who has light in the body have in the spirit also more light than others?"

**Phinuit:** "Yes, indeed."

**Newbold:** "Tell me how George made you know whom he wanted."

**Phinuit:** "He described him."

**Newbold:** "And his influence?"

**Phinuit:** "Of course."

**Newbold:** "You know it is very hard for us to believe in spirits at all. Do you remember your life on earth, doctor?"

**Phinuit:** "Oh yes, but I've been here a very long time."

**Newbold:** "Did you believe in spirits while on earth?"

**Phinuit:** (Phinuit gave a short, derisive laugh) "Not much, Not I."

**Newbold:** "Then you should sympathize with us."

**Phinuit:** "Oh, I can't put myself in your place." [9]

The communications with Moses were deemed a failure as his answers to Newbold's questions, and later Hodgson's, were vague and indistinct, clearly not evidential. G.P. explained to Hodgson that both Imperator and Moses were too high, or too advanced, to be effective in their ability to communicate, that they "cannot handle the machine as we can," meaning that spirits at lower levels can better control the medium as they are closer in vibration.[10] On March 24, 1897, Moses communicated to Hodgson:

> I have passed through so many stages since I came to this life, that to return through the light of the medium and recall all the names of friends is an impossibility until, at least, I have become fully accustomed to everything, viz., light, medium, yourself, surroundings, articles, etc. It is a strange and interesting experience at first I can assure you. At first we see the imprisoned spirit of some friend on earth but very vaguely, and at the moment we wonder what it all means, and before we can realize where we are or to whom we are speaking, our thoughts become a mass, as it were, of confused and half-registered and incoherent (pause)...It is not painful, however, to ourselves, but we see that it is distressing to those to whom we are trying to speak. Why, H[odgson], my dear fellow, you have no conception of what it is like, and how earnestly, truthfully, and sincerely we are struggling to reach our friends.[11]

After reading Hodgson's reports concerning his study of Leonora Piper, James Hyslop was inclined to accept the spiritistic hypothesis. "But there were certain difficulties connected with the mistakes and confusions and with the dramatic play of personality, as I afterward called it, that made me still suspend judgment," Hyslop wrote in his 1905 book, *Science and a Future Life*.[12]

Upon receiving his Ph.D. from Johns Hopkins University in 1887 and his LL.D. from University of Wooster, Hyslop taught philosophy at Lake Forest University, Smith College, and Bucknell University before joining the faculty of Columbia in 1895. He authored three textbooks, *Elements of Logic* (1892), *Elements of Ethics* (1895), and *Problems of Philosophy* (1905). His interest in psychical research was a result of his friendship with Professor William James.

Hyslop contacted Hodgson to arrange for some sittings with Mrs Piper. "When I entered the house with Dr. Hodgson he introduced me as 'Mr. Smith,'" Hyslop recorded. "I bowed in silence, did not shake hands, nor utter a word, and during the seventeen sittings published in my report Mrs. Piper did not hear my voice in her normal state, except twice when I changed it into an unnatural tone to utter a sentence, in one case only four words. My object was to conceal my identity, because I had been present at a sitting in 1892 for fifteen minutes, and met Mrs. Piper after the sitting. The present occasion was in 1898, and I had grown a full beard in the meantime." [13]

By that time, Mrs. Piper had changed from primarily a trance speaking medium to an automatic writing medium, while Rector had replaced Phinuit and G.P. as her primary spirit control. After Mrs. Piper went into the trance state, Hyslop took his place behind and to the right of her, from where he could see the automatic writing. Hodgson sat nearby and recorded the session. Some years after his first series of sittings with Mrs. Piper, Hyslop described the conditions and process:

In the first place, there are no resemblances to the traditional trappings and arrangements for so-called mediumistic performances, no cabinet, no curtains, no darkness, and no physical phenomena of any sort. Everything is done in broad daylight and every feature of the experiments is visible as in all normal experience. Mrs. Piper goes gradually into a trance and her head rests on a number of pillows lying on a table in front of her. Her face is turned to the left. Her right hand rests on another table at the right, and at an appropriate time this hand shows its readiness to write. A pencil is then placed between her fingers and the hand writes what purports to be messages from the dead. The sitter reads aloud the writing and asks questions or makes answers to the 'communications,' as the circumstances permit or require.

Mrs. Piper purports to be 'controlled' by a group of alleged discarnate spirits calling themselves by the name of Imperator, Rector, Doctor,

Prudens and possibly some others. These are the same alleged personalities that claimed to 'control' the automatic writing of the Rev. Stainton Moses before his death in 1892. Rector is the usual amanuensis for the writing and also the speaking when this method is employed. Imperator does not often 'control' and the other two seem not to serve as amanuenses but to exercise some other functions in the work. But in some way all 'communications' seem to come through the 'control' or amanuensis, and this, as I have remarked, is usually Rector, tho in my own records George Pelham (G.P.) often assumed this function.

The 'communicator,' in some way not definitely known, sends his message to Rector, or is aided by Rector in influencing the automatic writing, whether it be by telepathic transmission of his thoughts to the subconsciousness of the medium or to Rector or by direct 'possession' of the organism of Mrs. Piper. At times apparently the 'communicator' has to send his message to a third person, and he to transmit them to the more direct 'control.' Thus, George Pelham sometimes acts as an intermediary between the 'communicator' and Rector, the direct 'control.' There are also indications at times of other persons aiding in the results.[14]

The first part of the first sitting was full of confusion, Hyslop wrote, mentioning that Mrs. Piper's husband, William, had suffered some sort of paralysis a few days before and she was in a very anxious state of mind. While several names and relationships were correctly given, he then received a series of names which meant nothing to him. Toward the end of the session the name "Charles" was spelled out with the claim that it was his brother who had died of typhoid fever after suffering a very bad throat problem. He further communicated that he had died in the winter when snow was covering the ground and then changed the cause of his death to scarlet fever, although it was initially diagnosed as typhoid. He also reported seeing their mother, who had died after him.

"My brother Charles died at four and a half years in 1864 of scarlet fever and measles, so diagnosed, with a very putrid sore throat of a diphtheritic character," Hyslop recorded. "It was in March and a heavy snow fell on the day before and on the morning of his death, a fact which I remember because I was sent on an errand that morning. My mother died five years after my brother Charles."[15]

In an attempt to trick Mrs. Piper (or Rector), Hyslop asked Charles if he had seen their brother George. The fact was that George was still alive. The reply came through Mrs. Piper's hand that George would not be over there "for a while yet."[16]

At his second sitting with Mrs. Piper, Hyslop was immediately addressed with "James, James, speak to me," by someone claiming to be his father, Robert Hyslop. But he was not able to write anything else before Charles communicated again, confirming that it was their father, who had died some two years earlier. At the end of the sitting, as Mrs. Piper was coming out of trance, she uttered "Hyslop" and then "Tell him I am his father."[17] Hyslop's Aunt Eliza, who was still alive, was mentioned along with some incidents in her life, which Hyslop felt were characteristic of her.

In the third and fourth sittings, Hyslop's father communicated more fluently and talked about the discussions he had had, before he died, with his son about the afterlife. "What do you remember, James, of our talks about Swedenborg?" the father asked. "Do you remember of our talking one evening in the library about his description of the Bible?"[18] The father also referred to a discussion they had had about hypnotism and about apparitions near the point of death. The son recalled it all except discussing Swedenborg, but when he talked with his stepmother about it, she remembered it well, as she did not know who Swedenborg was and discussed him with her husband after James left that day.

The father further mentioned that James's voice was the last he heard before he died, also confirmed as fact by the son. As another test, Hyslop asked his father what medicine he had gotten for him in New York on his last visit with him. With some difficulty, Mrs. Piper's hand wrote "Himi" and "strychnine." In fact, Hyslop brought Hyomei for him, but did not bring strychnine. However, his father was taking strychnine with the Hyomei at the time. Hyslop further reported:

> He mentioned a black skull cap which he finally said had been made for him by 'Hettie's mother,' Hettie being the name of my half-sister. This was correct. The names of the members of the family were given as they were used in life, and many incidents indicated in connection with them. Thus my sister Lida was mentioned in connection with the organ and the statement made that he, my father, wanted her to sing. My father had brought an organ and wanted my sister by that name to learn to play and sing.[19]

Many other evidential facts were communicated by the father. He asked what happened to his old horse, giving the horse's name, Tom. He said that his old friend, Steele Perry, had moved west. He referred to another friend, Harper Crawford, being involved in a dispute over putting an organ in their church. The latter two facts were outside the scope of mental telepathy as Hyslop knew nothing about them, although he later checked with relatives and found them to be true. The senior Hyslop also mentioned a walking stick with his initials cut in the top, another verifiable fact.

Hyslop continued to sit with Mrs. Piper periodically over several years. While some of the messages were confusing and didn't make sense to Hyslop, there was much more in the way of evidence coming to him from deceased relatives. At one sitting, his uncle, James McClellan, communicated and mentioned that Hyslop was named after him, which Hyslop confirmed as correct. The uncle also said that he "despised the (nick) name Jim," which Hyslop knew nothing about. However, when Hyslop checked with his cousin, one of the uncle's daughters, he was informed that his uncle did, in fact, dislike being called Jim.

Charles, the deceased brother, asked him what happened to the chimney after he died. Hyslop recalled that an especially tall and ungainly chimney was built over the family kitchen at their old home in Ohio during 1861, three years before his brother died, but it was destroyed by a cyclone in 1884.

Hylsop noted that there were times when Rector struggled with the verbiage and G.P. would step in to help, but even with G.P., the grammar was sometimes faulty. In one message, the word "is" was used instead of "are," and Hyslop questioned G.P. on that knowing that G.P. would never have made such a mistake. G.P. replied to Hodgson, who was recording. "If I fail grammatically, Hodgson, it is owing to the machine…Cannot always make it work just right." In another sitting, G.P. was again questioned on his grammar. He replied:

> Cosmical weather interests both he and I –me –him—I know it all. Don't you see I correct these. Well, I am not less intelligent now. But there are many difficulties. I am far clearer on all points than I was shut up in the prisoned body. [Hodgson suggested he should have said "prisoning" or "imprisoned."] No, I don't mean to get it that way you spoke – perhaps I have spelled it wrong. Prisoned body. Prisoning. See here, Hodgson. Don't view me with a critic's eye, but pass my imperfections by. Of course, I know all that as well as anybody on your

sphere. Well I think so. I tell you, old fellow, it don't do to pick all these little errors too much when they amount to nothing in one way. You have light enough and brain enough I know to understand my explanation of being shut up in this body [referring to Mrs. Piper's body], dreaming as it were and trying to help Science.[20]

There was confusion and difficulty with names at times. In one sitting, reference was made to Hyslop's stepmother, who went by Maggie, as "Mannie." And later she was referred to as "Nannie," which confused things even more since Hyslop had an Aunt Nannie. After Hyslop asked for clarification, there was further confusion and dramatic play, during which G.P. took control and said that he would get the correct name. Near the close of the sitting, G.P. came back with Margaret as Maggie's given name, which was correct.

In another sitting, Hyslop's deceased cousin, Robert McClellan, was attempting to communicate, but Rector struggled to get his name, first saying "Allen," then "McCollum" and "McAllen." It was never given correctly in that sitting, but Hyslop understood who it was. At a later sitting, the name still not given, the cousin said that G.P. was assisting him to "communicate." Then, G.P. suddenly interrupted and said, "Look out, Hodgson, I am here, George Pelham. Imperator sent me some moments ago." G.P. said that the name sounds like "McLellen" (written out), which was close enough. The cousin then said, "Yes, I am he."[21]

In still another sitting, Hyslop's father tried to give the name James Carruthers, but Rector could not get it. As Rector continued to struggle with the name, G.P. again broke in and said that Imperator had sent him to assist. He said that he would return later. As Mrs. Piper was coming out of the trance state, she gave something very close to the name but not exactly. More than two years later, the name was given very distinctly four different times, but the next day it was again mispronounced, Rector writing "Carbes" and "Carleths." Some years later, after many years of psychical research, Hylsop analyzed the confusion of words:

We must not forget, in placing the emphasis of the spiritistic theory on the evidence for the personal identity of certain persons, that all the communications purport to come though discarnate spirits who do not attempt to prove their identity but serve as necessary intermediaries for the communications of those who do make this attempt. Hence, not only do we have the physical, and perhaps the mental subject of the medium to reckon with, but we have also the alleged mental subject of the 'control' to reckon with in the same results. Why this should be so can receive only the most general consideration, and the answer would be that only an occasional spirit can endure the conditions or retain consciousness long enough to serve as an intermediary. But dismissing this as either conjectural or as unnecessary and irrelevant to our present problem, and contenting ourselves with the real or apparent presence and mediation of such agencies, we have a condition that inevitably suggests a possible source of difficulty and confusion in the transmission of communications, and it would remain to see whether we could discover evidence in the record that such an hypothesis received any confirmation in the facts. We must remember too that we are not always limited to one such intermediary, but at times we have at least two, and possibly more than two. Rector was usually the 'control' in my sittings, but occasionally George Pelham (G.P.) acted as 'control,' and sometimes he acted as intermediary between Rector and the communicator endeavoring to establish his identity. In this way the opportunity for much dramatic play occurs as well as for the modification of messages.[22]

Hyslop went on to give another example, referring to a sitting in which his father used the word "Sunday." When alive, he always said "Sabbath." Further, in other communications, Rector also used "Sabbath." However, since it was said that G.P. was assisting, Hyslop concluded that he somehow translated the word "Sabbath" to "Sunday." Similarly, where his father would have said "carriage," the word "coach" was given.

Many comments concerning the confused mental state of the communicators were made. Early in the first sitting, Robert Hyslop communicated, "I am working to keep my thoughts clear," and later, "It will help to keep my thoughts from rambling." When his uncle communicated, he could not respond to a question put to him and said, "I will tell you when I return. I am dazed somewhat." On another occasion, the uncle said, "My head is troublesome. In thinking I hope to be clearer soon." In Hyslop's fourth sitting, his father commented, "I seem to lose part of my recollections between my absence and return, just before I had this change." Later, when he could not recall something, he said, "I know everything so well when I am not speaking to you." And still later, Robert Hyslop communicated, "If I fail in my memory, do not say well if that is my father he must have forgotten a great deal. I really forget nothing, but I find it not easy to tell it all to you. I feel as though I should choke at times and I fail to express my thoughts, but if fragmentary, try and think the best of them will you?" As G.P. had earlier explained, the communicating spirit had to put himself in a condition something like our sleep in order to communicate.[23]

Fraud was clearly ruled out, Hyslop concluded. Even if Mrs. Piper knew he was coming to sit with her, which she didn't, she would have had to employ a private investigator to dig up obscure facts in a town nearly a thousand miles from where she lived, this at a time when travel and communications were slow and relatively expensive. And she would have had to assume that none of Hyslop's relatives would mention that a private investigator was there asking about the names of horses, nicknames, church disputes, etc., etc. And the investigator would have had to somehow have found out about private conversations Hyslop had with his father.

The fact that information unknown to Hyslop but later verified as true was communicated seemed to rule out simple person to person telepathy. As for a more cosmic telepathy – one in which the medium taps into minds and memories anywhere in the world or into some cosmic computer and then relays the information back to the sitter in a conversational manner – Hyslop felt that there was no adequate scientific evidence for such a theory and that it represented a process far more incredible than spirits. He wrote:

> Telepathy does not explain dramatic play of personality, the mistakes and confusion, or the vast mass of unevidential matter involved in the records. Secondary personality of a most remarkable character has to be added to the process to give it even the appearance of rationality, while the spiritistic hypothesis, with such adjunctive suppositions as abnormal psychology supplies us, gives unity and rationality to the whole result."[24]

Having read Hodgson's reports before beginning his own study of Mrs. Piper, Hyslop noted that most of the failures on record were connected with persons who had only one sitting. "If I had passed final judgment on the phenomena as a result of my first sitting, I should have had a less favorable verdict to pronounce, as the first experiment, though by no means a failure in regard to the supernormal, did not supply enough for any scientific man bent on proving a vast theory," he offered. "In this subject we must not expect the supernormal to be on tap always and everywhere and for every one."[25]

When Hyslop was criticized by academic colleagues for his interest in psychical research, he asked "Why is it so noble and respectable to find whence man came, and so suspicious and dishonorable to ask and ascertain whither he goes?" [26]

---

[1] Holt, 513 (SPR Pr. XIII, 323f)

[2] _____, 514

[3] _____, 515

[4] _____, 570-571

[5] _____, 519 (SPR PR XIII, 360)

[6] _____, 523

[7] _____, 514

[8] _____, 532

[9] _____, 541-542 (SPR Pr XIV, 36f)

[10] _____, 583

[11] _____, 581

[12] Hyslop (1905), 212

[13] _____, 213

[14] Hyslop (1910), 22

[15] Hyslop (1905), 215

[16] _____, 215

[17] _____, 216

[18] _____, 218

[19] _____, 219

[20] Holt, 598-599

[21] Hyslop (1905), 277

[22] Hyslop (1910), 230

[23] Hyslop (1905), 258-270

[24] _____, 264

[25] _____, 288

[26] Blum 247

# -Seven-

# The Re-Education
# of Bennie Junot

*I do see and know a great deal about you and the things you do.*
**– the discarnate Bennie Judah**

On June 19, 1899, Bennie Junot struggled to communicate with his father through the mediumship of Leonora Piper. Dr. Richard Hodgson observed and recorded: "I hear…I hear some thing. Where is my mother – I want very much to see her. I can breathe easier now. I want to go home now…And take up my studies and go on…I see some one who looks like my father – I want to see him very much."[1]

Bennie Junot is the pseudonym assigned for privacy concerns by Hodgson to Bennie Judah, who died in a boating accident on September 5, 1898 at the age of 17. His parents were Noble R. Judah, a Chicago lawyer, and Kate Hutchinson Judah, a member of a well-to-do Chicago family. Mr. Judah was a member of the American branch of the Society for Psychical Research. Bennie was born in 1881, his brother Noble, Jr. in 1884 and his sister Helen in 1887.[2] Noble, Jr. is called "Roble" in the research records, while Helen keeps her given name. Noble Jr. would become a lawyer and Ambassador to Cuba. In all, there were 65 communications from Bennie over a period of some six years, with Hodgson present at all but one. In some of them, only Hodgson was present. (The Judahs are hereinafter referred to by the pseudonyms.)

Bennie's death took place while the family was vacationing in Osterville, Massachusetts, near Hyannis. The boat Bennie and his brother were on capsized, causing the mast to hit Bennie in the head. The blow was not immediately fatal, but he died later that day as a result of inflammation of the brain.

At that point in Mrs. Piper's mediumship, Rector was the chief control, although G.P. often assisted Rector and occasionally substituted for him. After Rector gives his usual sign, a cross, the transcript reads (punctuation added):

> **Rector:** "Hail thou friend, why come to us in sorrow? Why needst thou weep when all is well and ever will be? We will find thy friends for thee and bring them here....We see among our friends here a young man who seems dazed and puzzled. He is not near enough to us for us to give him much help at the moment but will be presently." (Hodgson tells Mr. Junot to respond.)

> **Mr. Junot:** "Yes, I understand."

> **Rector:** "George (G.P.) is here with him and trying to urge him to come closer...that he may see into thy world more clearly."

> **Bennie:** "I hear...I hear some thing. Where is my mother? I want very much to see her. I can breathe easier now. I want to go home now... And take up my studies and go on...I see some one who looks like my father – I want to see him very much."

> **Mr. Junot:** "Speak on, Bennie, tell us all about yourself."

> **Bennie:** [Much excitement in hand] "I...I want to see you awfully... I..." [Mr. Junot noted that "awfully" was a word frequently used by his son.]

> **Hodgson:** "Take your time. Take your time. Be quite calm."

> **Bennie:** "Father...papa...papa...Pa...father, I hear something strange... can it be your voice?"

> **Mr. Junot:** "Yes, Bennie, it's daddy."

**Bennie:** "I…You hear me…do you hear me? I…wonder how I can reach you as I long to do. I heard all you said…And I want to tell you where I am. (Hand moves toward Hodgson.) You are not my father."

**Hodgson:** "Kindly listen one moment. I am with your father, and I have brought your father here for you to free your mind to him."

**Bennie:** "And can I do so now?"

**Hodgson:** "Yes, fire away, take your time and be quite calm."

**Bennie:** "I want to see father more than any one except mama."

**Mr. Junot:** "Bennie, tell me what to say to your mother."

**Bennie:** "Oh, she is so sad, tell her I called her the other day and I could not make her hear me. I love her so, but…wait till I think it over and I will say it all."

**Mr. Junot:** "Are you happy where you are?"

**Bennie:** "I wish I could hear you. You were so good to me. Do you ride any now?" [Apparently, G.P. is passing on the messages from his father and Bennie does not hear his words directly.]

**Mr. Junot:** "Yes, sweetheart, yes, sweetheart, and think of you every day when I ride."

**Bennie:** "I often think how I used to go with you."

**Mr. Junot:** **"**Do you remember your ride in the West?"

**Bennie:** [Again, much excitement in Mrs. Piper's hand.] "I do very well. Yes, I do. I remember it all and do you remember what happened to me? Do you remember anything about a storm, dad…."

**Hodgson:** "Write that word again, Rector, please."

**Rector:** "Sounds like StORM – Rain."

**Mr. Junot:** "Let me ask him a question."

**Bennie:** "Oh, so many things are going through my head."

**Mr. Junot:** "Who went with you on your ride in the West?"

**Bennie:** "Will you say it again...who was with me...I..."

**Hodgson:** "The father says, 'Who was with you in your ride in the West?"

**Bennie:** "Father says...I...who I want to know about Harry."

**Mr. Junot:** "That's right." [Mr. Junot later informed Hodgson that Harry was a cowboy friend of Bennie's with whom he took a long horseback journey in the West.]

**Bennie:** "Tell him I remember him well...I..."

**Mr. Junot:** "Yes, he wrote your mother lately. Harry's gone South. He's gone away South."

**Bennie:** "And he is a good fellow and do you know I liked him very much and I thought he sent the photograph to her."

**Mr. Junot:** "He did, yes, he did." [Mr. Junot later explained that Harry sent a photograph of himself to Mrs. Junot.]

**Bennie:** "I heard her say it looked like him. I am very happy now, better than ever before. I saw her when she was so ill." [Mr. Junot explained that his wife suffered an illness after Bennie's death.]

**Mr. Junot:** "Bennie, what are you doing now? What are you doing now, Bennie?"

**Bennie:** "What am I doing, why, pa, dear, I am doing everything – writing, reading, studying, and am generally happy. Do you hear me I am getting...clearer, I think. I often...I often think I hear you calling me."

**Mr. Junot:** "Yes, we call for you often, dearie."

**Bennie:** "And when mother sits in that chair by the window I hear her say—Oh, if I could only see you dear. Ask her....Did Harry say he would send me any message. Speak slowly, dad, or I cannot hear all you say."

**Mr. Junot:** "Mama wrote and told Harry that you had gone away and left us."

**Bennie:** "I wonder what he thought when he heard that. Give him my love and tell him I will never forget the good times we had together...who was that who tried to call me back? I did not like her. Who was that who tried to call me back?" [Mr. Junot did not understand the reference at the time, but upon returning home was told by Mrs. Junot that an old nurse had attempted to contact Bennie through a medium and took his harmonica as an influence.]

**Mr. Junot:** "Do you see mother and papa drive out South sometimes?"

**Bennie:** "Of course I do. I told...out to where they took my body."

**Mr. Junot:** "Ah, sure, Bennie, your mind's clear enough."

**Bennie:** "And I see the flowers mother put there...they..." [Bennie went on to describe the flowers and arrangements.]

Also, the names of Frank and Charles, very close friends of Bennie, were given by him at that first sitting, and they were constantly referred to in later sittings. Bennie also mentioned seeing his father get "the hair clipped" a few days earlier. Mr. Junot took this to refer to his having the hair of a horse clipped. He further mentioned playing "Home Sweet Home" and "Swanee River" on his harmonica for his mother, also confirmed as fact.

At Mr. Junot's second sitting, Bennie told his father that there were two or three letters written to him by "L," apparently a girl friend, that were left in his little case and he was concerned that others would read the letters. He asked that his mother retrieve the letters and not let anyone else read them. [The letters were never found.]

Bennie continued: "I want you to remember...Af...Alfred...where is he...at home?" [Mr. Junot informed Hodgson that Alfred was a near-neighbor and a good friend of Bennie's.]

Over the next six-plus years, until November 22, 1905, a month before Hodgson's death, Bennie would continue to communicate, offering much in the way of evidence while also giving Hodgson and other researchers a better understanding of the difficulties in communicating. Here are some of the more interesting messages, exchanges, and observations:

**March 5, 1900:** Mrs. Junot told Bennie that she often feels him around and wonders if it is him. "Yes, indeed I do and mama there is no doubt about it. I do see and know a great deal about you and the things you do. I see all the pictures of myself and all my own work." [Mr. Junot informed Hodgson that there are many pictures of Bennie around the house and various pieces of his handiwork.]

When asked to write his name, he spelled out "Benjamin Roble Junot." However, Roble was his father's name, as well as his brother's name, not his middle name. When Mrs. Junot informed him of this, Bennie struggled with the name, writing, "H...H...Haer...Hher" before giving up. His middle name was "Harrison."

Bennie later communicated that Miriam, his cousin, was the first to greet him after he crossed over. Mr. Junot noted that Miriam passed only a few weeks before Bennie's death.

Mr. Junot asked Bennie if he had seen his mother, Bennie's grandmother. "Yes, I did and she told me to tell you dear Dad that she had taken care of you ever since she came here, and no matter what you do she will still watch over you.

At the end of the sitting, Bennie signed his initials, "B.H.J." and Mrs. Junot noted that the writing was very much like Bennie's.

As Mrs. Piper was coming out of trance, she said she saw a young man with light hair singing "Swanee River," a song that his parents had recalled him singing when in the flesh.

**March 6, 1900:** Bennie told his parents that he is frequently with them when they are driving and that the "Good Priest" (Imperator) is helping him keep his thoughts clear. He then mentioned that he and his maternal grandmother had noticed that "Aunt Helen" was having a lot of problems with her teeth, a fact confirmed by Mrs. Junot.

**March 7, 1900:** Bennie recalled the new stall that his father had built for his pony, but he could not remember the name of the pony. "I know everything so well before I speak, then I lose it," he commented, then recalling the "long things that used to grow" which he picked and gave to his sister, Helen, but he could not remember the name of those either. Mrs. Junot reminded Bennie that they were cat o'nine tails. When told this, Mrs. Piper's hand became very excited.

Rector then intervened and said that Bennie was leaving for a moment. After a short time, Bennie announced that he had returned. "My head is getting clear since that man named ...called George went away with his father." Hodgson then gathered from Rector that his (Hodgson's) deceased father had come to deliver a message to him (Hodgson) and this had confused Bennie.

**March 19, 1900:** Hodgson sat alone with Mrs. Piper when Bennie came and asked if he was his father's friend. Bennie said he could hear Helen (his sister) playing the piano. Hodgson noted the time as 11:26 a.m. and sent a telegram to the Junots after the sitting, asking if Helen had been playing the piano that morning. Mrs. Junot replied by telegram that Helen had been playing the piano that morning between 11:15 and 11:30. By letter, Mr. Junot explained that Helen would have been in school that morning except that she had been allowed to stay home because of bad weather. Bennie told Hodgson that they have great music where he was and asked if he could hear it. Hodgson told Bennie that he could not hear it as his senses were too shut in. Bennie then said he forgot that Hodgson was still "in the body."

**March 28, 1900:** Again, Hodgson was sitting alone with Mrs. Piper when Bennie communicated. Hodgson noted that this was the only time Bennie acted as "control," i.e., actually took over Mrs. Piper's body and wrote himself, not requiring Rector or G.P. as intermediaries. Hodgson reported his interesting observations as Bennie took control:

> Movement in hand, not violent, suggesting new control. Same pencil given. Finds it, feels it, places it on block-book, so that it lies flat on book, lift it up and down a little, tapping various times with it lengthways transversely across book, then raise it and cast it to the front across the room. Fresh pencil offered, not accepted, but hand pats block-book cover, round the edges and over surface with hand slightly hollowed, palm down, patting with distal joints of fingers. Then hand is held up as if the book were being inspected by some one just behind it, then turned round as if showing the palm for inspection, then bent backwards and forwards at the wrist, all as if for the inspection of a person just behind. Finally the hand took up the ordinary writing position on the block-book. The time occupied by those movements was about

from three to five minutes. I was about to place the fresh pencil in the usual place, between first and second fingers, but the hand moved a little, as if rejecting that position, and seized the pencil between the second and third fingers, so that it passed between the proximal joints of the second and third fingers, and was held near the point by the ends of the thumb and first finger.

"Yes, here I am...and he is teaching me how to speak, this is a queer place I think and I am wondering how I got here with you," Bennie wrote. "I feel quite happy to know I can come myself. I am Bennie and you are Mr. Hodgson. They tell me I am doing well...Tell me if you hear me, do you hear me or do you see me or how do you do?"

Hodgson explained to Bennie that he was using Mrs. Piper body and writing through her hand, to which Bennie replied, "Well that is queer too because I hear you and I see you very clearly and I talk to you because I am using my own mind and I see just what you are wishing me to do...I like you pretty well already because I think you are a friend of dad's, aren't you?" Hodgson noted that the hand of the medium stretched forward, as if someone were standing in front of her. "Did you hear that spirit tell me to look up when he spoke to me?" Bennie asked Hodgson, apparently referring to Rector or G.P. Hodgson wondered if "looking up" corresponded to stretching up the hand to spirit.

Referring to a letter he had received from Mr. Junot, Hodgson asked Bennie if he had seen Sammy. "Well, yes, I have and Sport also," Bennie replied. Hodgson would later be told that Sport was the name of their stable dog who had died some years before.

Hodgson then asked Bennie if he would look up [Hodgson's] cousin Fred Hyde, who had died many years earlier. He suggested that G.P. could probably help him find Fred.

**April 3, 1900:** "I saw Mr. Hyde and I like him mighty well," Bennie communicated to Hodgson, who was again sitting alone with Mrs. Piper. "He is a very bright fellow and has been helping me in many ways." Hodgson then remembered his request to locate his cousin. "Oh, you mean my cousin Fred?" Hodgson replied. "Yes he is your cousin Fred and the gentleman (G.P) who is speaking for me helped me to find him."

**October 29, 1900:** Bennie broke in at another solo sitting by Hodgson and said he had just one thing to communicate – that he had cured Helen's throat problem. Hodgson later found out from Mr. Junot that Helen had an "ugly sore throat" during September and it had caused much anxiety.

**February 18, 1901:** With Mr. and Mrs. Junot present, Bennie referred to a "wall" that was being put up behind the house. Mr. Junot said it was a fence, not a wall. Bennie said that is what he was referring to and that "you will forget the names of things when you get here."

Bennie asked his mother if she heard him when he called her the other night. Mrs. Junot replied that she wasn't sure and asked what he said to her. "I said to write to Roble," Bennie responded. Mr. Junot recalled that evening when his wife "suddenly started up and proceeded to write to Roble. Her motions were so unusual in some way as to attract comment from others of the family. She said, 'I must write to Roble'."

**February 19, 1901:** Mrs. Junot asked Bennie what he does when not communicating with them. "Do...well the things I care for most are those I left behind in the body," he responded, "but I am most contented here, dear and I live with grandpa and grandma Junot...I am learning all the time the conditions of this life, the reality and truth of our having to live in one life to be able to in this."

Mrs. Junot asked why Grandma Junot never comes to the sittings. "But she has dear, only I fear I am a little greedy and take up all the light dear mother, but I do not mean to," Bennie answered, the "light" referring to the medium.

**February 20, 1901:** Bennie told his mother that George, her cousin, sends his love and commented that he was such a jolly fellow when alive. Mrs. Junot did not agree. "This is a joke, dear mother, because he was never known to smile...and we often remark...we remark it here," Bennie replied. "And I speak it in particular that you may know just who I mean."

Bennie then passed on a message from another male cousin who had recently passed over and asked that it be given to his mother: "I was I thought as happy as I could be when I owned the body, but after I left I found I did not know what happiness was...I saw you almost as soon as I lost control of my body, and I was so happy, and I was told that I should see clearer and clearer as time passed and so I have, and when I have seen you grieve I have said, 'Oh well it is not for long, and it is only a condition of the body'."

**February 11, 1902:** Frank Junot, Bennie's uncle, communicated, speaking to his brother. "I am delighted to see you – I took Bennie's place for a moment, a good boy...one of the best I ever knew. Tell Alice (Frank's widow) I am sure I can remember everything soon..." Frank told his brother that he had tried to communicate earlier but "could not understand the whys and wherefores." He also said that he had been met by his deceased son and that they are now together. "I found it all better than I had ever dreamed," he added. Hodgson noted that the handwriting from Frank was larger and more emphatic than with Bennie.

Bennie then returned and told his father that he had brought Hugh Irving, their old servant. In a previous sitting, Mr. Junot had asked Bennie if he could find Hugh and determine what ever happened to Rounder, the Junot's dog. Apparently, when Hugh left their employment, he took Rounder with him. Hugh told Mr. Junot that he lost Rounder, but that he would attempt to find him and see that he is returned. Mr. Junot noted that Hugh referred to Bennie as "Mr. Ben," just as he had when alive, but referred to him by his first name when he had always called him "Mr. Junot" when alive.

Grandpa Junot then communicated briefly, telling his son that even though he died when his son was young there is very little about his life that he did not know.

**February 12, 1902:** Bennie brought Sam, the son of some Junot friends who had died not long before. Sam asked Mrs. Junot to tell his mother to keep the Mansfield photographs. When Mrs. Junot later relayed the message to Sam's mother, she understood what was meant.

**April 2, 1902:** Hodgson was sitting alone with Mrs. Piper when Bennie broke in. "John Welsh has Rounder." Hodgson did not understand. "John Welsh has Rounder. Tell this....tell...tell...John Welsh has Rounder." Hodgson still didn't understand and repeated "John Welsh *is* round her?" Apparently frustrated, Bennie replied: *"Has...has...*It's I, Benny, don't you see me? I, Benny."

**February 23, 1903:** The subject of Bennie's horse came up again and Bennie said he could still not remember the name, but then he wondered if the name started with a "K." Mr. Junot told him that was correct and urged him to try and get the rest of the name. Bennie then proceeded to spell it out, "K-L-O-N-D-I-K-E," which Mr. Junot confirmed as correct.

Bennie told his father that he saw some men working around the old barn. Mr. Junot confirmed that for the past three days workmen had been moving the old barn at their farm, although he had not been home since the moving began.

Bennie then gave way to Hugh, the old servant. However, the writing involved curious looping and neither Hodgson nor Junot could make it out. Rector then communicated that Hugh "speaks queerly" and this was responsible for the strange writing. But Hugh managed to ask how

Rounder is doing. Apparently, Mr. Junot found John Welsh and got his dog back. "Rounder is all right, Hugh," Mr. Junot said. "He's so glad to get back." Mr. Junot then asked Hugh if he gave Rounder to Welsh. "No, I saw him at Welsh's house in the body, and prayed him to send him to you," Hugh explained. "Then Mr. Bennie got hold and we worked to get him back. I hope you keep him now – look out for him."

After some confusing remarks, Bennie said, "When I get here and they don't always understand what I do say. You will know when you get here how hard I try to tell you all that you may [know] it is really I."

**February 24, 1903:** Mrs. Junot said she had concerns about communicating with Bennie, wondering if it was holding him back in his progress. "…now let me tell you one thing," Bennie told her. "Don't question the right and wrong of my returning because there are no wrongs in it."

Bennie then informed his mother that he could see Helen having more throat problems in a couple of days, but not to worry. Upon returning home, Mrs. Junot reported to Hodgson that they found Helen quite ill with a sore throat and under the doctor's care.

Mrs. Junot asked Bennie if he knew all that happens to them. "All to my immediate family, yes – you, dad, Robie, Helen," he responded. Mrs. Junot then asked him if he knew what was going on with others that he knew. "Yes and no," Bennie answered. "I can if I think specially about any one friend and wish to know. Otherwise, I do not."

In a sitting the previous day, Mrs. Junot asked about Bennie's cousin, Mary, the daughter of Frank and Alice Junot who had died some time before Bennie. Bennie said he had brought her for this sitting but she was unable to communicate as she did not yet understand this method of speech. However, he assured her that Mary was often around Aunt Alice. Mrs. Junot asked what Alice was doing in that world. "She looks after some of the other children here," Bennie replied, but added that he could not get Rector to communicate exactly what she does. As he talked about Mary, he said she was standing there and laughing at his words about her.

Mrs. Junot asked Bennie if he hears her when she asks for his help. "Yes, I often do," Bennie replied. "I know a great deal that goes on with you, dear, and when grandma says you humor Helen I think she don't (sic) understand…I help you with her often." Bennie said that he was also helping Roble as much as possible.

Bennie asked his mother if she understood the philosophy of prayer, to which Mrs. Junot asked what he meant. "How necessary it is to pray for what you wish," Bennie told her. "I understand it since I came to this life…prayer is everything to us here."

**December 16, 1903:** With Hodgson sitting alone, Bennie asked him if Roble got his hat into the paint. Hodgson wrote to the Junots and found out that Roble had painted his old straw hat green and wore it about the farm all summer.

Bennie also said that he saw Roble "fussing about his clothes" recently while also trying on a new suit which he did not like. Checking on this, Hodgson was told by Mr. Junot that Mrs. Junot bought Roble a new suit at Thanksgiving time and it was exchanged at Roble's request.

Bennie said that Rounder appeared to be getting very stiff in his legs and that he often pats him and talks to him. He wags his tail and sniffs at him. "I think he sees me, really, I do."

**February 22, 1904:** "Music is the inspiration of the soul," Bennie told his father, asking him to tell Helen how much he loves to hear her play and practice. He then asked his father if his coat is blue. Mr. Junot acknowledged that it was blue with red inside. "Do you understand what a beautiful place this is dad?"

**February 24, 1904:** With Hodgson sitting alone, Bennie said, "Here is George (G.P.), perhaps you would better greet him too. He has been a good friend to me, and when the light (Mrs. Piper) has been especially drawn upon by myself he has been my support." Hodgson then told George that he was grateful for all his support. "Just say good morning that will do," George communicated. "You know I understand. It is only to please the boy, understand."

**June 27, 1904:** Bennie told his mother that he could see some one in the body with her but couldn't make out who it was. They moved closer to the table. "It is my sister (Helen)," Bennie exclaimed. "Oh I am so glad you are here." After discussing her music and school, Bennie asked Helen what made her let Klondike run away. Mrs. Junot then corrected Bennie and said that it was Roble's horse that ran away. "So it was," Bennie responded. "That's so. I remember now but mine kicked up a good deal." Helen agreed and said that Klondike was becoming very mean in his old age.

Bennie said that he does not like the girl his sister calls Edith at school. Helen asked if he meant Edith Waterman and asked why he did not like her. Bennie replied that he saw her as insincere.

**June 28, 1904:** Roble had just graduated college and attended with his mother. "Say Roble, what was the matter with your foot," Bennie asked. "I cut my toe in swimming," Roble responded. "I thought so,"

Bennie said. "I heard you sing out but I saw it bleed...Was that your handkerchief you put on it?" Roble told him that it was one borrowed from another boy. "I thought so," Bennie continued. "I saw the influence but it didn't look just like yours. Do look out."

Bennie then mentioned that his father, who was not present at the sitting, seemed very troubled over some railroad business. Mr. Junot confirmed this with Hodgson, informing him that the issue with the railroad had caused him great anxiety for weeks.

**February 27, 1905:** Bennie told his father that he would be there to meet each of them when they came over. "I heard you talking about my going a long way from you," he communicated. "Not so, dad. I am growing all the time in knowledge of this new life but not that I shall leave you. Don't forget that. Did you understand that I heard you talking about my going so far away?" Mr. Junot told Hodgson that he and his wife had talked of the possibility that Bennie might have to pass on and away from remembrance of them.

Mrs. Junot then told Bennie that he should do nothing to prevent his own progress. "No, how could I, dear mother?" Bennie responded. "There are laws connected with this life and its conditions which enable me to progress constantly yet. While progressing I am better able to, if possible, help you."

Mr. Junot asked Bennie if he had any messages from his father and mother. "Grandma is so interested in my talks with you that when I finish here she gets close to me and asks me all sorts of questions," Bennie answered his father. "And I have to tell her everything about you, all as I hear from you."

**February 28, 1905:** Bennie asked about the condition of his horse, but again struggled with the name, getting only "KLON." Mr. Junot informed him that he went bad and had to be sold to the butcher.

Mrs. Junot asked Bennie if all the people in his life help those on their side. "Invariably, except the children here and we have to help them ourselves," Bennie told his mother. She then asked him if his appearance had changed. "I look about the same. You will not have any trouble recognizing me when you come." Mrs. Junot said she had often wondered if people change appearance in that life. "That depends, mother dear, on the conditions under which they passed over and the condition of their lives while in the body."

Mrs. Junot asked if they grow old. "No, not in spirit, mother...Old people grow younger in a sense while children grow to the years of maturity as you would express it...We look as we did when in the body with the exception of looking old. I do not grow wrinkles, lose my hair, etc. I retain my looks so you would know me."

**November 21, 1905:** Mrs. Junot asked Bennie if he had any regrets about leaving this world so early. "Why no, mother," he replied. "I have nothing to regret, dear. I am very happy here and I have greater privileges than you can possibly have. I can see you all just as often as I wish and I understand you are coming to me some day. Therefore, I am not only glad I came over but I am supremely happy, if you can understand it." Mrs. Junot said she thought everyone should have a long life. "But god (sic) thinks differently," Bennie replied. "And this is the way of all – all must come sooner or later. He knows better than any of us on our side or yours. I get dad's thoughts sometimes when he is surrounded by curious influences giving advice and help, and I say...Oh how much better off I am and how I wish he could see me as I am."

Although the Junot sittings took place under the direction of Dr. Hodgson, Professor Hyslop summarized them in the May 1911 issue of the ASPR Journal. "It will be apparent to most readers that, however, we might suppose guessing to account for any single incident this hypothesis would hardly account for the uniform success, especially in the names of his three friends, the sending of the photograph, sitting of the mother at the window, and the names of the tunes so often played on the harmonium for the father and mother," Hyslop opined, going on to mention that Bennie gave the name of the dog, Dandy, and a cow, Spot, and three other acquaintances, Lawrence, Lydia, and Major. When Bennie talked about Major, he asked his father to let Major know that he had seen his father on his side and to ask him if he remembered Thomas and his sister Mary Ellen. In fact, Major had an Uncle Thomas who had died many years earlier and two sisters, Mary and Ellen, both deceased.

"They are rich in two kinds of incidents," Hyslop concluded, 1) those spontaneously given and without suggestion of topic; and 2) those instigated by associations connected with the topic suggested and having varying degrees of evidential value. Taken collectively the facts make an impressive arrangement for a spiritistic interpretation, and all such incidents should be taken collectively rather than individually."

Referring to one critic's comment that there is nothing in the evidential part of the communications which provably transcends telepathy between living minds if we suppose this faculty "to possess the necessary scope and extension," Hyslop offered that guessing, chance coincidence, and every other possible alternative might explain it with the proper "scope and extension," whatever that meant.

---

[1] The sole reference for this chapter is Chapter XLIX (pages 785-829) of On the Cosmic Relations, by Henry Holt. Dr. Holt drew from the Volume XXIV of the SPR Proceedings. Also, the case is summarized in the May 1911 issue of the ASPR Journal.

[2] Thanks to Bruno Molon of Chicago for digging up background information on the Judah family.

# -Eight-

# Boston Mayor Describes
# Afterlife Conditions

*We advance until we feel that we have perfected ourselves according*
*to God's will and idea.*
**– the discarnate Augustus P. Morgan**

S itting with Leonora Piper on January 17, 1900, Anne Manning Robbins heard directly from Imperator, the high spirit who headed the band of 49, including Rector, who did most of the communicating and go-between work from that side of the veil. "We see thee and him writing a book together," Imperator communicated through the hand of Mrs. Piper, the "him" referring to Augustus P. Martin, a former mayor of the city of Boston, Massachusetts, with whom Robbins had worked for eight years. When Robbins asked what the book was to be about, Imperator replied, "It is concerning the natural things in life and many different conditions of thy life, which will be put together in a form of philosophy. *It will be so* in spite of anything which thou mayst think to the contrary." [1]

While Robbins, a graduate of Mount Holyoke College, was a competent writer and worked well with Martin, she could not imagine the two of them collaborating on a book of any kind. At a later sitting, she told Imperator that she had no desire to write a book. "Friend, to write a book, it is thy doom or duty, one and both combined," Imperator replied. [2]

Robbins's first sitting with Mrs. Piper was during the winter of 1884-85, not long after her mediumistic ability was discovered and before

Professor William James was introduced to it. Robbins recalled that Mr. Piper, his father, and a small group of friends were present. She had not known Mrs. Piper before that, but had been invited by a Piper family friend. "The personality of Mrs. Piper, then a young woman, with her sweet, pure, refined and gentle countenance, attracted me at once," Robbins wrote in the book that Imperator predicted, a 1909 publication titled *Both Sides of the Veil*.[3]

At the time, Mrs. Piper was reluctant to have people watch her go into the trance state, and so she retired to a separate room for that purpose, after which others were admitted. After Mrs. Piper entered the room, Robbins heard the sound of someone talking in a low tone and was told by Mr. Piper that it was the poet Longfellow. But shortly thereafter, Dr. Phinuit took over from Longfellow. After she was admitted to the room, Phinuit, controlling Mrs. Piper's body, put his hand on Robbins's shoulder and told her that she was very harmonious.

Robbins does not further report on that first sitting, but it apparently impressed her enough to schedule a private sitting with Mrs. Piper during April 1885. She had hoped to hear from a friend, Hiram Hart, who had died three months earlier, but Phinuit told her that it would take about another eight months before Hart was able to effectively communicate. She returned in that time and heard from Hart. In fact, Hart was able to take complete control of Mrs. Piper's organism, i.e., not requiring Phinuit as a go-between. She noted that Hart's handwriting was similar to what it was like when he was alive in the flesh and dissimilar to that of Phinuit's and to Mrs. Piper's when she was not in trance and being controlled.

Over the next 10 years, Robbins had a number of sittings with Mrs. Piper and "talked" regularly with Hart. But Robbins also had many conversations directly with Phinuit. "I found that Dr. Phinuit understood me," she wrote, "and who does not flatter himself that he is not ordinarily understood? He seemed to know all about my good points and somehow to have a special knowledge of my failings, and from that time (first private sitting) on he sustained the relation of adviser and friend. I was altogether too proud to impart my secrets to even the closest living acquaintance, yet, confession being good for the soul, I found myself confessing freely to Phinuit."[4]

While visiting the office of the Society for Psychical Research during February 1888, Robbins met Dr. Richard Hodgson, who, at the time, was interviewing various people who had had sittings with Mrs. Piper.

Upon learning of Robbins's stenographic abilities, Hodgson solicited her help in recording and transcribing the sittings.

It was in 1894, that Robbins first met Martin, who had become Boston's police commissioner 10 years after serving as mayor. Robbins became his administrative assistant or secretary for the next five years and later worked with him when he became the water commissioner. She remembered him as a man of "dignity, sweetness and light." She recorded that he listened patiently to the complaint of the poorest petitioner for justice and was like an old Roman patrician might have been, a father to all young people who worked for him. "The geniality of his nature and the kindly courtesy of his manner made themselves felt like sunlight in the quarters which he occupied daily, and during all my experience in office life I have never known a man more loved by other men than was he," Robbins wrote.[5] Martin was usually referred to as "General," after Massachusetts Governor John Long commissioned him an honorary brigadier general because of his distinguished service during the Civil War, especially at the Battle of Gettysburg.

When Robbins told Martin about her sittings with Mrs. Piper and how she had communicated with deceased friends and relatives, Martin courteously smiled and shrugged. Although he apparently didn't really approve of her "dabbling in the occult," he was too much of a gentleman to criticize her.

After Martin's death on March 13, 1902, Robbins wrote off Imperator's prediction as "failed prophecy." But she had had too many meaningful and evidential sittings with Mrs. Piper to discount everything because of that. She still trusted in Imperator and Rector, who had replaced Dr. Phinuit and G.P. as Mrs. Piper's spirit controls in 1897, some 12 years after Robbins's first sitting with her. The *modus operandi* as observed by Robbins was for Mrs. Piper to go into a trance and then for either Imperator or Rector to take over her body and communicate by means of automatic writing. Imperator, who was said to be a very high spirit, would communicate only when he had some profound wisdom to relate. When deceased relatives and friends wanted to communicate with the sitter, Rector would take over and relay the messages from the various spirits through Piper's hand.

At times, when the spirit control seemed to be talking to another spirit, Robbins noted that Mrs. Piper was mumbling, her lips moving slightly. When coming out of trance there were brief remarks and utterances, some clear, some in a whisper, and some of them unintelligible.

"The appearance is as if she were taking a last look at spirits standing near, and as if these spirits, while she is returning to her body, were impressing upon her mind words and messages for her to repeat to the sitter," Robbins explained. "Some of her broken utterances also indicated her returning perception of her surroundings in the room where the sitting was taking place."

On May 21, 1903, Hodgson was informed by Rector that a spirit there was constantly calling for a lady in the body. After some struggling to get the name, he wrote "Robbins." The spirit was identified as having been Augustus Martin, but it was said that he was not yet ready to speak, though he would be soon. However, it wasn't until December 23 that year, some 21 months after his passing that Martin actually began to communicate. Imperator asked Hodgson to arrange for a sitting by Robbins on that date. The transcript of that sitting reads (punctuation added):[6]

**Rector:** "Art thou here? Art thou present?"

**Robbins:** "I am."

**Rector:** "In God's holy name we greet thee this day and this hour. We sent for thee to return to us that we might make all clear to thee, bring messages from those who seek thee on our side and teach thee the divine and holy will of God. Hearest thou me?"

**Robbins:** "I do. I am glad I have not been dropped from the fold."

**Rector:** "Dropped, friend? Not one lamb who cometh unto us, who seeketh us in the highest, who have faith in God, will depart from us or will we allow them to drift from the fold unprotected or unguided. Thy friends on this side hath sought thee often."

**Robbins:** "Friend?"

**Rector:** "Friends. They have sought thee, they have called us to seek thee, to find thee out, to bring thee unto us and unto them. Hearest thou me?"

**Robbins:** "Yes."

**Rector:** "Friend, oh those of little faith know not the workings of the Allwise…I am Rector, servant of God. I bring to thee first thy friend known as Hiram." (Hiram Hart)

**Hiram:** "I am bringing another friend who seeks you, who knows you as you are. He would speak also, but the awakening of his soul was the most remarkable I have ever known. I sought him and found him. He sought me. We found each other. We are together. We clasp hands, we are friends. They call him on our side 'General.'"

**Robbins:** "I see."

**Hiram:** "I know not his other name so well, but he is known by this and we call him this, and he is happy but longs to meet you. Do you hear?"

**Robbins:** "Yes."

**Hiram:** "Now here comes the General. Will you speak to him?"

**Robbins:** "Oh, I would be delighted."

**General:** "I want to see you. I want everything to be understood between us, and until it is I do not feel satisfied. Can't you help me? Can't you see the obstacles in my way? Can't you see that God's will was better? Oh, you are not so weak as I thought in your belief. Why didn't I know better? Well, because I was grappling with the world. That is it."

**Robbins:** "Is this Hiram talking, or is he talking for the General?"

**Unidentified Control:** "No, he is talking for the General. He is quoting the General's words. You remember the little poem, 'Tell me, ye winged winds, That round my pathway roar, Do ye not know some spot…" (Unable to record all the words.)

**Unidentified Control:** "You remember that?"

**Robbins:** "Yes."

**Unidentified Control:** "You remember, 'Some lone and pleasant dell, Some valley in the West, Where free from toil and pain, The weary soul may rest'"?

**Robbins:** "General, you used to repeat a lot of poetry, didn't you?"

**General:** "Oh, I forgot,...yes, I did. I have found that peace, that rest, the beautiful awakening of the spirit. I have longed for a talk with you, but I did not understand the conditions."

**Robbins:** "Yes, I have been only waiting patiently for you to come."

**General:** "You have called for me in your spirit. I knew it and felt it, but I could not reach down until the conditions were arranged for it. Do you know what they all mean? Perhaps you know better than I do. But these good priests opened the way, who showed me the Light, opened the door for me and there I am. Would to God you could see me as I am! I am quite the man that I was, only my ideas are all changed. They are more now I think in harmony with your own...Oh, it is beautiful, it is ideal, just over the river, lift the Veil and you know all. Tell me something of yourself."

**Robbins:** (Reply about herself not recorded.)

**General:** "But, oh, why was I so blind? It was because of the thickness, the thickness of the flesh."

**Robbins:** "General, do you know what I am doing?"

**General:** "Yes, I know it well. Do you mean the nature of the work, or the private work?"

**Robbins:** "I mean this minute."

**General:** "This present minute?"

**Robbins:** "Yes."

**General:** "Why, aren't you registering something?"

**Robbins:** "Yes."

**General:** "I can see your hand move and I can see your spirit, too, so plainly, and the spiritual hand guides the material hand, and it seems as though it was registering something. Is it what I am saying?"

**Robbins:** "Yes."

**General:** "Well, that is natural."

**Robbins:** "Well, I guess so."

**General:** "That is natural, and how rapidly you worked with that for me. I shall never forget those days. And do you remember the last time I saw you in the body?"

**Robbins:** "Yes."

**General:** "You remember what you said to me? Do you remember saying, 'I think you are getting better'?"

**Robbins:** "I think I said that, that time." [Robbins recalled saying that during a number of visits.]

**General:** "Yes, you did. You were so hopeful and you helped me so much, but I could not tell you all I felt. Do you hear?"

**Robbins:** "Yes." [She later noted that she assumed that he would recover because of the prophetic statements made by Imperator, believing then that he would have to be alive for them to reach fulfillment.]

From this point on, the exchange is abridged, to include only the more meaningful, interesting, or evidential comments:

Robbins asked Martin if he remembered that she used to tell him of messages she had received through Mrs. Piper. Martin remembered the messages, but didn't seem to realize that they were from Mrs. Piper or that Mrs. Piper was the medium he was currently using.

**General:** "Oh, I remember there was a friend of yours, a lady in the body – now who was she? I can't think what her name was, but she lived somewhere in some other town, and you used to go and see her and then come and bring me messages from the priests who are helping me now. But I can't remember who she was, but I remember the messages perfectly, the nature of the messages, and they really helped me. They gave me great encouragement, and that is all I needed, was encouragement, until time helped me over."

Robbins noted that Arlington Heights, where Mrs. Piper then lived, was about eight miles from the center of Boston in an opposite direction from where Martin lived.

**General:** "…Oh I wish you knew how I felt, how light I am, how I can see, how I can read and how I can move about, how free I am from encumbrance, how clear my mind is, how really supremely happy I am. You would be delighted for my sake."

Some discussion then took place about Martin's family. He said that his grandson Augustus, who was named after him and who died at age two, about six months after his death, was with him. Also, another grandson was born just a week prior to the sitting. Martin said he thought that the newborn was also named after him. Robbins told him she didn't know the name. When she later checked with the mother, she was told that the given name was William Everett, but they called him Augustus, as he seemed to replace the little Augustus whom they had lost.

**General:** "It is just the little details of the material life which I cannot grasp and [in] which I long to have you help me, but the actual life, and the actual life of the children, and all that, is well known to me, but the details of the material life I cannot see."

Robbins again asked if Martin was speaking directly to her or if Hiram Hart was relaying his words to her. Martin replied that Hiram was doing it for him as he does not yet know how to take possession of the medium. Robbins asked if he might be able to take possession at some time.

**General:** "Yes, but not just now. I am trying to understand the laws and the workings of the machine, and they put me up here so I could see. Just like a schoolboy being sent to the board to figure out a multiplication table. I am set up here, I am held here, and there are three clergymen, one behind me, and one on either side of me, holding me up here and telling me to talk, and I am talking to Hiram, and Hiram is repeating it after me, and I am trying to do a sum in geometry. That is just what I am trying to do. And since I am not fully equipped in that problem perhaps you can understand something of the difficulty."

Robbins told him that he seemed to be doing wonderfully well for his first attempt at communicating.

**General:** "They have been preparing me for months and months to make me understand it. They have put me up here and taken me away again. They have held me up and showed me the Light, and said, 'do this and do that, and see this and see that,' and shown me the details, and the ins and outs and the whys and wherefores, and why shouldn't I learn something after having it hammered into me all that time. Then I said, well, I must reach her. It is an utter impossibility for me to [let go?] until I do. [I will] move heaven and earth, but I must reach her. And they said: 'Wait, you have got to learn. You must go here with us, you must stand on this side, hold up your hands, bow your head, speak in this kind of a way, speak slowly, articulate distinctly.' But without the preparation there is a good deal of confusion. But they are very, very good to me, and they know – what they don't know about the details of this Light is not worth knowing. I assure you that, if you can grasp me. With your clear mind you can grasp it pretty well, I think."

Martin then talked about Poland Springs, a place he loved when alive and from where he was supplied with what he called the finest water in the world. Robbins said she had not thought of the place until he mentioned it. Martin added that little Augustus was now there by his side. He asked Robbins if she had any special questions for him before his thoughts began to wander. She asked about the moments after he left his body.

**General:** "When I first passed out my mind was cloudy, rather confused. I felt as though I was going into space, did not know where, drifting as it were, for a few hours – that was all – and then I felt as though there was a strong hand grasped me and said to me: 'It is all right, it is all over.' And I said: 'What is over?' I could not seem to understand what it all meant, and after a little while, perhaps an hour, possibly an hour or two, I saw oh such a light! You cannot imagine it, cannot conceive what it is like. It is the most brilliant and yet the softest moonlight that you ever saw, and I thought, what a beautiful light it was! And all of a sudden I saw people moving about. I saw their heads, their figures. Then they seemed all clad in white, and I could not seem to make them out. They were moving in the air.

"And I said: 'What is this place?' Where am I? What has happened?' It was all such a puzzle to me. When I get strong I will tell you about it. I can't tell you any more. Now what do you want me to do, think over the few days – and when I come back, to tell you what my experience was. I tell you one thing, the clergyman who is talking for me now was the best friend I ever had, and he said: 'Come along, it is all right,

131

I will show you the way; it is all right, you will get over this confusion in a minute, and I will help you.' And I said: 'Who are you? Where am I? Where am I going? What am I doing? What does all this mean?' He said: 'Never mind, it will all be clear to you in a few minutes. Just wait patiently and come with me.' And he stood ready to welcome me."

Robbins asked who the "clergyman" was and, much to her surprise, was informed that it was Hiram Hart. Though not a clergyman in the physical life, he apparently was acting in that capacity in the afterlife.

**General:** "I know who you know, you know who I knew, now we will be friends together, and this is all right; I have had experience and I know, and I will explain it to you in a few minutes. I thought I saw the doctor bending over me and I wanted him to go away. He seemed to be in my way as I was going out. I wanted to get away from him, and all of a sudden I was going through this misty, cloudy way, and then I went past [possibly "fast"] until I got to this light, and it was like going up, up, up in the air, in a balloon as it were. You could not conceive of anything more strange and beautiful, in a sense – the confusion was not so beautiful, but because it was so I could not seem to retain my consciousness and could not seem to be released from the burden that hung over me, and all of a sudden, the moment I realized this hand was on my arm, then I began to see clearly; and from that moment I have been advancing and going on, and I have seen everybody I ever knew, and I have had the happiest time you could imagine. I have a mansion all my own and live in it just the same as you live in your place there, just the same. I have walls, I have pictures, I have music, I have books, I have poetry, I have *everything*...It is not a *fac simile* of that life, but that life is a miserable shadow of what this really is, and when I get strong, as I become stronger, and, that is, more accustomed to using this line (light?) I can tell you more clearly about it."

Martin wondered how long he had been there. Robbins answered that it had been nearly an hour.

**General:** "An hour in the earthly world? Well, I don't know how long that is, but I am too weak to remain; that is, I am afraid I can't use this Light any more."

Robbins heard Martin tell Augustus, his grandson, to come with him, and they left. Rector returned and Robbins asked if Martin would be able to come again through Mrs. Piper.

**Rector:** "At times he is. He is a marvelous personality and he has a very clear mind and he has a very earnest desire to work for God and humanity."

At a sitting on May 24, 1904, Rector introduced Robbins to a physician, who gave her some advice on her health. He told her that he formerly lived in Boston, but that he had died in Paris a year or two earlier. Robbins later determined that a physician by the name given her had lived on Beacon St., Boston and died in Paris the preceding September. After the doctor left, Martin communicated and told her that he saw the doctor going out as he was coming in.

**General:** "...I have been studying into this thing, studying the laws of our nature – that is, its problems on our side – and I am perfectly delighted with the conditions. I am perfectly delighted with the thought of returning. I seek you out and follow you night and day. I am often standing by your side when you don't realize it, and I stand there and laugh at myself to see how utterly unconcerned you are in regard to my presence, but I say but if her spiritual eyes could open and she could see me as I am I know she would be delighted..."

Robbins asked Martin if he was talking now or if Rector was acting as an intermediary.

**General:** "Oh, Rector is holding the Light. I could not, they would not allow me to do that. Not quite now, but I may be able to later. But they have to support the Light, some friend has to look after it."

Robbins asked Martin if he remembered any of the public officials who used to work with him.

**General:** "I think I should. Many names have gone from me, naturally, and new ones have come up to me. Names of places, names of people whom I knew in the mortal world, have gone from me to a certain extent, and as I go on they go still farther from me, but I shall never forget you. I remember when I was suffering so, I remember the little councils we had together, and they have lasted in my memory and will to the end of all life."

Robbins asked him if the spiritual sympathies are the only ones remembered.

**General:** "Yes, well, those are the real vital ones, those are the real ones. And when you understand better the conditions of life and the conditions of passing from that life to this, the changes in the life as it were, you will understand more clearly what that means. But until then it will be difficult for you to understand it fully. I have got to go out a moment – you will excuse me – I must go for a little change. My thoughts begin to wander, and if I stayed you would be displeased with my wandering thoughts, so I will just go out and get refreshed and return instantly."

After about a minute of silence, Martin returned. Robbins told him that she had assembled many of his speeches and put them together in one complete copy. She wondered if Martin knew anything about it.

**General:** "Well, yes, I knew the outline, but the work itself, the actual work as it was going on, I could not fathom. But I knew the work concerned my mortal life and things that transpired in it. But the nature of it I could not define. We know generally what takes place in a general way, but if we were to define it, condense it and give utterance to it, it would be difficult. But such is the law of this life. Remember, now, if you could see me you would say I was a mere film, and you would say, 'how transparent and peculiar and how light and how strange you look to me;' and you would say, 'where is your body? You look like a shadow, as it were,' but still I could talk with you, we could converse with each other, and you would be surprised to see how real I am. The passing out is really beautiful, just after you once get beyond the border, it is perfectly beautiful. You know the meaning of the word heaven? Well, it is heaven indeed. But the coming back is a little confusing at first and we have to learn."

Robbins asked him if he knew anything about his funeral.

**General:** "Yes, I knew it and saw the body and saw the flowers. I saw the way in which it was laid out. I saw – don't you think it looked well? I looked as though I was asleep, don't you think so? And I don't think the face showed suffering – that is, the clay did not show the suffering, the body itself – but I felt, oh, I was so pleased to be out and away from the atmosphere, I felt so choked and so distressed for breath, and the moment I was released from the imprisoning body then I could breathe perfectly. I felt – I could not describe it to you."

After they further discussed the funeral service, there were several remarks of a personal nature, followed by Martin's explanation of his ability to influence Robbins's writing.

**General:** "I want to say this, that when you are working I sometimes dictate thoughts to you, and it is surprising to me to see how clearly you register them, and I think sometimes you are surprised to think that you have done what you have, and if you just stop and give me a thought you would know why it was that you did those things, registered those thoughts. Sometimes there seems to be a barrier between you and your thoughts, they are not clear, and they seem to be a little obscure, and then they clear up, and you have always attributed that to the condition of your brain, and now if you just give me credit for a little bit of help you would do the right thing. Not that I am egotistic, but the point is that I am really with you. And I want to say one thing, that you have not grown old in spirit and not in the flesh. It looks so clear to me, so free, so bright and so young, and I think your body looks the same. I can't see much change. Yes, I think you look about the same. I can't see the body so clearly as I can the spirit."

After discussing the building they once worked in, Martin asked about Orinton Hanscom, one of the higher officials in the police department, with whom he had had some differences when they were working together. Martin mentioned that he now had a higher opinion of him "because I see his principles."

When Martin had to leave briefly to again "get my breath," Hiram Hart communicated, saying that he saw Martin leaving and thought he would "come in" and say "how do you do?" Martin returned quickly and Hart departed.

Robbins again queried Martin as to what happened immediately after he passed out of his body. He repeated much of the earlier conversation and added to it.

**General:** "…And we are taken up by perhaps a priest, or man that acts in the capacity of what you would understand as a clergyman, and they say: 'This is a state of transition. You are now in the real life, in the new life. You will not see the face of the Father for many, many years, but He will give you strength and power to go back if you wish and see those whom you have left behind.' And the feeling of ecstasy is beyond description, and no spirit that ever returned to earth could begin to describe it for the understanding of the mortal mind. And then I was surrounded by friends, by acquaintances, by old war veterans, by my intimate friends whom I know, members of my family and all, surrounded by them, welcoming me. Why, I felt I should be enveloped by them, the delight was so great, but when I tried to call them by name I was at a loss to do so. They had to tell me who they were. I knew their faces, not one failed to me. I knew them and understood them well. I saw them and recognized them, but to call them by name, believe me, I could not. And when I tried to speak I found instead of it being an effort and difficult for me to speak, I found that my thoughts were understood, actually understood, and their thoughts were returned to me. There was a perfect communion between us.

"And then I was taken – would you believe it if I should tell you? I was taken to an actual mansion. It would be what you would call a palace. There is a garden, walks about it. It is divided into rooms, actual compartments. I was taken to that and [they] said: 'Here is your home; occupy it, live in it; have what friends you choose with you, what relatives you choose with you, and as those whom you have left behind follow you, you may welcome them to this home as you may see fit.' Do you understand it?"

Upon "gliding in" to the mansion, Martin saw beautiful pictures and flowers, and heard beautiful music, the harmony of which he had never heard in the earthly world. Robbins asked him what he does with his time.

**General:** "Well, now I will tell you. What would correspond with your morning – we have no morning – that is, it is all morning in a sense, in a way – there is no daylight and darkness with us, it is all daylight – and what corresponds with your morning – I find that there are always entering into this life, there are spirits entering constantly from your life, and each one needs help, needs to be shown the way, and I enter the multitude, the throng outside of my own home; I pass through, I see the veil uplifted, I see a spirit passing in, perhaps millions of spirits. And I was told when I entered it that I must make this life here useful by helping others and by reverencing God, offering up gratitude in a prayerful spirit to Him who created me and gave me the privileges of life here. And I do that through the so-called day, without fatigue, with perfect delight, assist some one spirit or more who have left the body and entered this life. And until they are fully conscious and realize where they are – some are taken from us, we are not allowed to see them at all, they are taken into another sphere; those are passed beyond us, we have nothing to do practically with them – but there are spirits that enter our own sphere, and we each lend a hand, show them their homes, settle them in it, go back and help another, and we are constantly doing that.

"And then I feel sometimes that I would like to help in something that corresponds with your writing. I find in my home everything for which I ask. If I wish a pencil, what corresponds with your pencil, I have it. If I wish to write my thoughts I can write them, if I wish to speak them I can do so, and every thought is granted, every desire is granted. And if I wish to lecture, as I often do, I can do so without fatigue, and it is helpful to those who enter this life. If I wish to write , I can write, if I wish to walk, I can walk, if I wish to sing, I can sing, if I wish to speak I can speak. That makes the life, as you would understand it, perfect. It is a perfect life. And in order to live this perfect life you have got to live in the imperfect life, and the more you undertake to prepare for this life the less you have to go through when you pass it and the clearer your thoughts become when you enter it. Have you got the idea?"

Martin further explained that it was pretty much beyond her comprehension, and said that if her eyes were opened to the spiritual life she could see him as he stood there talking with her, observing every gesture which is copied by Rector. Robbins asked him about his "afternoons."

**General:** "...sometimes I write a lecture, I go out and look at my flowers, enjoy them; I go and visit others, they visit me. I learn to play on the instruments, the different instruments. I am absorbed in music, and I love the flowers and birds.

"Then I feel as though I would like to take up some intellectual pursuit, and then I begin, and I am studying with those who have been here longer than myself the actual conditions of this life and what go to make up the life here, and as I learn I give it out to others, interpret my knowledge to others. Therefore, our intellectual capacity is unlimited in a sense, and constantly being educated....there are lectures and concerts of all kinds and descriptions going on, so that our lives are completely filled..."

Robbins asked about sleep.

**General:** "Have no sleep, no rest. What corresponds with your rest is activity on our part. And then after the devotional exercises we are ready for what would correspond with your day for our work again. Can you conceive of anything more beautiful or more perfect, or more to the liking of a man with my tastes and my ideas?"

Martin went on to say that man should live his allotted time to prepare for the spirit world, otherwise he remains a "child" when he gets there, having to "unfold, bud, and flower" there when it should have taken place during the person's earth life.

Robbins asked how long it takes for him to come through to her at a sitting.

**General:** "I would seem some distance from you if you could see me as I am. When you have a desire to speak with me – there are spirits here who know every mortal on the face of the earth; this is, the same one does not know, but the different ones know every mortal – and they say: 'Here is a friend, I think she is a friend of yours; there the Light is beginning to burn; it is open; we have attached the ethereal cord and we will remove the spirit from the Light, take it to our world or out on the cord, attach the cord to the shell, as it were, fill it with our ethereal light, and you can enter into it and see if it is your friend, and if so follow Rector, follow those that are used to the cord and go to the end of it and speak over it to Rector, who is actually within the shell himself, and he will transmit your messages to your friend. It takes in all, I suppose, of your time five or ten minutes perhaps for me to reach you."

The next sitting took place on December 20, 1904. Robbins was told that Imperator was away and left Prudens in charge. Hodgson was not at this sitting. At the end of the sitting, which took approximately two hours, Robbins was asked to take a message to Hodgson to the effect that the surgery had gone well. As Robbins came to understand it, another of Mrs. Piper's regular sitters was undergoing surgery of some kind and Imperator was near her to give healing. Robbins knew nothing about it at the time the message was given.

Rector said that Martin would try to speak directly to her, meaning that Martin was allowed to take control and Rector would not be relaying the messages. When Martin began communicating, Robbins asked Martin if he was doing so without assistance.

**General:** "For the first time, I am, yes. Dear creature, he is here to help me, he stands beside me watching me to see that no harm comes to the instrument over which I speak. [Robbins asked if it was hard.] No, not hard, but if you were to question me one question after another it might confuse me, but you ask your questions so clearly, so slowly and in moderation, that I can understand them and reply. But if you were to fire questions at me, so to speak, volley after volley, it would confuse me so I should be obliged to go out. You understand?"

Martin mentioned having seen Robbins at a "green place" where she was attending lectures and sitting in what looked like a tent, since her last sitting. Robbins took this to mean a place called "Greenacre" in the town of Eliot in the state of Maine, where she had attended a conference. Martin also referred to seeing her swinging in a hammock, something she had rarely done. Robbins confirmed the experience and said she had fallen asleep in the hammock. She recalled it being an especially peaceful sleep and wondered where she was then.

**General:** "The spirit, your spirit, goes out upon an ethereal cord, just the same as the spirit of the Light here departs. Now I see the spirit of a woman going out, and it is the same in sleep, and I talk with your spirit just the same as I am talking with you now. Sometimes I almost feel that you will remember it, but when the spirit becomes active and fully possessed of the body and mind, then it forgets."

Robbins asked if she could learn to leave her body at will. Martin told her that it not always wise to do so, nor healthful, but he was still studying such matters. The conversation then changed to Martin's attitude about spiritual matters before his death. Robbins wondered if his closed-mindedness relative to the spirit world and his "have to see it to believe it" mindset retarded his awakening.

**General:** "You realized, I think, that my desire was for the advancement of mind, and you remember how I used to love poetry, and that I had a vein of sentiment, as you used to express it. Well, all that is fine spiritual perception; and it is really beautiful to me, now when I realize that I possessed that at all when in the physical body, and it has been a great benefactor to me in this life. You understand what I mean...

"I loved life for what life gave, and I loved the pleasures, and I loved the physical and all that the physical gave, but still I was large enough in heart, I feel, and in spirit not to allow physical temptations to drown my soul."

The conversation went back to his ability to communicate.

**General:** "Well, there are so many restrictions. This great spirit, this man here who leads, he is the noblest spirit I know, and there are so many restrictions – he understands the conditions so well, and he has his everlasting eye upon watching constantly that no harm shall befall anything or anybody connected or associated with the Light or the spiritual influences who work through it. Why, it is really marvelous."

Robbins asked if he was referring to Imperator, and he said that they refer to Imperator and his band as "the saints." He said that Imperator was in the seventh sphere, what Robbins might call "heaven." She asked him what sphere he was in.

**General:** "I am in the third now. We have to pass through the third sphere in order to return, one might say, and therefore I could not return immediately directly [when] I passed out of my body...It is like going from one room to another. We advance until we feel that we have perfected ourselves according to God's will and idea, and then [when] we are satisfied with ourselves, and not until we have [satisfied ourselves]."

Robbins asked if he went into the first sphere when he first passed out.

**General:** "Entering the material life is one sphere of life; that is the first, because life comes with the creation of the mortal body; life comes, it is the breath of God, and you are a branch of His great tree, you understand, and then the spirit grows, advances. Sometimes it does not advance in the mortal because it is hampered by physical ill, etc. If not, it is removed after a time and enters our life and then begins to develop and grow."

Robbins asked if everyone leaves here just when right for him or her to go, whether he is young or old.

**General:** "Yes, yes, yes, that is all in the hands of God, and although we never see God – I have never seen Him and never hope to – He rules us all and reigns over us all, and we are a part, a branch of Him, and your question will make that clear.

"Perhaps you know that in the earthly Bible, the material Bible, 'In my Father's house there are many mansions'; do you remember that?"

The subject turned to age. Robbins asked how old he was compared with Imperator.

**General:** "Well, Imperator is – in fact, no spirit is ever old, there is no such thing as age with us. We enter this life according to our acts in the mortal life. If we have advanced and grown, we have gained so much when entering this life, but if we are hampered by physical ills or physical infirmities, or perhaps some may inherit imbecility or something of that kind, when the spirit leaves the body it enters this life and grows, in a sense, as a child. It rests, it is released. The moment it is released from the body it assumes a condition of happiness, as it were. There is a peacefulness about it that permeates the whole spirit, and a certain power of understanding, and then it advances and grows until we are – we might put the age, for your understanding, to fifty, and we are never older than that in spirit...The body grows old simply but the spirit never grows old. The spirit remains young and beautiful always...But the conditions of the spirit and its happiness [do] depend somewhat upon his advancement and growth and understanding and desires of right and wrong in the physical life"

Robbins asked if a person who was not spiritually developed when he died would be able to see and talk with him.

**General:** "Well, he would be – for your understanding – he would be in a somewhat lower plane upon entering this life, but if he has a great desire to reach me there are certain conditions through which he must pass in order for that desire to be accomplished, and if he lives according to the restrictions and the laws which are mapped out for him here, then he might be able to see me in what you might term a few days. Then his desire would be fulfilled and he would be made happier in consequence."

The subject turned to frequency of communication through a medium.

**General:** "...I have learned from Imperator, who knows all there is to know and prepares his messengers to give such light as he deems that they are fitted to give – he says too frequent communication on our side is not wise, and it is wiser for the spirit to store up its knowledge and learn all the conditions of its life and then return occasionally, imparting that knowledge to his friend on the earthly side occasionally, but not too frequently, as the spirit loses by too frequent communication."

The subject returned to Martin's ability to communicate.

**General:** "My thoughts keep clear, as you ask your questions so clearly and beautifully that they are not confusing to me. If you were to say, 'Now, General, I want you to find a name for me, get it now if you can,' – in searching for that name, or switching my thoughts from the track on which they are flowing at the present time, over which they are flowing, it would confuse me so that I should lose the whole thread of my individuality and thought."

Imperator was again discussed.

**General:** "I am never left alone when I am speaking with you. Imperator comes and goes, keeps coming and going, to see that all is going on well, and Rector or Prudens, some of them stand here and watch me to see how I get along, and if I fail for words or light they supply it. It comes over a line."

Martin again lamented his lack of spiritual enlightenment when in the body.

**General:** "The only thing I regret is the absolute imbecility on my part of the truth of an eternal life, but sometimes we have not the keenest spiritual perception into the higher things while in the mortal body, especially when the mind is troubled and disturbed with all that the earthly world places before us, and while life [lasts] we have not the time, perhaps, or the keen appreciation, and I may say apprehension, of the possibilities of the future. Therefore, I made my mistakes in that line [life] – not exactly mistakes, but I lost a great deal."

At a sitting on December 20, 1905, the book they would write together came up.

**General:** "I am very anxious, since I have learned so much about this beautiful life and realize the truth and reality of it by having the actual experience, that the world should though your hand and brain be made cognizant in part of the unfoldment, of the true development of the soul after it leaves its environment; that it is an active consciousness, that it is in the state of higher development, that it is able to reach the physical plan and act through such voices as your own, we would say, to give expression and utterance to the truth and reality of in part what this life contains. Is that clear to you?"

Later in that same sitting, Martin said that there was someone there who was trying to use the light, but it was not open to him. His name, Martin said, was Myers or Myer. Robbins took it to be Frederick W. H. Myers, the pioneering English researcher who had died in 1901. She felt certain that Martin knew nothing about Myers when he (Martin) was alive.

**General:** "...he comes here, he finds the Light unopen – a very active, brilliant, fine man, keen perceptions, finest type of mind – and he comes here, he finds the Light not burning, he departs, he goes and looks after his family – he has family in the mortal body – and he goes to find them and remains with them, and often times when the Light is burning he fails to appear, but you can understand that because of his absence from the Light and being among those he loves...He goes to other worlds and other planets. He is constantly studying – he is a great student – he is studying the conditions and the changes and the whys and the wherefores of communication, and the laws of life in the spirit, in the body, and the ways of God and the ways of man and spirit in general."

Hodgson died of a heart attack later that same day and it was left to speculation as to whether Myers came to alert Hodgson, his old associate in psychical research, as to what was about to happen.

Sittings by Robbins with Mrs. Piper became less frequent after Hodgson's death, but she did sit with Mrs. Piper on June 17, 1908. She again asked about his activities. Martin again told her of his home and reminded her that their homes are as real to them as ours are to us. He told her that their world is the real world and earth objects are simply imitations of those in the real world.

**General:** "If we bathe in the river our garments are not wet, but still we are purified, we are cleansed...We come out and it is light and dry, the garments are dry, but the soul is purified by bathing in the waters. Is that clear to you? We walk about the lakes, we walk in the gardens, we meet friends, we commune with friends, we hear music, we hear sermons, and we pass our time glorifying God and living in His presence, in a sense – understanding what His hand hath created and what He has blessed us with, eternal life."

Robbins wondered if there is a sky above him or if sees stars. Martin described it as a beautiful, soft moonlight effect, which she would not be able to comprehend. He said there were no stars, but that they at times see a face in the light.

**General:** "The face appears over us and we know it is the face of Christ. We hear the swishing of the garments, as it were, and then it passes off and some one else receives the vision...We see these little rays all about us, this beautiful figure passing, we see another face and then another as it passes. Why do we not come into closer proximity with them, as we say? Because they are superior even to ourselves, they have progressed, they have gone on to a higher, even, sphere than our own. That is, they are the controlling, the ruling forces, and govern our own life and our own world. Do you understand?"

---

[1] Robbins 57-58

[2] _____, 59

[3] _____, 31

[4] _____, 34

[5] _____, 49

[6] this and all subsequent dialogue and quotes are from Chapter XI, pages, 100-212

# -Nine-

# Hodgson Returns

*Well if I am not Hodgson, he never lived.*
**– the discarnate Richard Hodgson**

D r. Richard Hodgson, who had been studying Leonora Piper for
some 18 years, died on December 20, 1905, at age 50, while playing handball. Although he apparently did not anticipate a pre-
mature death, he jokingly told friends that if he were to die early enough
he would communicate through Mrs. Piper much more effectively than
others had because of his familiarity with the *modus operandi.*

Alta Piper, who wrote a short book about her mother, described
Hodgson as "brusque, quick and bluntly outspoken, [yet] there was
something so likable about [his] whole personality that his friends esteemed him greatly." She added that he enjoyed playing the violin and
that his bluff jovial exterior came to the fore "by the fine, beautiful precepts and counsels of Imperator."[1]

Over those 18 years, Hodgson gradually moved from debunker to
skeptic to believer. Hereward Carrington, another psychical researcher
and Hodgson's close friend, wrote that during the latter years of his life
Hodgson would allow no one to enter the privacy of his small apartment
as he was concerned that it would upset the "magnetic atmosphere." According to Carrington, Hodgson began receiving direct communications
from Imperator and Rector, the spirit controls who succeeded Dr. Phinuit
and George Pellew and were apparently from a much higher realm than

their predecessors. Hodgson kept these communications a secret because he feared it would affect his standing as an objective researcher.

In a letter to a friend, Hodgson wrote: "It adds a great deal to life, of course, to be assured of the nearness and help of particular discarnate spirits, but, apart from this, there is no necessity for anyone who believes in God doubting the absolute persistence of the moral order throughout the whole of existence." [2]

In a letter to Anne Manning Robbins (see previous chapter), written on November 24, 1901, Hodgson wrote:

I should have replied to yours of 17 earlier, but could not find any copy of the notes which I now enclose on T sheets.

But apart from all this we must remember that nothing can be regarded as infallible, and I tried to put my general view about this in the notes, a copy of which I enclose. About what Imperator and his group are in their world I have no doubt. They have done for me and some others also – more than everything, but the final written or spoken results though Mrs. P.'s inadequate organism surrounded by our earthly make-ups generally can only afford us faint glimpses of the great holies from which they take their origin. We cannot pray too much to do and suffer the will of God, whatever it be. I went through toils and turmoils and perplexities in '97 and '98 about the significance of this whole Imperator regime, but I have seemed to get on a rock after that – I seem to understand clearly the reasons for incoherence and obscurity, etc., and I think that if for the rest of my life from now I should never see another trance or have another word from Imperator or his group – it would make no difference to my *knowledge* that all is well, that Imperator, etc., are all they claim to be and are indeed messengers that we may call divine. Be of good courage whatever happens, and pray continually, and let peace come into your soul. Why should you be distraught and worried? Everything, absolutely everything – from a spot of ink to all the stars, every faintest thought we think up to the contemplations of highest intelligences in the cosmos, are all in and part of the infinite Goodness. Rest in that Divine Love. All your trials are known better than you know them yourself. Do you think it is an idle word that the hairs of our heads are numbered? Have no dismay, fear nothing and trust in God.

**Yours sincerely,**
**R. Hodgson**[3]

In a letter dated December to Robbins, he wrote:

Of course we get misrepresented and misunderstood in all sorts of ways. In the old years when I was prominent in exposing fraudulent mediums, Spiritualists generally used to revile me as a gross materialistic skeptic who had no other object but the persistent determination to disprove Spiritualism. Nothing could have been further from the truth even then. And now, as you rightly say, in recent years, with the Imperator regime, another influence has come which I trust, even to the end and after—with all my darkness and weakness and blunderings and bruteness – I shall not escape, which I trust will abide with me ever, for it is law and love and peace and freedom and joy and God.

**Yours ever,**
**Richard Hodgson**[4]

Eight days after Hodgson's death, Miss Theodate Pope, a good friend of Hodgson's, was having a sitting with Mrs. Piper. Rector was writing something when Mrs. Piper's hand dropped the pencil and started shaking. When the hand steadied itself, it wrote the letter "H," after which the point of the pencil was broken. When a new pencil was placed in Mrs. Piper's hand, it wrote "Hodgson." It started to write something else, but only rapid scrawls followed.

Rector then took back control of the medium and explained that Hodgson was there, but that he was too "choked" to write. It wasn't until another sitting by Pope five days later that Hodgson communicated again, beginning with a poem. However, he added that he felt confused and could write no more. At a third sitting, on January 8, 1906, Hodgson came again and explained that it was extremely difficult for him to communicate, suggesting that he had not yet awakened enough or that he had not yet learned how to handle the "mechanism" [Piper's body].

As Hodgson grew stronger in his new environment and learned how to "use the light" (the medium), he communicated with Professor William James, other members of the ASPR and SPR, and several friends. A number of his messages were very evidential, but James remained skeptical as to whether it was really Hodgson communicating.

James and his wife Alice sat with Mrs. Piper on May 21, 1906. After Hodgson greeted them, he asked William James if he had solved the problems yet. The transcript, here abridged, reads:[5]

**James:** "Which problems do you refer to?"

**Hodgson:** "Did you get my messages?"

**James:** "I got some messages about your going to convert me."

**Hodgson:** "Did you hear about the argument that I had? You asked me what I had been doing all those years, and what it amounted to… Well, it has amounted to this – that I have learned by experience that there is more truth than error in what I have been studying."

**James:** "Good!"

**Hodgson:** "I am so delighted to see you today that words fail me."

**James:** "Well, Hodgson, take your time and don't be nervous."

**Hodgson:** "No. Well, I think I should ask the same of you! Well, now, tell me – I am very much interested in what is going on in the Society, and Myers and I are also interested in the Society over here. You understand that we have to have a medium on this side while you have a medium on your side, and through the two we communicate with you."

**James:** "And your medium is who?"

**Hodgson:** "We have a medium on this side. It is a lady. I don't think she is known to you."

**James:** "You don't mean Rector?"

**Hodgson:** "No, not at all. It is…do you remember a medium whom we called Prudens?" [Prudens is apparently another spirit reporting to Imperator. Exactly why Prudens was assisting and not Rector is not made clear.]

**James:** "Yes."

**Hodgson:** "Prudens is a great help. Through Prudens we accomplish a great deal. Speak to me, William. Ask me anything. What I want to know first of all is about the Society. I am sorry that it could not go on."

**James:** "There was nobody to take your place...Hyslop is going to, well, perhaps you can find out for yourself what he is going to do."

**Hodgson:** "I know what he is going to do, and we are all trying to help Hyslop, and trying to make him more conservative, and keener in understanding the necessity of being secretive."

**James:** "You must help all you can. He is splendid on the interpreting side, discussing the sittings, and so forth."

**Hodgson:** "I know he is, but what a time I had with him in writing that big report. It was awful, perfectly awful. I shall never forget it. [James noted that Hodgson wanted it much shorter than Hyslop thought it should be.] William, can't you see, don't you understand, and don't you remember how I used to walk up and down before that open fireplace trying to convince you of my experiments?"

**James:** "Certainly, certainly."

**Hodgson:** "And you would stand with your hands in your trousers pockets. You got very impatient with me sometimes, and you would wonder if I was correct. I think you are very skeptical."

**James:** "Since you have been returning I am much more near to feeling as you felt than ever before."

**Hodgson:** "Good! Well, that is capital."

**James:** "Your personality is beginning to make me feel as you felt."

**Hodgson:** "If you can give up to it, William, and feel the influence of it and the reality of it, it will take away the sting of death."

The two continued to discuss Society business and mediums. At one point Hodgson had to excuse himself. Rector then communicated that Hodgson had to go out and get his breath. When he returned, they talked about passwords which Hodgson claims he left behind for

James, Lodge, and others, but James said he had not been able to find any such password. James then asked Hodgson if he recalled an incident in which he was playing with children at the Putnam Camp in the Adirondacks.

**Hodgson:** "Do you remember – what is that name, Elizabeth Putnam? She came in and I was sitting in a chair before the fire, reading, and she came in and put her hands, crept up behind me, put her hands over my eyes, and said, 'Who is it?' And do you remember what my answer was?"

**James:** "Let me see if you remember it as I do."

**Hodgson:** "Well, it feels like Elizabeth Putnam, but it sounds like – "

**James:** "I know what you mean."

As James recalled the incident, her name was Martha Putnam, not Elizabeth. One day after breakfast, little Martha climbed on Hodgson's back and sat on his shoulders, clasping her hands over his eyes, saying, "Who am I?" Hodgson laughing, responded "It sounds like Martha, but it feels like Henry Bowditch (who weighed around 200 pounds). James considered this very evidential as he doubted that anyone but himself remembered the incident. James pointed out the error in the name to Hodgson and asked if he could remember the correct name of the girl.

**Hodgson:** "I have got it now in my mind. I could not think of it at first. Well it has gone from me at the moment. Never mind. That is less important than the thing itself."

**James:** "Do you remember another thing? We played a rather peculiar game. Possibly you may recall it. Had great fun."

**Hodgson:** "I remember playing leap-frog with the boys. Do you remember that?"

**James:** "Yes, that was frequent."

**Hodgson:** "Yes, that is a very... – and then do you remember how I played bear."

**James:** "Yes, bear is first rate. I was not there, but I heard them talking about your playing bear...."

The conversation went back to the passwords and Hodgson was unable to remember exactly where he left them. They then discussed his personal effects that were to be sent to his sister in Australia and James assured him that John Piddington was taking care of it. Hodgson lamented the fact that James was unable to completely "get hold of the spiritual side of this thing and not only the physical side." James complained that Hodgson was too fragmentary in his messages and hoped he could grow more continuous. Hodgson responded by saying that James should not expect too much from him but to take things little by little and put the pieces together and make a whole out of it. He further explained that in a sense it was like a telephone call in which there were things the person couldn't remember at the time but might be remembered after the call was over. Near the end of the sitting, Alice James told Hodgson that she was so glad that he could come at all.

**Hodgson:** "Well, you were always a great help to me, you always did see me, but poor William was blind. But we shall wholly straighten him out and put him on the right track...I am sorry to be off so soon, but I know there are difficulties in remaining too long. They often told me that frequent communication was not good for anyone. I understand what they mean now better than ever..."

At a sitting on June 12, 1906, Alice James asked Hodgson if he recalled an argument he had with Margie, her sister, in their library. She no sooner asked the question when Mrs. Piper's arm was raised and her fist shaken threateningly. "Yes, I did this in her face," Hodgson replied, referring to the shaking of the fist. "I couldn't help it." William James remembered the scene well, noting that his sister-in-law defended some slate-writing medium she had seen in California, much to Hodgson's opposition to it.

In analyzing his sittings, James stated that the only evidential point is the anecdote about the Putnam child as he doesn't think anyone else knew about the playful incident. While having concluded that the conscious Mrs. Piper was not trying to put one over him, James still saw the possibility that someone told her about the incident and that her subconscious memory was now reproducing it.

One of the more interesting sittings in which Hodgson communicated involved Professor William Newbold, whom we met in Chapter Six. Professor James pointed out that some persons make for better "sitters" than others and said that Newbold appeared to be one of the best. A good friend of Hodgson's, Newbold sat with Mrs. Piper on June 27 and July 3, 1906. George Dorr, another ASPR member and also a good friend of Hodgson's, was present. After Mrs. Piper went into trance, Rector communicated briefly and turned it over to Hodgson. The SPR script reads, in part and slightly abridged:[6]

**Hodgson:** "Well, well, of all things! Are you really here! I am Hodgson.

**Newbold:** "Hallo, Dick!

**Hodgson:** "Hello, Billy, God bless you.

**Newbold:** "And you, too, though you do not need to have me say it."

**Hodgson:** "I wonder if you remember the last talk we had together –"

**Newbold:** "I do remember it, Dick."

**Hodgson:** "I can recall very well all I said to you that glorious day when we were watching the waves."

**Newbold:** "Yes, Dick, I remember it well." [Newbold documented that it was on a splendid afternoon of July 1905 at Nantasket Beach.]

**Hodgson:** "I told you of many, many predictions which had been made for me. I told you I hoped to realize them but I would not consent to give up my work."

**Newbold:** "First rate, Dick, you told me just that."

**Hodgson:** "I would give up almost anything else but my work – my work and my pipe."

**Newbold:** "Dick, that sounds like you...Do you remember something I told you on the boat going to Nantasket?"

**Hodgson:** "Yes, of course. Long ago you wrote me of your happiness and I wrote back and asked you if you were trying to make me discontented." [This was not what Newbold had in mind, but he confirmed that Hodgson often spoke to him about his happiness.]

**Newbold:** "I don't remember, but I have your letters and will look it up."

**Hodgson:** "Look over your letters and you will find my memory better than yours."

**Newbold:** "Like as not! Like as not!"

**Hodgson:** "I have hoped to boss things on this side."

**Newbold:** "Yes, Dick, so you [told me.]

After some further conversation with Newbold, Hodgson began speaking with Dorr. Dorr asked for clarification as to whether Hodgson was communicating directly or Rector was relaying messages from him.

**Hodgson:** "It is wholly done by Rector and it will continue to be. I shall take no part in that."

**Dorr:** "Then it is he who is speaking?"

**Hodgson:** "It is Rector who is speaking and he speaks for me. I have no desire to take Rector's place. I trust him implicitly and absolutely."

**Dorr:** "And he constantly reports for everyone?"

**Hodgson:** 'Everyone. There is no question about that. In the first place he is more competent to do it, he understands the conditions better than any individual spirit; he is fully capable and is under the constant direction of Imperator…"

On July 3, Newbold and Hodgson again dialogued. After some initial greeting, the transcript reads:

**Hodgson:** "I am trying my level best to give you facts."

**Newbold:** "Very good."

**Hodgson:** "I said my pipe and my work would not be given up even for a wife. Oh how you have helped me, Billy. Yes, in clearing my mind wonderfully. [Newbold noted that Hodgson made a very veridical remark at this point, but he had to omit it for some unexplained reason.] You said you could not understand why so many mistakes were made, and I talked you blind trying to explain my idea of it."

**Newbold:** "Dick, this sounds like your own self. Just the way you used to talk to me."

**Hodgson:** "Well if I am not Hodgson, he never lived."

**Newbold:** "But you are so clear."

**Hodgson:** "Of course I am. I am drawing on all the forces possible for strength to tell you these things. You laughed about the ungrammatical expressions and said, why in the world do they use bad grammar?"

**Newbold:** "Yes, Dick, I said that."

**Hodgson:** "I went into a long explanation and attributed it to the registering of the machine. You were rather amused but were inclined to leave it on my better understanding." [machine = medium's brain]

**Newbold:** "You mean, I think, that you understood the subject better than I and I took your explanation?"...

**Hodgson:** "I think I do. I find now difficulties such as a blind man would experience in trying to find his hat. And I am not wholly conscious of my own utterances because they come out automatically, impressed upon the machine."

**Newbold:** "Perfectly clear."

**Hodgson:** "Yes, I am standing beside you." [This may have been in response to Newbold mentally wondering if Hodgson was actually there in the room.]

**Newbold:** "Can you see me, Dick?"

**Hodgson:** "Yes, but I feel your presence better. I impress my thoughts on the machine which registers them at random, and which are at times difficult to understand. I understand so much better the *modus operandi* than I did when I was in your world. Do you remember you said you could faintly understand – faintly understand the desire on the part of a friend after coming to this side to communicate with his friend on the earthly side?. But why he would choose such methods were most perplexing things to you."

**Newbold:** "No, Dick you are thinking of someone else. I never told you that."

**Hodgson:** "Yes, you did in the case of the man I am talking of, who pretended to give manifestations, and you were right in your judgment."

**Newbold:** "Yes! I think I did say in that case."

**Hodgson:** "While in other cases you were open and clear to my explanations – and agreed with me, especially regarding G.P."

**Newbold:** "Right! First-rate! That is all very characteristic."

**Hodgson:** "You were a good listener always, Billy, always…I remember when you were with me I got very much interested in some letters you wrote me after your return home – your saying some things puzzled you very much" [Newbold noted that another first-rate veridical statement had to be omitted here.]

**Newbold:** "By jingo! That is true, Dick. It was ten years ago…Do you remember telling me that day that when you got on the other side you would make it hot for me?"

**Hodgson:** "I do indeed remember it well. I said I would shake you up – shake you up!"

**Newbold:** "That is just the word you used, Dick." [Newbold later noted that he was not sure that "shake you up" was what Hodgson had said, but that it was such a colloquial expression.]

**Hodgson:** "Yes, I did. Oh – I said, won't I shake you up when I get over there if I go before you do! And here I am, but I find my memory no worse than yours in spite of the fact that I have passed through the transition stage – state. You would be a pretty poor philosopher if you were to forget your subject as you seem to forget some of those little memories which I recall, Billy. Let me ask if you remember anything about a lady in Chicago to whom I referred."

**Newbold:** "Oh, Dick, I begin to remember. About eight or nine years ago, was it, Dick?" [Newbold recalled a woman from Chicago that Hodgson wanted to marry, but could not recall her name and wasn't sure Hodgson ever told him the name. Hodgson gave the last name as "Densmore" (a pseudonym for privacy purposes), which Newbold still didn't recall.]

**Hodgson:** "Do you remember my little talk about the satellites?"

**Newbold:** "Yes, I do."

**Hodgson:** "And about the inhabitants of Mars?"

**Newbold:** "I do indeed, I remember very well." [Newbold noted that these discussions took place in 1895.]

**Hodgson:** "That is what I am reminding you of. I heard you and William – William discussing me, and I stood not one inch behind you."

**Newbold:** "William who?"

**Hodgson:** "James."

**Newbold:** "What did William James say?" [Newbold recalled this talk with James the prior week.]

**Hodgson:** "He said he was baffled but he felt it was I talking – at one moment – then at another he did not know what to think." [James confirmed this as "perfectly true."]

**Newbold:** "Did you hear anything else?"

**Hodgson:** "Yes, he said I was very secretive and careful."

**Newbold:** "Did you hear him say that?"

**Hodgson:** "He did. He said I was – I am afraid I am."

**Newbold:** "I don't remember his saying so."

**Hodgson:** "I tell you Billy, he said so." [James remembered it.]

**Newbold:** "Did he say anything else?'

**Hodgson:** "He paid me a great compliment. I fear I did not deserve it. However, I am here to prove or disprove through life. Amen. Good-by. God bless you and your good wife. Remember me to her. Adieu. R.H." [Newbold remembered the compliment.]

Newbold wrote his impression to James: "The evidence for H's identity, as for that of other communicators, seems to me very strong indeed. It is not absolutely conclusive; but the only alternative theory, the telepathic, seem to me to explain the facts not as well as the spiritistic. I find it, however, absolutely impossible to accept the necessary corollaries of the spiritistic theory, especially those connected with the Imperator group, and therefore am compelled to suspend judgment."[7]

James noted that the two sittings with Newbold contained less bosh matter than other sittings and that the two omitted communications would have greatly increased the veridical effect.

Mrs. R. Bergman sat with Mrs. Piper on December 31, 1907 and again on January 1, 1908. In the first sitting, the communications were in writing and there was difficulty in reading them. In the second sitting, the voice was used and things went more smoothly. The below extracts are from the second sitting. Hodgson related what seems to have been a near-death experience, although not so named at the time.

**Hodgson:** "Do you remember my description of luminiferous ether, and of my conception of what this life was like? I have found it was not an erroneous imagination." [Mrs. Bergman recalled the discussion with Hodgson.]

**Hodgson:** "I remember telling you about my dismounting and sitting and drinking in the beauty of the morning."

**Bergman:** "Tell me any experiences that befell you while riding."

**Hodgson:** "Oh, I told you about the experience with the fiery horse. You remember he dismounted me. It was the first experience I had in seeing stars. I lost consciousness. I experienced passing into this life. I remember my being unconscious and recovering consciousness. I remember telling you about this at the hotel."

Mrs. Bergman recalled how Hodgson had related this very experience to her at the Parker House in Boston in 1904. She remembered that Hodgson spoke of being in a "spiritual universe" during the time he was unconscious.

**Hodgson:** "When I found the light (Mrs. Piper), it looked like a tremendous window, open window. The canopy – do you remember how they used to talk about the canopy? It is an ethereal veil. If your spiritual eyes were open you could see through this veil and see me talking to you perfectly."

Mrs. Bergman also recalled Hodgson discussing the "canopy" with her when he was alive.

James concluded that this was a very evidential sitting. "It is improbable that such unimportant conversations should have been reported by the living R.H. to Mrs. Piper, either awake or when in trance with other sitters; and to my mind the only plausible explanation is supernormal. Either it spells 'spirit return,' or telepathic reading of the sitter's mind by the medium in trance." [8]

Another curious and interesting observation by James had to do with one of the sittings by Miss Theodate Pope. Hodgson asked Miss Pope if she recalled a story he told her about his old friend Henry Sidgwick, one of the founders of the SPR. Pope did not understand and asked for clarification. Hodgson explained that he imitated Sidgwick, who stammered frequently. "I said s-s-s-should be i-n the t-r-i-c-k," Mrs. Piper's hand wrote. Miss Pope then remembered the story, with Hodgson quoting Sidgwick at the time, "H-Hodgson, if you b-b-believe in it, you'll b-be said to be in the t-trick."

At a sitting by Anne Manning Robbins, Hodgson said, "There is a man named Child passed out suddenly, wants to send his love to William James and his wife in the body." Miss Robbins, apparently confused as to whether he meant Alice James or Child's wife, asked for clarification. Hodgson replied, saying that Child said, "I hope 'L.' will understand what I mean." Hodgson did not know who "L." was.

When told of the sitting, James explained that "L." was Child's widow. Moreover, he recalled Professor F. J. Child as a colleague at Harvard University. James was reasonably certain that Hodgson had never met Child during life and that Mrs. Piper knew nothing of him. Also, Miss Robbins did not know him.

Still another seemingly evidential sitting was by "Mrs. M.," who, before Hodgson's death, talked to him about getting an endowment for the American branch of the SPR and adding both Professor (Billy) Newbold and Dr. Schiller to the staff. She asked Hodgson if he remembered the conversation. "Buying Billy!!" Hodgson responded with some excitement. "Buying only Billy." Mrs. M. reminded him that she wanted Schiller too.

In all, there were eleven such communications that James considered evidential to some degree. However, he remained on the fence relative to the spiritistic hypothesis. He wrote:

> These eleven incidents sound more like deliberate truth-telling, whoever the truth-teller be, than like lucky flukes. On the whole they make on me the impression of being supernormal. I confess that I should at this moment much like to know (although I have no means of knowing) just how all the documents I am exhibiting in this report will strike readers who are either novices in the field, or who consider the subject to be pure 'rot' or 'bosh.'

> It seems to me not impossible that a bosh-philosopher here or there may get a dramatic impression of there being something genuine behind it all. Most of those who remain faithful to the 'bosh' interpretation would, however, find plenty of comfort if they had the entire mass of records given them to read. Not that I have left things out (I certainly have tried not to!) that would, if printed, discredit the detail of what I cite, but I have left out, by not citing the whole mass of records, so much more mannerism, so much repetition, hesitation, irrelevance, unintelligibility, so much obvious groping and fishing and plausible covering up of false tracks, so much false pretension to

power, and real obedience to suggestion, that the stream of veridi-
cality that runs throughout the whole gets lost as it were in a marsh
of feebleness, and the total dramatic effect on the mind may be little
more than the word 'Humbug.' The really significant items disappear
in the total bulk. 'Passwords,' for example, and sealed messages are
given in abundance but can't be found. (I omit these here, as some of
them may prove veridical later.) Preposterous Latin sentences are written, e.g., 'Nebus merica este fecrum' – or what reads like that (April
4, 1906). Poetry gushes out but how can one be sure that Mrs. Piper
never knew it? The weak talk of the Imperator band about time is reproduced, as where R.H. pretends that he no longer knows what 'seven
minutes' means (May 14, 1906). Names asked for can't be given, etc.,
etc. All this mass of diluting material, which can't be reproduced in
abridgement, has its inevitable dramatic effect; and if one tends to hate
the whole phenomenon anyhow (as I confess that I myself sometimes
do) one's judicial verdict inclines accordingly.

Nevertheless, I have to confess also that the more familiar I have become with the records, the less relative significance for my mind has
all this diluting material tended to assume. The active cause of the
communications is on any hypothesis a will of some kind, be it the
will of R.H.'s spirit, of lower supernatural intelligences, or of Mrs.
Piper's subliminal...a will to say something which the machinery
fails to bring through. Dramatically, most of this 'bosh' is more sug-
gestive to me of dreaminess and mind-wandering than it is of humbug. Why should a 'will to deceive' prefer to give incorrect names so
often, if it can give the true ones to which the incorrect ones so frequently approximate as to suggest that they are meant? True names
impress the sitter vastly more. Why should it so multiply false 'passwords' ('Zeivorn,' for example) and stick to them? It looks to me more
like aiming at something definite, and failing of the goal...That a 'will
to personate' is a factor in the Piper phenomenon, I fully believe, and
I believe with unshakeable firmness that this will is able to draw on
supernormal sources of information. It can 'tap,' possibly the sitter's
memories, possibly those of distant human beings, possibly some cosmic reservoir in which the memories of earth are stored, whether in
the shape of 'spirits' or not.....

.....*Prima facie*, and as a matter of 'dramatic' probability, other intelligences than our own appear on an enormous scale in the historic

mass of material which Myers first brought together under the title of Automatisms. The refusal of 'modern enlightenment' to treat 'possession' as a hypothesis to be spoken of as even possible, in spite of the massive human traditions based on concrete experience in its favor, has always seemed to me a curious example of the power of fashion in things scientific.

The plot of possibilities thus thickens; and it thickens still more when we ask how a will which is dormant or relatively dormant during the intervals may become consciously reanimated as a spirit-personality by the occurrence of the medium's trance.[9]

Meanwhile, Professor James Hyslop was also hearing from Hodgson. After leaving his professorship at Columbia University and then battling some health problems, Hyslop organized the American Institute for Scientific Research, which was to be devoted to the study of abnormal psychology and psychical research. Following Hodgson's death, the ASPR became a section of Hyslop's organization and he dropped the study of abnormal psychology from his objectives, deciding to focus strictly on psychical research.

During the summer of 1904, Hyslop and Hodgson met at Putnam's Camp in the Adirondacks to talk over the formation of an American Society independent of the London organization. It was their intention to again meet at the same place during the summer of 1905 to finalize their plans, but Hodgson was unable to make it. Less than two weeks before his death, Hodgson wrote to Hyslop in New York and proposed that they meet after the holidays.

At a sitting with Mrs. Piper some two months after his death, Hodgson communicated and mentioned the meeting they were to have had in New York as well as the place they were to meet. He also mentioned the report he had planned to publish in which he would address the concerns of Mrs. Henry Sidgwick of the London SPR about the "possession" theory of the trance process. While Hyslop considered the possibility that he had mentioned all of this to Mrs. Piper, he doubted it as it was not his policy to discuss such matters with her.

On February 27, 1906, Hodgson asked Hyslop if he remembered when he told him that if he got to the "other side" first and was able to communicate through a medium, he would talk with the fervor of a [southern preacher]. Hyslop replied that he remembered no such conversation, to which Hodgson said he must have said it to someone else. The sitting was reported to William James who recalled telling Hodgson that if he made it to the "other side," the tone of the Imperator group would change to that of [southern] minstrels.

On March 16, 1906, Hyslop had a sitting with a prominent New York City woman with psychic abilities. Because of her standing in the community, he could not mention her name and referred to her as "Miss X." Hodgson communicated with some pertinent information, though not necessarily evidential. Hyslop then went on to Boston to sit with Mrs. Piper. "Soon after the beginning of the sitting, Rector, the trance personality usually controlling, wrote that he had seen me 'at another light,' that he had brought Hodgson there, but that they could not make themselves clear, and asked me if I had understood them," Hyslop documented. "I asked when it was and received the reply that it was two days before Sabbath."[10] This coincided with the date of Hyslop's sitting with Miss. X.

When Hodgson began communicating, he asked if Hyslop had received his message though Miss X, and when Hyslop told him that he was uncertain, Hodgson asked him to try again. Hyslop then arranged for another sitting with Miss. X. on March 24. Here again, Hodgson communicated and used phraseology similar to that coming through Mrs. Piper. After the sitting, Hyslop wrote to Henry James, Jr. in Boston and asked him to sit with Mrs. Piper and, if Hodgson communicated, to ask him what he had told him in New York. Henry James, Jr. did so and "stated with some approximation to it the message, which I had received on the evening of the 24th."

At a sitting with another woman of social standing, given the pseudonym "Mrs. Quentin," Hyslop heard from George Pellew (G.P.) on the Ouija board. The following dialogue took place:

**Hyslop:** "Well, George, have you seen any of my friends recently?"

**George:** "No, only Richard H."

**Hyslop:** "How is H?"

**George:** "Progressive as ever."

**Hyslop:** "Is he clear?"

**George:** "Not very."

**Hyslop:** "Do you mean when he communicates or in his normal state?"

**George:** "Oh, all right normally. Only when he comes into that wretched atmosphere he goes to pieces. Wonder how long it will take him to overcome this."

Then, on October 10, 1906, Hyslop again had a sitting with Mrs. Piper. The transcript reads:

**Hodgson:** "I am Hodgson."

**Hyslop:** "Good, Hodgson, how are you?"

**Hodgson:** "Capital. How are you, Hyslop, old chap?"

**Hyslop:** "Fine."

**Hodgson:** "Good to hear it. Did you receive my last message?"

**Hyslop:** "When and where?" [Hyslop had in mind the sitting with Mrs. Quentin.]

**Hodgson:** "I told George to give it to you."

However, while Hyslop thought he was referring to George Pellew, Hodgson then said it was George Dorr whom he had asked to give the message. Hyslop said he had not heard from George Dorr. But Hodgson acknowledged the sitting with Mrs. Quentin. As a test, Hyslop asked Hodgson how the messages came. Mrs. Piper's hand ceased writing and began to move about the sheet of paper exactly as if she were spelling out words on the Ouija board.[11]

Three hours after a sitting with Mrs. Piper, Hyslop visited another medium, "Mrs. Smith," who did not know he had been experimenting that day with Mrs. Piper and had heard from Hodgson. Mrs. Smith was a trance-speaking medium. After saying a few words about a person recently deceased, Mrs. Smith said: "Beside him is Dr. Hodgson. It is part of a promise to you today as he had just been to say to you he was trying not to be intense, but he is intense. I said I would come here. I am. I thought I might be able to tell different things I already told. Perhaps I can call up some past interviews and make things more clear."

As Hyslop saw it, there were just three hypotheses capable of explaining such facts: 1) fraud; 2) telepathy; and 3) spirits. He summed it up:

> As to fraud, that has been excluded from consideration in the Piper case for fifteen or twenty years, and only unintelligent men would talk about it any longer...

> I do not think that telepathy as an explanation will fare any better. In fact I should be ashamed, as one who has tried to be scientific, to advance telepathy as an explanation of any such facts. Any man who knows what he means by the use of this term would not venture to suppose it as an explanation...

> As to the third hypothesis, namely, that of spirits, I shall not undertake any dogmatic defense. It is obvious to me that it is the most rational hypothesis after eliminating fraud from such matters...[12]

---

[1] Piper, 122-125

[2] Baird, 296

[3] Robbins, 86-87

[4] _____, 87-88

[5] Holt, 725-728 (PR XXIII, 80f)

[6] _____, 719-723 (Pr. XXIII, 61-78)

[7] Murphy, 174

[8] _____, 194

[9] Holt, 733-736 (PR XXIII, 115-118)

[10] De Vesme, 537-538

[11] _____, 540-541

[12] _____, 543-544

# -Ten-

# Return to England & The Cross Correspondences

*It was full of intelligence and could be described as more like an intelligent person than a hand.*
**– Sir Oliver Lodge**

At the invitation of Sir Oliver Lodge, who was knighted in 1902 for his contributions to science in the fields of electricity and radio, Leonora Piper returned to England in November 1906, accompanied by her daughters, Alta and Minerva, by then young women. (William Piper died in 1904). Lodge immediately took note of the change in her mediumship since he had observed her in 1889-90:

> The dramatic activity of the hand was very remarkable: it was full of intelligence, and could be described as more like an intelligent person than a hand. It sometimes turned itself to the sitter, when it wanted to be spoken to by him; but for the most part, when not writing, it turned itself away from the sitter, as if receiving communications from outside, which it then proceeded to write down; going back to space – i.e., directing itself to a part of the room where nobody was – for further information and supplementary intelligence, as necessity arose…In the old days the control had styled itself 'Phinuit'; now Phinuit never appears, and the control calls itself Rector…

In the old days, undoubtedly, the appearance was sometimes as if the actual control was changed – after the fashion of a multiple personality; whereas now I think it is always Rector that writes, recording the messages given to him as nearly as he can, and usually reporting the first person, as Phinuit often did. I do not attempt to discriminate between what is given in this way and what is given directly, because it is practically impossible to do so with any certainty...If a special agency gets control and writes for a few minutes, it does not seem able to sustain the position long, but soon abandons it to the more accomplished and experienced personality, Rector. In the recent series there appeared very little evidence of direct control other than Rector...

We shall speak of the 'Gurney control,' the 'Hodgson control,' etc., without implying that these agents – even assuming their existence and activity – are ever really in physical possession of the organism; and, even when they are controlling as directly as possible, they may perhaps always be operating telepathically on it rather than telergically – operating, that is, to say, through some stratum of the mind, rather than entirely on any part of the physical organism.[1]

Lodge mentioned the earlier exchange in America between George Dorr and the discarnate Richard Hodgson (See Chapter Nine) in which Hodgson said that Rector does all the speaking and is under the constant direction of Imperator. Thus, Lodge concluded that the changes of control are more dramatic than real.

Hodgson communicated frequently at the England sittings, but was seldom the most prominent communicator, saying that he was helping Myers and others to communicate and thought it best to remain in the background. At the 13th sitting, on December 3, 1906, the following exchange occurred:

**Hodgson:** "Hello, Hello, Lodge. How are you on that side?"

**Lodge:** "Hullo, Hodgson. I want to ask you something."

**Hodgson:** "Fire away at me, I am in the witness box."

**Lodge:** "Well, you told me to give a message to Billy Newbold."

**Hodgson:** "Right."

**Lodge:** "About the title of a Hindustani poem, but you did not tell me anything in Hindustani. That is, I expect, what he wanted."

**Hodgson:** No, I beg your pardon; he asked me to translate into English the name of a poem I wrote, now in his possession."

**Lodge:** "Very well; and is that all I am to say to him?"

**Hodgson:** "Yes, about that. But you will please tell him that he is not to feel disturbed about that medium's message; it is all rot. He will understand about it, i.e., his going to the bottom with his wife, going to the bottom of the sea. U.D.? ["U.D." was Rector's usual abbreviation for "understand."] Myers has had very little opportunity or encouragement to prove his identity."

**Lodge:** "Yes, that is fairly true so far."

**Hodgson:** "And now if the opportunity can be given him, no one, no one on our side is more desirous of proving his identity than Myers.. U.D?"

**Lodge:** "Yes, I quite understand ..."

**Hodgson:** "We cannot remain here; our utterances are fragmentary, but they are earnest and sincere. This must be the case, however, until the veil is lifted, with all made clear to you. Your mind cannot help us. If you think of a thing seriously it cannot convey anything to us. We go, and may God be with and watch over you always. Farewell." [It was signed with a cross and an "R," the usual closing for Rector.] [2]

The eighth sitting began:

**Hodgson:** "I am Hodgson, but I cannot take Rector's place today. However, I will make a poor attempt to speak through him."

**Lodge:** "Very glad to see you."

**Hodgson:** "Here's ditto."

It was noted by researcher Henry Holt that "Here's ditto" was a frequent expression of Hodgson's when alive, although not especially evidential since Mrs. Piper had no doubt heard him say that at least a few times. A very curious comment followed:

**Hodgson:** "Do I understand that Mrs. Piper is in England?" [3]

Lodge commented on the differences between Mrs. Piper's trance state in 1889-90 and 1906, mentioning that from four to six cushions or pillows were placed on the table in front of her, and that after going into trance she would turn to the left side so as to be able to breathe. Writing material was placed on the right side of the pillows, either on the same or on a subsidiary table, usually 100 blank sheets, all numbered in order, and four or five pencils of soft lead. It was the duty of the experimenter to record all that the sitter said. He also had to arrange the pad so that the hand could conveniently write upon it; and to tear off the sheets as they were filled. The automatic writing was large and scrawling, and often did not begin at the top of the page. There were times when one page was filled with an abundance of material, but other times when only a few sentences, or even just a few words were written. When a page was being torn, the hand would sometimes show impatience at the interruption.

The tone was, Lodge observed, much more dignified and serious now than in the Phinuit days. In 1889-90, going into trance appeared to be a painful process, or at least one involving muscular effort. Mrs. Piper's face was contorted and sometimes there was a slight tearing of the hair. Now, after some heavy breathing, she just slipped into trance without effort – "a sleep with the superficial appearance of that induced by chloroform; and the return to consciousness, though slow and for a time accompanied by confusion, is easy and natural." [4]

About 30 seconds after going into trance, the right hand "woke up," slowly rose, made the sign of the cross in the air, and indicated it was ready to write. The experimenter placed a pencil in Mrs. Piper's hand and had to place it between the fore and middle fingers, at which time it was grasped and the writing began. First a cross was drawn, and then the word "Hail" was written, followed usually by "We return to earth this day with joy and peace," or "We greet you friend of earth once again, we bring peace and love," followed by "R" for Rector.

In one sitting, the communicating spirit was asked if he recognized the room he was in. At that point, Mrs. Piper's hand went up and scoped the room for some time, as if there were eyes in the hand.

In 1889-90, the sittings lasted no more than an hour, but in 1906, they would sometimes last as long as two hours. On one occasion only, in 1906, Mrs. Piper could not achieve the trance state. The coming out of trance was gradual and semi-consciousness lasted for several minutes, during which time Mrs. Piper often muttered sentences and her eyes, if opened at all, glared in sleep-walking fashion. However, even after out of the trance, it took her about 30 minutes to regain normal composure. During that time, Alta would tend to her, usually just sitting by her and doing needlework. When Mrs. Piper was herself again, one of her daughters would take her for a walk in the garden. Then, they all had lunch together with nothing said of the sitting.

At one sitting, Lodge asked Rector for the whereabouts of Dr. Phinuit.

**Lodge:** "May I ask a question? Does 'Phinuit' mean anything to you?"

**Rector:** "You mean Dr. Phinuit? Oh yes, we see him occasionally, friend; he is in another sphere of this life, no longer earth-bound, and he is very well and very happy."

**Lodge:** "He was a friend of mine." [Lodge noted that he was referring to 1889-90 and that he was on affectionate terms with Phinuit at that time.]

**Rector:** "Could you by any possibility be the friend on earth whom he called 'Captain'**?**

**Lodge:** "Yes, indeed, that is me."

**Rector:** [Excitement in hand] "Would you like to see and speak with him?"

**Lodge:** "I should if it did him no harm."

**Rector:** "Oh no harm in the least; he is beyond harm, friend; he has so progressed. He will no doubt be glad to return. We will speak with him and report his doings."

**Lodge:** "Will you give him my love?"

**Rector**: "I will give him your love certainly with great pleasure. He is a much better spirit than he was thought to have been. He fell in with the wrong element to begin with...I will see him and report at our next meeting. R." [5]

At the next meeting, Rector reported that he found Phinuit and gave him Lodge's message, and that Phinuit also gave his love and would endeavor to return through the "light" at the next meeting. However, recalling the stresses involved when Mrs. Piper went into trance before Phinuit communicated in 1889-90, Lodge questioned whether it would be a good thing. Rector agreed and said that since Phinuit is not in the least bit anxious to return, he would leave it at that.

During Mrs. Piper's 1889-90 visit to England, Lodge's neighbor, Isaac Thompson, had a fairly evidential sitting with her. He died in 1903, and during a 1905 visit to America, Edwin Thompson, Isaac's son, who was only eight years old during Mrs. Piper's first visit to England, had a sitting with her in hopes of hearing from his father. The sitting took place in Boston on December 11, nine days before Hodgson's death. Hodgson introduced Edwin anonymously after the trance began. Although Isaac Thompson seemed to communicate and wonder how his son found him, the sitting was mostly a failure. Eleven months later, on November 10, 1906, Susan Thompson, Isaac's widow, and Edwin sat with Mrs. Piper, with Lodge opening and recording the session. After Imperator gave the sign of the cross in the air and wrote "Hail," the sitting proceeded:

**Rector:** "A spirit is present whom we have seen before; he is imploring us to let him speak."

**Lodge:** "Yes, we wish to speak to him."

**Rector:** "We understand you very well, friend, and you are understanding me also. [Lodge trades places with Edwin at this point.]

**Isaac:** (Excitement in hand, many scrawls) "I am so very glad to return again. I have longed to speak once more."

**Edwin:** "Have you ever communicated with me before through this medium?"

**Isaac:** "Are you any possibility my son?"

**Edwin:** "Yes, have you spoken to me before?"

**Isaac:** "Oh yes, do you not remember how difficult it was for me to reach you under those new and strange conditions? (Apparently referring to the Boston sitting.) I am so delighted to see you again. I cannot think fast enough. God bless you my boy. I have been helping you and Theodo…."

**Edwin:** "Can you give me your name?"

**Rector:** "What name? R."

**Edwin:** "I do not know who it is yet."

**Rector:** "Neither do I. R." [The words "Theoder. T H E." are then written, but it is unclear as to who is now writing.]

**Edwin:** "Oh, you mean Theodora."

**Isaac:** "All the time I am helping her."

**Edwin:** "Do you remember speaking to me before?"

**Isaac:** "God bless you. Not long ago, but it was not here…I am your father, I am, and I sent several messages to you through a friend who came with you and who is now on our side. [Apparently referring to Hodgson, who was alive and present at the Boston sitting.] Do you understand my son?…How is it you do not speak?"

**Edwin:** "Can you give me any message that I can tell mother?"

**Isaac:** "Tell her I am sorry I did not understand about coming here. Had I, I should have arranged things differently for her. Take good care of her will you?"

**Edwin:** "She is here, would you like to speak with her?"

**Isaac:** "Oh yes, oh yes, oh yes. Why did you not tell me before?"

**Susan:** "Do you see me?"

**Isaac:** "I hear her speak." [Excitement, pencil breaks.]

**Susan:** "Do you see me?"

**Isaac:** "I do, I do, I do, I do."

**Susan:** "Can you call me by my name?"

**Isaac:** "S s s a. Let me free my mind and tell you how I feel. I am not dead now, but I am speaking with you. Isauc (sic) I am he. Do you remember Issa, Issa, Susa, Susa..."

**Susan:** "Can you help me about Theodora?" [Theodora was not well.]

**Isaac:** "Yes, I can now, but I did not before. Dear, are you tired? Are you tired and discouraged at times?"

**Susan:** "Yes, Isaac, since you went."

**Isaac:** "Better I came. Think it so. Can't you see me?"

**Susan:** "No, I cannot."

**Isaac:** "Susar, Susan, Susu, Susin [Excitement, scrawls]

**Susan:** "Shall Theodora come in? Would you like to see her?"

**Isaac:** "Yes, more than you think."

**Susan:** "Here is Theodora."

**Isaac:** "She is going to get well and get stronger and better than ever before in all her life. She has light, she has light, but do not use it. It isn't good for her."

**Susan:** "You mean she could write automatically but is not to try?"

**Isaac:** "Correct. Do not let her do so, I beg of you. Father. Papa." [Last two words are signatures.] I wish you could get all good out of that life: that, let me desire for you. Dear Theo, you have a claim to health – it is your right."

**Theodora:** "Can you tell me anything I should do to get strong?"

**Isaac:** "Yes, I'll ask the Doctor, I'll call the doctor."

Lodge then recorded that there was a change of control as the control calling itself "Doctor" (not Phinuit) gave many medical details and precepts, after which Isaac Thompson returned and talked business matters with his son. He was especially interested in knowing the results of a lawsuit that had been filed before his death. Isaac was apparently pleased with the results of the lawsuit and said something to the effect that he had tried to tell the man who helped him in America and who was now with him.

**Edwin:** "Who is that?"

**Isaac:** "His name is Hodgson."

**Edwin:** "Oh yes, Dr. Hodgson. I understand."

**Isaac:** "And he is helping me now…"

At a later sitting, Isaac Thompson informed his wife and son that he had a new friend on that side. He struggled to get his name, spelling it "Chares" twice and finally "Charles." It was Charles E. Stevens, Susan Thompson's brother, who had died some six weeks before the sitting. They dialogued:

**Charles:** "I didn't realize I was coming over. Oh dear. I am so glad to understand it now…I want you to look up a picture I ordered before I left, and it never came."

**Edwin:** "Can you tell us from whom you ordered it?"

**Charles:** "That would be difficult to get through to thee [Lodge noted that he was a Quaker], but I ordered it from a friend of mine, who used to take my orders and get them for me…"

**Susan:** "Yes, Charlie, the picture did come after you left, and Mary sent the bill of it to Mrs. Alsop to pay." [Edwin knew nothing of this.]

**Charles:** "Oh I am so glad to understand."

**Susan:** "Is there any other message thou would like to give about anything?"

Charles asked Susan to look after Mary, their sister, and said something to the effect that Mary would be joining him. Susan asked for clarification, wondering if Mary would be joining him soon. Charles did not give a definite answer, and said he had good reason to ask Susan to take good care of Mary. He then discussed business matters with Edwin, correctly mentioning some names of business associates and detailed knowledge on some of the business matters. At the conclusion of that discussion, Isaac returned, commenting that he was there to greet Charlie when he went over to his side and helped him find his way. In the ensuing conversation, Rector broke in to say that he was using "you" rather than "thee" to be better understood.

One of the reasons Lodge invited Mrs. Piper to England was to see if she might add to the intriguing "cross-correspondences" and "cross-references" coming through several other mediums, including Margaret Verrall, Helen Verrall, and Alice Fleming, the latter referred to in the SPR records as "Mrs. Holland," a pseudonym for privacy purposes.

Mrs. Verrall, Miss Verall, and Mrs. Fleming were all automatic writing mediums who received messages in the privacy of their homes. There were no "sitters" or researchers present. Their forms of mediumship did not involve the deep trance of Mrs. Piper.

Basically, the cross-correspondences involved fragmentary messages coming through two or three mediums, which when joined together, formed a coherent message. It was a scheme purportedly devised by the discarnate Frederic W. H. Myers (See Chapter Three), who had died on January 17, 1901. The objective was to show that an independent intelligence was influencing the different mediums, thereby ruling out telepathy. As an over-simplified example of a cross-correspondence, one medium might get the Latin word *Veni*, another medium unknown to the first one might get the word *Vidi*, and a third medium, unknown to the other two, the word *Vici*, the three combined forming the famous quotation attributed to Julius Caesar, meaning "I came, I saw, I conquered."

Somewhat akin to the cross-correspondences were cross-references, in which a message was given to Myers or another discarnate by the researcher with one medium and asked to communicate it through another medium. Or Myers would attempt to get the same word or phrase through two different mediums.

One such cross-reference experiment was carried out by Hodgson, before his death, at a sitting with Mrs. Piper on January 28, 1902, when he asked the discarnate Myers to attempt to have Helen Verrall in England record a hand holding a spear. However, Rector, who was controlling Mrs. Piper at the time and acting as the go-between with Myers and Hodgson, thought Hodgson said "sphere," and asked for clarification. After Hodgson repeated the word and spelled it out, the control agreed to give it a try. At the next sitting, on February 4, Myers claimed to have been successful but he spelled the word "sphear" in communicating with Hodgson during that sitting. As Hodgson was to find out, the Greek word for "sphere" and the Latin word for "spear" came through in Margaret Verrall's script three days after the January 28 sitting with Mrs. Piper.[6]

Myers, a classical scholar, was fluent in both Latin and Greek, while Margaret Verrall lectured in the classics at Newnham College and also knew some Greek and Latin. Why it came through Margaret Verrall and not Helen Verrall was not made clear by Myers or Rector, but it was deemed likely that Myers could not get it though Helen Verrall's hand and so successfully used her mother's hand. "The significant point here," Professor Hyslop wrote in his summary of the case, "is that what was started in English was translated into Greek and Latin when delivered in England, with the same mistakes there that had been made in Boston."[7]

On September 19, 1903, soon after reading *Human Personality and Its Survival of Bodily Death,* Myers's seminal work on psychical research, Mrs. Fleming, the sister of author Rudyard Kipling, began receiving messages purportedly coming from Myers via automatic writing. The initial messages were short and apparently an attempt by Myers to convince her of his identity. He told her that much of what he would write through her was not meant for her, that she was to be the reporter. Mrs. Fleming, who was living in India at the time, was asked to send the messages to Margaret Verrall at 5, Selwyn Gardens, Cambridge. Mrs. Fleming had read Verrall's name in Myers's book, but had no knowledge of her address. Myers had been good friends with both Dr. A. W. and Margaret Verrall. A. W. was also a classical scholar at Cambridge.

In a subsequent message, Myers told Fleming not to worry about being made a fool or dupe. "It's a form of restless vanity to fear that your hand is imposing upon yourself, as it were," Myers communicated to her. "If it were possible for the soul to die back into earth life again I should die from sheer yearning to reach you – to tell you that all that we imagined is not half wonderful enough for the truth…If I could only reach you – if I could only tell you – I long for power and all that comes to me is an infinite yearning – an infinite pain. Does any of this reach you – reaching anyone – or am I only wailing as the wind wails – wordless and unheeded?"[8]

On another occasion, Myers wrote that "to believe that the mere act of death enables a spirit to understand the whole mystery of death is as absurd as to imagine that the act of birth enables an infant to understand the whole mystery of life." He added that he was still groping… surmising…conjecturing.[9]

Mrs. Fleming also received messages from Edmund Gurney and Roden Noel, both unknown to her. A message from Noel said to ask "A.W." what the date May 26, 1894 meant to him, and if he could not remember, to ask Nora. Not knowing what to make of the message, Fleming sent the message to the SPR in London, where it was recognized that A. W. was a reference to Dr. A. W. Verrall and Nora to Dr. Eleanor (Nora) Sidgwick. May 26 was the date of Noel's death.

On February 26, 1907, as Mrs. Piper was coming out of trance, she repeated the word "laurel" several times, followed by "I gave her that for laurel." The following day, Myers communicated, "I gave Mrs. Verrall [a] laurel wreath." When Margaret Verrall's scripts were examined, it was discovered that on February 6, she wrote, "Apollo's laurel bough" twice, as well as "Laureatus," the Latin for laurelled, and "with laurel wreath his brow serene was crowned, and a laurel crown." There was also a drawing of a laurel wreath.[10]

One of the more simple experiments began on January 16, 1907, in London, when SPR researcher John Piddington, communicating with Myers through Mrs. Piper, asked Myers to attach a sign to any message he might get through another medium, suggesting a circle with a triangle in it. Such a sign came through the automatic writing of Margaret Verrall in Cambridge on January 28, 12 days after Piddington's request. Then, on May 8, Mrs. Fleming, still living in India, recorded a circle and a triangle in her script, although the triangle was not in the circle.

Another fairly simple cross-reference is known as the Euripides case. On March 4, 1907, Margaret Verrall wrote "Hercules Furens," a play written by Euripides. This was followed by a message from Myers to A.W. Verrall about the play, and then, "Ask elsewhere for the bound Hercules." On March 25, Myers again made reference to the play and wrote that "the clue is in the Euripides play if you could only see it." On April 8, communicating through Mrs. Piper, Myers mentioned several words and phrases, including Euripides, as having been given as a cross correspondence. On April 16, Mrs. Fleming's script also referred to Euripides.[11]

One of the more famous and complex cross-correspondences was referred to by the researchers as the "Hope, Star and Browning case." On February 11, 1907, Piddington was sitting with Mrs. Piper and communicating with Myers when Myers asked him if Margaret Verrall received the word "evangelical" and told Piddington to look out for "Hope," "Star," and also "Browning." Piddington then examined Margaret Verrall's recent scripts and found in her January 23 script: "Justice holds the scales. That gives the words, but an anagram would be better. Tell him that — rats, star, tars, and so on..."

In Mrs. Verrall's script of January 28, Myers wrote "Aster" (Latin = star). It was followed by reference to "Abt Vogler," a poem by Robert Browning containing the word "hope." When, in his next sitting, Piddington asked Myers about the intent of the word "evangelical," Myers explained that it was a botched attempt to get the name "Evelyn Hope" through. Evelyn Hope was the title of another of Browning's poems. The words, "the hope that leaves the earth for the sky," were also written by Myers.

On February 17, Helen Verrall's script contained a drawing of a star, followed by, "That was the sign she will understand when she sees it... No arts avail. And a star above it all rats everywhere in Hamelin town." The latter was believed to have been Myers' way of getting the "Pied Piper" through, a reference to Mrs. Piper. Piecing it all together, Piddington was able to get the "Hope, Star, and Browning" suggested by Myers in the earlier sitting.[12]

Myers and Hodgson collaborated in several other messages. Lodge summarized the experiments:

> We have in the course of the last few years been driven to recognize that the controls are pertinaciously trying to communicate now one, now another definite idea by means of two or more different automatists, whom at the same time they are trying to prevent from communicating telepathically or unconsciously with one another; and that in

order to achieve this deliberate aim the controls express the factors of the idea in so veiled a form that each writer indites her own share without understanding it. Yet some identifying symbol or phrase is often included in each script, so as to indicate to a critical examiner that the correspondence is intended and not accidental; and, moreover, the idea thus co-operatively expressed is so definite that, when once the clue is found, no room is left for doubt as the proper interpretation.

That is precisely what we have quite recently again and again obtained. We are told by the communicators that there are other correspondences not yet detected by us; and by more careful collation of the documents this has already been found true. The evidence needs careful and critical study; it is not in itself sensational, but it affords strong evidence of the intervention of a mind behind and independent of the automatist.[13]

---

[1] Holt, 745-746 (Pr. XXIII, 131)

[2] _____, 743-744 (Pr. XXIII, 245f)

[3] _____, 743

[4] Lodge (1909), 262

[5] Holt, 758-759 (Pr. XXIII, 280-81)

[6] Hyslop (1919), 166-67

[7] _____, 166-167

[8] Barrett, 200

[9] _____, 200

[10] Saltmarsh, 59

[11] _____, 79-80

[12] _____, 68-69

[13] Lodge (1909), 336-337

# -Eleven-

# Later Years
# & The Return of
# Professor James

*The attitude of the Philistine is caused by a failure to reflect on
the situation in any alleged spiritistic phenomena.*
**– James H. Hyslop**

After returning home to Boston during the summer of 1907, Mrs.
Piper resumed sittings with Professor James Hyslop and other
researchers under the reorganized ASPR. Dr. Hodgson continued to communicate, often commenting on the difficulties he had in
making himself understood. Among the more interesting comments
relative to the communication, as recorded by Hyslop, before and after the England trip were:

> In leaving the body the shock to the spirit knocks everything out of
> one's thoughts for awhile, but if he has any desire at all to prove his
> identity he can in time collect enough evidence to prove his identity
> convincingly.

> The change called Death which is really only transition is very different from what one thinks before he experiences it. That in part explains why Myers never took a more active part after he came over
> here. He had much on his mind before he came, which he vowed he
> would give out after he came over, but the shock [was such] that many
> of his determinations were scattered from his living memory. This is

a petty excuse but a living reality – a fact. It is unmistakably so with every one who crosses the border lines.

...when expecting the best results the poorest may be given, unless this is fully understood by those living in the mortal life. It is only by simple recollections that real proof of identify can be given.

It is, I find, most difficult to use the mechanism and register clearly one's recollections. I have much sympathy for George (G.P.) whom we badgered to death, poor fellow. He gave me all I had to hope for in spite of my treatment of him. Now just keep your patience with me and you will have all you could ask for. Understand?

...I am more awake than asleep, yet I cannot come just as I am in reality, independently of the medium's light.

It is so suffocating here. I can appreciate their difficulties better than ever before.

There is no telepathy in this except as it comes from my mind to yours.[1]

Here is an interesting dialogue between Hodgson and Hyslop in which they further discuss the difficulties:

**Hodgson:** "I cannot forget anything if you give me time to recall. You must have great patience with me as I am not what I hope to be later."

**Hyslop:** "All right, Hodgson. Do you find that we conjectured the difficulties fairly well?"

**Hodgson:** "We did surprisingly well. I was surprised enough. Is my writing more difficult than it used to be?"

**Hyslop:** "It is about the same."

**Hodgson:** "Do you remember anything about it?"

**Hyslop:** "Yes, I do."

**Hodgson:** "I remember your comments about it, and much was left to me to explain."

**Hyslop:** "Yes, that is true."

**Hodgson:** "Of course it's true. Think I am less intelligent because I am in the witness box?"

**Hyslop:** "No, I understand the difficulties."

**Hodgson:** "I hope you do, but this is the happiest moment of coming over here. I mean in meeting you again."

**Hyslop:** "All right, Hodgson. I feel that it would have been better for you to lead on this side." [referring to the leadership of the ASPR]

**Hodgson:** "Perhaps, but I am satisfied. Do you remember how I said to you I sometimes longed to get over here?

**Hyslop:** "Yes, I expect that was true and I have heard persons say you said it."

**Hodgson:** "I did often. I longed to see this beautiful country if I may so express it." [2]

Hyslop documented his report by commenting that he never heard Hodgson say he was anxious to pass over, but that he had heard others say that he had this wish. As for Hodgson's handwriting, Hyslop said that there were several times when he had to write to Hodgson in Boston to tell him that he could not read his handwriting. Hyslop also recalled a comment by Hodgson about what a difficult time he would have in reading his messages if he were to pass first and be able to communicate.

In the May 1910 issue of the *ASPR Proceedings*, Hyslop wrote:

The difficulty of communicating anything intelligible regarding a supersensible world through sensible media will always give rise to statements that will often seem absurd and trivial. An analogy of this difficulty can be found in the difficulties which a man born deaf and dumb must encounter in the attempt to communicate his visual experiences to a man born blind. It is in fact absolutely impossible to do this intelligibly. Nothing but the most obscure analogies are accessible for the purpose and possibly even these analogies would have to be reduced to common emotional experiences as a means of suggesting the intelligible. Unless, therefore, the transcendental existence affords some clear analogies to the earthly, such as space relations or ethereal replicas of the present existence, there would be very little to make the use of terrestrially acquired concepts distinctly useful in imparting knowledge and attempts at it might possibly degenerate into the really or apparently trivial. This would certainly be the case if the condition for communicating be anything like our secondary personality. In a clear state of mind, if analogies permitted, some intelligible communications might be made about the supersensible world, but this would not be probable in an abnormal mental condition involving dreamlike or delirious action, and no one knows what else not familiar to us.[3]

In 1909, G. Stanley Hall, president of Clark University, persuaded Hyslop and William James to let him and his assistant, Dr. Amy Tanner, study Mrs. Piper in a series of six sittings. Since Hall had been a total disbeliever in Mrs. Piper's ability, they questioned his motives but apparently thought he might be persuaded to see Mrs. Piper in a new light if he were to observe her more closely. However, they later concluded that Hall had only one objective – to debunk her. He mixed up a slightly toxic compound and dripped it into Mrs. Piper's mouth during her trance. This resulted in blistering and swollen lips the next day. He attempted another experiment, resulting in injury to her arm.

As other researchers had already learned, an antagonistic attitude by sitters results in poor phenomena, if any. And that is apparently what Hall and Tanner got. They concluded that Mrs. Piper's phenomena were nothing more than a secondary personality of an unusual kind. In a 1910 book titled *Studies in Spiritism,* Tanner attempted to expose Mrs. Piper and bring an end to the whole idea that spirits exist and are able to communicate.

"The refrain of the whole book, with its sneering and criticism of psychic researchers is that they do not know how to conduct experiments of the kind," Hyslop wrote of Tanner's book. "These authors would have readers believe that they are exceedingly wise about these things and that all others have been credulous fools who have conducted the experiments."[4] Over some 99 pages in the January 1911 issue of the ASPR Journal, Hyslop explained why he thought Hall and Tanner were the fools and why their lack of understanding of the proper protocol in such research defeated Mrs. Piper and gained a "victory" for them, or so they felt, since their objective clearly was to debunk her. He likened their research to a man with a butcher knife trying to perform a delicate operation or a man with a pitchfork trying to sew a button on a shirt.

Nevertheless, some damage was done to Mrs. Piper's reputation, as well as to those of James, Hodgson, Lodge, Hyslop, and other psychical researchers. Those stuck in the muck and mire of scientific fundamentalism embraced the findings of Hall and Tanner and felt that they were justified all along in their disbelief.

In fact, a decade earlier, on October 20, 1901, the pseudoskeptics celebrated when the *New York Herald* carried a story in which Mrs. Piper supposedly "confessed" that she was not in touch with spirits of the dead. What she said, however, was that she was more inclined to believe that the messages coming through her were some form of telepathy rather than spirits of the dead communicating, but she admitted that she had no recollection of what went on while she was in trance and was not qualified to be a judge in the matter. Indications were that she was trying to take the "intelligent" approach, the one advocated by Professor James, or to show herself as being very objective in the matter. But to many who did not want to believe in spirits, it was clearly a "confession."

Whether the Hall-Tanner sittings resulted in Mrs. Piper' declining health is uncertain, but it seems to have begun around that time. A third visit to England was made in October 1909, but she was sick much of the time with a cold or the flu and there was little in the way of good phenomena. Coming out of trance was especially difficult. She remained in England despite the poor health, and in a sitting on May 24, 1911 Imperator made it known that they were suspending her mediumship. Upon returning to the United States, she was able to do some automatic writing while not in the trance state, but Hyslop and the ASPR had already gone on to more dedicated research with other mediums, primarily Minnie Soule (referred to as "Mrs. Chenoweth") and Mrs. Willis M. Cleaveland (referred to as "Mrs. Smead"), both of whom he had been studying for several years. Thus, since Mrs. Piper was no longer a subject of scientific research, little, if anything, was recorded of Mrs. Piper's sittings over the next 10 years. Interestingly, Imperator also controlled Mrs. Chenoweth, while Hyslop continued to communicate with Hodgson, Myers, and G.P. through her.

Not long after his death on August 26, 1910, Professor William James began communicating with Hyslop through both Mrs. Smead and Mrs. Chenoweth. In each case he identified himself with the sign of Omega. At a sitting with Mrs. Chenoweth on September 26, 1910, Hyslop heard from both G. P. and Hodgson concerning James. The transcript read, in part:

**G.P.:** "Hodgson is busy preparing conditions for our new experimenter at this work. It looks easy now but we can tell nothing sure until some effort has been made. Allow me to send James' greetings to you and he has asked me to tell you that it will be his pleasure to do all he can to make his records complete and clear."

**Hyslop:** "Give him my greetings and I shall be patient."

**G.P.:** "It was not a surprise to us when he came but to him, and when he found it was all over his first interest was in regard to this expression. He is very careful and is trying to hold his energy until the time is perfectly evident as the best time. It is good to see you again and the summer has made somewhat of a hole in your stack of work, but it has piled up some new work, so you are no farther ahead."

**Hyslop:** "That's correct."

**G.P.:** "But the world waits for an expression now as never before and if it is possible we will make our dash for liberty and settle some of these misunderstood problems. I think I am always tempted to recall some of my own past every time I return for I can never quite recover from the awful grilling which Hodgson gave me after my most respectable and sudden departure. You are not such a fiend as he was or we would all be in the deep, deep sea."

**Hyslop:** "Thank you."

**G.P.:** "You get the evidence just the same and we are not so distressed. The sittings with you are so much pleasanter, so much more social. Hodgson says that will do. He wants to hear no more of such compliments."

**Hyslop:** "I understand."

**G.P.:** "It is perfectly true just the same."

**Hyslop:** "I learned my lesson from him and what he said afterward."

**G.P.:** "Yes, he is all right and he saw after he got the light but a minute before and unlike some people he placed a guide post telling which way not to go."

Hyslop saw this conversation as somewhat evidential, as even though Mrs. Chenoweth knew of Hodgson and the Piper sittings as well as having heard of G.P., he was fairly certain that she did not know about Hodgson's "grilling" methods. Hodgson followed G.P.

**Hodgson:** "I did not think when you were here in the spring that the next time you came I would have William with me. He is very happy and confident. Chaffed me a good bit on my inability to talk definitely to him and insists that with the conscious life as he is enjoying, he can make a better showing than I did. He is happy to find that the life is clear and livable, not a phantom existence as he sometimes thought. You remember the suggestion of shadows on the brain, aura, panto-mimes, some such weird expressions of a past existence unreal and unnatural. You must recall the conversation when these doubts were in his mind. He has referred to it several times since he came here. It was after I had made such havoc of my identity."

Hyslop saw this statement as especially evidential as very few people knew that William James feared that the afterlife would be some sort of "phantom existence" – a scenario that did not appeal to him. Two days later, James communicated with Hyslop through Mrs. Chenoweth:

**James:** "I cannot lose consciousness. Life is communicable. I still ex-ist as an individual with power to recall the past and I do not desire to question how or why just yet but to keep my hold on the opportunity until I am convinced of the possibility of definite communications." [5]

On November 11, James communicated with some trivial informa-tion, including his favorite evening snack of bread, milk, and berries, in order to establish his identity. It was followed by:

**James:** "I can see the headlines in the newspapers now if this were given out, but if I had said I had broken bread with the Saviour or Saint Paul there would have been many who would have believed it a part of the life of a man of my reputation in my new sphere. How stupid and insane the world always appears en masse to the thinking and studious brain."[6]

On November 19, 1910, James was able to communicate better:

**James:** "Do you recall coming to me once in the winter when snow was on the ground and we talked over these things and I gave you something to take away?"

**Hyslop:** "I recall that event very well."

**James:** "At that time we talked of the clergyman's wife who had the power of talking automatically." [The reference was to Mrs. Smead.]

**Hyslop:** "Yes."

**James:** "Since then I have seen her or rather since I came into this life."

**Hyslop:** "Yes, good."

**James:** "And I have made an effort to write with some success but not for long at a time. She does better when you are present."

**Hyslop:** "Good."

**James:** "Altho I find enough power to make some good expression when you are not there."

**Hyslop:** "Good."

**James:** "It is more spasmodic than here but that is largely a question of environment and companionship and desire. At that visit at my home you had to hurry away at last and some things were left for another time. I had been planning for a long time to see you. Indeed I was always planning for a time to talk more with you."

Hyslop recalled the long talk he had with James during the winter of 1906, when heavy snow was on the ground. They discussed Mrs. Smead, who was the wife of a clergyman. Hyslop confirmed the fact that Mrs. Smead did better when he was present. James continued the dialogue, trying to remember the first time he had met Hyslop at a certain house in Cambridge. Hyslop couldn't remember for certain if that was the first time, but deemed it likely. Then:

**James:** "I think so and I was impressed with your fervor and laughed with Richard (Hodgson) about it afterwards."

**Hyslop:** "I expect you did."

**James:** "I said to him that you would have that high hope shattered after a while."

**Hyslop:** "Yes, I was converted long before Hodgson and you knew it."

**James:** "We had been through the stages of Imperator wonder and worship and still had the problem of Moses' identity unsolved. You remember how we were harassed by the conflicting statements and contradictory evidence?

**Hyslop:** "Yes, perfectly."

**James:** "It was enough to make us swear but we stuck to the task and hid our chagrin as best we could."

Hyslop considered this a very evidential sitting as he felt certain that Mrs. Chenoweth had no knowledge of that first meeting with James or the discussions about Imperator and Stainton Moses. There were other pieces of evidence coming through, including the mention of a photo of Hodgson which James had framed in his house, something unknown to both Hyslop and Mrs. Chenoweth but later confirmed by Hyslop.[7]

At a later sitting, the transcript read:

**James:** "I am a conscious being with body of expression and capacities normal and rational, and I have found fewer limitations than I expected."

**Hyslop:** "What kind of limitations do you find?"

**James:** "A lack of power in impressing what is in my mind. You remember a short talk we had about telepathy and you were impressed with the lack of power to impress on a sensitive mind the thought of yours. I am studying the problem from this view point. The light presents me with a dead brain or at least an inactive one. I cannot use the hand as if it were a hatchet, but must have it function as nearly normal as possible. One may pull the tendon of the leg or a dead fowl, but the foot makes only spasmodic response."

**Hyslop:** "I understand. Then.....[unable to finish before James continued]

**James:** "The brain is a dead planet, reflecting only, but I can infuse sufficient life into it then I write normally, do you see?"

**Hyslop:** "Yes, I imagine that the relation of the body to the light is like reincarnation. One has to get the same kind of adjustment that he had to his own organism before he left it. Is that right?"

**James:** "Yes, exactly and a point we all missed. Now when I once get that hold many limitations will disappear. That is what the familiar guide or control does, so Madame tells me."

And in still another sitting:

**James:** "It does not seem the least strange to discuss these things with you. I believe with you that the moral and ethical development of the world hangs on this spiritual knowledge."

**Hyslop:** "Good."

**James:** "It becomes an incentive for righteousness in its best and truest sense and makes the brotherhood a real and dominant note in the progress of civilization. Heretofore, the world has risen to new power on the neck of its fallen brothers, which at best is but volcanic progress."

**Hyslop:** "Yes, we want pacific movements to bring the world to its unity and sense of brotherhood."

**James:** "The emerging of one peak from the tumultuous sea of distress which sinks another portion of the fair land is not drawing the world to God."

**Hyslop:** "No, we should have universal peace for that."

**James:** "It can never come until men learn the truth of immortality. The struggle for the present day power is so tantalizingly universal. I am philosophizing, but my soul is optimistic, even if my world has a touch of the pessimistic."[8]

According to Alta Piper, her mother's trance returned in 1915 before what was to become known as the "Faunus" message came through her for Sir Oliver Lodge. As Lodge reported it, Anne Manning Robbins was having a sitting with Mrs. Piper on August 8, 1915 when she received a message from Hodgson to give to Lodge. "Now Lodge, while we are not here as of old, i.e., not quite, we are here enough to take and give messages. Myers says you take the part of the poet, and he will act as Faunus." When Miss Robbins told Hodgson she did not understand the message, he said that Lodge should check with Margaret Verrall, as she would understand. Hodgson added that Arthur said she would understand. This was taken to be Dr. Arthur W. Verrall, Margaret's husband, who also was deceased.

Alta Piper then posted the message to Lodge, it reaching him early September. Lodge didn't understand and wrote to Mrs. Verrall, who like her husband, was an authority on the classics. Mrs. Verrall referred him to a passage in "Horace" in which Horace gave an account of his narrow escape from death, from a falling tree, as a result of the intervention of the poet Faunus.

Actually, an earlier message came through Mrs. Piper on August 5, while doing automatic writing in a non-trance state. It read: "Yes. For the moment, Lodge, have faith and wisdom in all that is highest and best. Have you all not been profoundly guided and cared for? Can you answer, 'No'? It is by your faith that all is well and has been." This arrived by separate post on the same day as the Faunus message.

Knowing that a fallen or falling tree is a frequent symbol for death because of a misinterpretation of *Eccl. xi. 3* in the Old Testament, Lodge wondered if it would be a death in the family or some financial disaster that Myers, his old friend, wanted him to be ready for. It was not until he received a telegram from the War Office on September 17, informing him that his son, Raymond, had been killed on the battle-field in Ypres on September 14 that Lodge understood. He took it to mean that Myers wanted to lighten the blow by letting him know that his son still lives.

On September 25, Mary Lodge, Sir Oliver's wife, was having an anonymous sitting for a friend with Gladys Osborne Leonard, a trance medium much like Mrs. Piper, when a message came through from Raymond in which he said, "Tell father I have met some friends of his." Mary Lodge asked if he could give a name. "Myers" was the response. Lodge would later sit with Mrs. Leonard and hear from Raymond, who said that Myers was helping him adjust to his new environment. Much in the way of evidential information came through to convince Lodge that he was in fact communicating with Raymond.

One especially evidential message came through another medium, Mr. A. Vout Peters, on September 27. Raymond referred to a group photograph in which he was holding a walking stick. Neither Sir Oliver nor Mary Lodge could recall any such photograph. Then, in a sitting with Mrs. Leonard, they questioned Raymond about the photograph. Raymond was able to communicate that it was a group photo of his army unit, that he was sitting down while others were standing, and the person behind him was leaning on him. Four days after that sitting, they received a letter and photograph from the mother of one of Raymond's fellow officers. Raymond was sitting, a walking stick across his legs, and the arm of the man behind him resting on his shoulder. The photo had been taken on August 24, three weeks before Raymond's death.

Mrs. Leonard, who was just beginning her mediumship at the time, would go on to be frequently studied by the SPR and referred to as "England's White Crow."

Over the next five or six years, Mrs. Piper spent much of her time caring for her ailing mother, thus having little time for mediumship. Dr. Gardner Murphy of Columbia University, later president of the ASPR, had a number of sittings with her from 1922 to 1925, but reported that for the most part his sittings "were uneventful and lacking in the types of phenomena which characterized the zenith of her career."[9] There were, he added, some phenomena of interest, suggesting that they can be found in Jane H. Sagendorph's 1926 book, *A Vision and its Sequel.*

Possibly the last published communications coming through Mrs. Piper were set forth in a 1937 book titled *Personality Survives Death* by Lady (Dr.) Florence Barrett, the widow of Sir William Barrett, a professor of physics at the Royal College of Science in Dublin, and one of the founders, in 1882, of the Society for Psychical Research. Sir William died on May 26, 1925. On the last day of his life, still feeling well and happy in the morning, he sent a postcard to Mrs. Jervis, a family friend who had recently visited America and sat with Mrs. Piper. He asked Mrs. Jervis if she could come to tea on the 28th and tell of her experiences. Mrs. Jervis heard of Sir William's death on May 27, the same day she received the post card.

On June 6, Lady Barrett received a letter from a member of the London SPR informing her that Sir William had "manifested" at a sitting with Mrs. Osborne Leonard. He asked that Lady Barrett be told that his mother was with him at the moment he passed and that he is well and happy. He further stated that he sent a message from a place "a long way off and over the sea." He was unable to get any names through Mrs. Leonard, but recalled being somewhat familiar with the place from a visit there. Whether he was referring to Mrs. Piper could not be established with any certainty, but about the middle of June Mrs. Jervis received a letter from Mrs. Piper, passing on a message from Sir William. It read: "Tell Mrs. Jervis I am sorry I could not keep the appointment."

Lady Barrett, an obstetrician and dean of the London School of Medicine for Women, decided to sit with Mrs. Leonard and received much in the way of evidence from her deceased husband. Though none of it involved Mrs. Piper, it is interesting to compare some of Sir William's messages relative to the difficulties in communicating with those received through Mrs. Piper. One of those messages read:

> Sometimes I lose some memory of things from coming here; I know it in my own state but not here. In dreams you do not know everything, you only get parts in a dream. A sitting is similar; when I go back to the spirit world after a sitting like this I know I have not got everything through that I wanted to say. That is due to my mind separating again, the consciousness separating again. In the earth body we have the separation of subconscious and conscious. Consciousness only holds a certain number of memories at a time. When we pass over they join, make a complete mind that knows and remembers everything; but when one comes here to a sitting the limitation of the physical sphere affects one's mind, and only a portion of one's mind can function for the time being. When I withdraw from this condition one's whole mind becomes again both subconscious and conscious; my subconscious mind encloses my conscious one and I

become whole again mentally...I cannot come with and as my whole self. I cannot.[10]

Bearing on the harmony aspect discussed in prior chapters, Sir William had this to say:

We are extra-sensitive to the thoughts of those on earth, specially in the early days when our own minds hover between the earth we have left and the new land on which our feet are not held firmly planted. In that *between* conditions we need your thoughts, but we need right thoughts, constructive, helpful, loving thoughts.[11]

Mrs. Piper died on July 3, 1950, at age 91. Now, more than six decades later, more than 100 years since the peak of her powers, her name is recognized by only a few, and only a few of those few really appreciate the evidence offered through her that consciousness survives physical death. It is difficult for those who do appreciate the evidence to understand why there is so much ignorance of it or indifference to it. Frederic Myers, when still alive in the flesh, explained the resistance by science, as he saw it:

To the man of science the question has never yet assumed enough of an actuality to induce him to consider it with scientific care. He has contented himself, like the mass of mankind, with some traditional theory, some emotional preference for some such picture as seems to him satisfying and exalted. Yet, he knows well that this subjective principle of choice has led in history to the acceptance of many a dogma which to more civilized perceptions seems in the last degree blasphemous and cruel.[12]

Sir Oliver Lodge, one of the great scientists of his era, was somewhat more blunt when he said that the rejection of the Piper research and similar research with other mediums by his scientific colleagues was a "salutary safeguard against that unbalanced and comparatively dangerous condition called 'open-mindedness,' which is ready to learn and investigate anything not manifestly self-contradictory and absurd."[13] More diplomatically, Lodge later put it this way:

The aloofness of science is not really because the phenomena are elusive and difficult of observation; rather it is because they appear to run counter to preconception or prejudgments, or what may be called rational prejudices, based upon a long course of study of natural phenomena, with which these asserted occurrences appear to be inconsistent; so that favouring testimony has to be criticized, continually suspected, and frequently discarded, because it appears to be testimony in favour of what is *a priori* impossible or absurd. The aim of science has been for the most part a study of mechanism, the mechanism whereby results are achieved, an investigation into the physical processes which go on, and which appear to be coextensive with nature. Any theory which seems to involve the action of Higher Beings, or of any unknown entity controlling and working the mechanism, is apt to be extruded or discountenanced as a relic of primitive superstition, coming down from times when such infantile explanations were prevalent.[14]

[1] Hyslop (2008), 166-172,

[2] _____, 164-165

[3] Hyslop (1910), 166-167

[4] Hyslop (1911), 93

[5] Hyslop (1914), 227-232

[6] _____, 243

[7] Hyslop (1919), 235-236

[8] Hyslop (1914), 244-245

[9] Murphy, 200

[10] Barrett (1937), 56

[11] _____, 114

[12] Myers, 399

[13] Lodge (1909), 2

[14] Lodge (1929), 28-29

# Epilogue

# Examining the Alternatives

*I myself can perfectly well imagine spirit-agency*
**–William James**

s mentioned in the Preface, my objective in writing the book was to extract the most meaningful material from the whole gamut of the research into Mrs. Piper's mediumship and offer it independent of what Professor William James referred to as the "bosh" material, in the hope that it might be better understood and appreciated. The hard-core skeptic, or pseudoskeptic, would not approve of such an approach. He or she would say that it is not "scientific," that we need all of the material to properly weigh the evidence. But, as I also said in the Preface, this is not intended as a scientific treatise of any kind. I have approached it as a lawyer representing Mrs. Piper might present her side of the case. If it is seen as *apologia* for Mrs. Piper, so be it.

Basically, there are five alternatives when it comes to the Piper phenomena:

1. **Conscious Fraud:** Leonora Piper was a master fraud with a very exceptional memory and great dramatic ability;

2. **Unconscious Fraud/Secondary Personality:** The so-called "controls" of Mrs. Piper were just secondary personalities who were devious tricksters with highly developed telepathic abilities;

3. **Superpsi:** The medium or her "controls" were telepathically accessing the information from different minds anywhere in the world or from some cosmic reservoir;

4. **Impostor Spirits:** Devious earthbound spirits were pretending to be deceased loved ones and friends.

5. **Spirits:** The deceased loved ones and friends were in fact communicating

Let's examine these alternatives, while also keeping in mind the possibility that there is a sixth explanation – one that is beyond human comprehension.

### *Conscious Fraud*

To begin with, Dr. Richard Hodgson sat with Mrs. Piper on the average of three times a week for 18 years between 1887 and 1905. Add in dozens or scores of sittings by Professor William James, Sir Oliver Lodge, Professor James Hyslop, and many other distinguished scientists and academicians. All observed her under test conditions and attested to her character and integrity. James said that he would stake as much money on Mrs. Piper's honesty as on that of anyone else he knew and that he was willing to leave his reputation for wisdom or folly to stand or fall on Mrs. Piper.

Moreover, many of the veridical facts that were communicated through Mrs. Piper were beyond research, even if she had had the time to do background investigations or the money to hire a professional investigator. Most of the time, she was unaware of the identity of the sitter and often the researchers would not bring them into the room until she was already in the trance state. Many of the facts communicated were not recorded anywhere, and at times the sitters were unaware of things told to them and had to verify them as facts through others. At times "Mrs. Piper" spoke or wrote foreign languages she did not know.

Unless one is prepared to believe that all those esteemed researchers were complete dupes or participants in a senseless hoax, conscious fraud is not a consideration.

### Unconscious Fraud/Secondary Personalities

Professor James clearly had a difficult time accepting Phinuit and Rector as the spirits of deceased persons, but strangely he does not really discuss George Pellew (G.P.), who was Mrs. Piper's primary control between the Phinuit and Rector regimes. As indicated earlier, it was this G.P. control who convinced Hodgson that there was more than a secondary personality at work in Mrs. Piper's mediumship. Thus, it is a mystery as to how James was able to write off Phinuit and Rector as secondary personalities without also claiming that G.P., who was known to have existed, was a secondary personality. Indications are that James simply lacked the courage to offer anything in opposition to materialistic science.

But even if we assume that the "control" was a secondary personality rather than a spirit of a dead person, the question turns to how the secondary personality telepathically accesses the information it feeds back to the sitter, and more than that how it organizes all the facts and transmits them in a conversational manner. Thus, calling the "control" a secondary personality does not rule out the communicators (those for whom the control is relaying messages) being spirits of the dead.

And then, there is the question as to why the secondary personality would claim to be the spirit of a dead person. What was the "game"? Why was some alter ego or material consciousness representing itself as the spirit of a deceased person? Why was it so intent on deception? If Mrs. Piper was that good of an actress and had that good of a memory, she should have been on the stage or performing in more creative ways. And do we then assume that the spirit controls associated with many other mediums, such as Feda, the primary control of Gladys Osborne Leonard, enjoyed similar games of deception.

Professor James admitted that "most of us felt during the sittings that we were in some way, more or less remote, conversing with a real Rector or a real Hodgson."[1] He noted that Hodgson's "saucy" and "teasing" attitude toward Miss Pope was "absolutely characteristic" of Hodgson and that his expressions and phrases with a Dr. Bayley "were quaintly characteristic of R.H. in the body, as they appear, often rapidly and spontaneously, they give the almost irresistible impression that it is really the Hodgson personality, presiding with its own characteristics."[2]

The bottom line here is that even if a secondary personality, whatever that might be, is involved, an explanation is needed for the veridical information being communicated.

### Telepathy/Super ESP

It is one thing to telepathically determine the number and suit of a card in a deck held by a person in a separate room, quite another to instantly organize facts and make lengthy coherent statements in a give-and-take manner.

Simple telepathy, i.e., reading the mind of the sitter, is clearly ruled out in those many cases in which the sitter was unaware of the fact communicated. That leaves the much more complex form of telepathy, now known as *Superpsi.* As Dr. Minot Savage commented, "If anyone chooses to assume that the subliminal consciousness of somebody can do any conceivable thing; travel over the world and find out any conceivable item of knowledge; tell of things that nobody in the world knows; resurrect facts from a long-distant past, and move physical objects without contact – if, I say, anyone chooses to assume a theory like this, why there is nobody who can prevent his doing it. But if he claims that it is scientific, or that there are any known facts or adequate reasons for such an assumption, then I submit that he will be likely to place under suspicion his reputation as a sane, fair-minded, and careful investigator." [3]

Hodgson and Hyslop wondered why, if the medium was telepathically obtaining the information, there was so much information, including names, that Mrs. Piper did not pick up – facts which were known to the sitters. Why telepathically pick up certain facts and not others? And why, when Professor Newbold asked Hodgson if he remembered a particular conversation, would Hodgson have referred to a different conversation? If Mrs. Piper or her secondary personality had been reading Newbold's mind, she should have mentioned the one Newbold was thinking about.

And if there is some cosmic computer in the ethers into which the medium or a secondary personality can tap for information and then offer it up in a conversational manner, as Professor James theorized, why claim spirits? It would seem that the medium could gain even more fame and fortune if she were to credit it to her own brain power and ability to access this cosmic reservoir, rather than to spirits of the dead. Of course, it must be remembered that as late as 1901 Mrs. Piper never claimed spirits. In her so-called "confession" of that year, she said she didn't know if spirits were communicating, since she was in a trance state.

Weighing all the factors here, both simple and the more complex telepathy seem highly unlikely and without foundation in explaining the Piper phenomena. That is not to suggest that telepathy and other forms of extra-sensory perception do not exist independent of spirit communication, only that they do not conflict with or rule out spirits.

### Impostor Spirits

Many psychical researchers have reported the existence of impostor spirits – low level or earthbound spirits pretending to be someone else. "False personation is a ubiquitous feature in this total mass," Professor James stated. "It certainly exists [in other Piper sittings]; and the great question there is as to its limits." [4]

Impostor spirits were suggested in some of the "bosh" material not offered in the book, especially in communications purportedly coming from the spirits of authors George Eliot and Sir Walter Scott, as well as a bogus sprit in the Hall and Tanner sittings. Other research in the area of mediumship suggests that lower-level spirits can more easily communicate, since their vibrations are more in tune with earthly vibrations, and thus devious, earthbound spirits make their way into mediumship circles quite often, one of the reasons why mediumship is frowned upon by many and why we read in the New Testament under 1 John 4:1 that we should "test the spirits, whether they are of God."

But can impostor spirits access detailed facts known only to the spirits they are impersonating? If so, we go back to the arguments against *Superpsi*. Are they all then impostors? If Rector was in fact a benevolent control, why didn't he tell the researchers that the spirit wasn't who it claimed to be? Was Rector also an impostor? If so, who was he impersonating? Rector? Why should Rector have to impersonate someone who was unknown to any living person and whose existence could not be verified?

Calling it an impostor spirit does not, however, defeat the spiritistic hypothesis. Whether the spirits were who they claimed to be or earthbound spirits impersonating them, they were still spirits. Considering the fact that so much of the communication was good natured and not devious in any way, it does not seem very likely that the majority of communicators were impostors.

## Spirits

With all of the foregoing hypotheses ruled out, at least highly unlikely, it would seem that the spirit, or spiritistic, hypothesis makes the most sense. James did not totally disagree with Hodgson, Lodge, and Hyslop on that. "The records are fully compatible with this explanation, however explicable they may be without it...I myself can perfectly well imagine spirit-agency, and I find my mind vacillating about it curiously," James wrote.[5]

As Hyslop pointed out, the selective unity of consciousness, the dramatic play of personality, and the character of the mistakes and confusions all support the spiritistic hypothesis. "...when we say to the average man that we can communicate with the dead, or that we have obtained through apparitions or mediumistic phenomena facts which prove survival, they see that we are implying communication as well as survival of the discarnate, and with it they assume that the process of communication is as simple as our ordinary social intercourse," Hyslop wrote, going on to discuss the mindset of those who reject the spiritistic hypothesis:

> They read the records which we present as if they were merely jotted down conversations with the dead conducted very much as we talk with each other. They make no effort to investigate the complexity of the process, but take the phenomena at their face value and ask no scientific questions. They read an alleged message as they would a telegram or an essay. They make no account of the conditions under which the message is transmitted when it claims to come from another world, but recognize exactly what the conditions are in the physical world...If a message, however, claims to come from the dead, they set up objections as if they knew exactly what the conditions are for the receipt and delivery of the communication. There is, after twenty-five years of work on the problem by scientific men, absolutely no excuse for such conduct or ignorance...[Unfortunately], it is more convenient.[6]

Little has changed since those early years of psychical research. Science remains essentially materialistic, mechanistic, and reductionistic, arrogantly refusing to consider the research of those esteemed scientists and scholars of yesteryear, while seeing spirits and survival as a return to religious superstitions.

[1] Holt, 708

[2] _____, 711

[3] Savage, 104-105

[4] Holt, 707

[5] _____, 710

[6] Hyslop (1918), 208

# References

Baird, Alex, *The Life of Richard Hodgson*, Psychic Press Limited, London, 1949

Barrett, Sir William, *On the Threshold of the Unseen*, E.F. Dutton & Co., New York, 1917

Barrett, Lady Florence, *Personality Survives Death*, Longmans, Green and Co., London, 1937

Berger, Arthur S. and Joyce, *The Encyclopedia of Parapsychology and Psychical Research*, Paragon House, 1991

Blum, Deborah, *Ghost Hunters*, The Penguin Press, 2006

Carrington, H., *The Case for Psychic Survival,* The Citadel Press, New York, 1957

De Vesme, *Caesar, Experiments with Mrs. Piper Since the Decease of Dr. Hodgson*, The Annals of Psychical Research, London, July 1907

Edmonds, John W. & Dexter, George T., *Spiritualism*. Partridge & Brittan, New York, 1853

Gauld, Alan, *The Founders of Psychical Research,* Schocken Books, New York, 1968

Gauld, Alan, *Mediumship and Survival*, Paladin Books, London, 1983

Hamilton, Trevor, *Immortal Longings*, imprint-academic.com, Exeter, UK, 2009

Hardinge, Emma*, Modern American Spiritualism*, University Books, New Hyde Park, NY, 1970 (reprint of 1869 book)

Hare, Robert, M.D., *Experimental Investigation of the Spirit Manifestations*, Partridge & Brittan, New York, 1855

Hodgson, Richard, *A Record of Observations of Certain Phenomena of Trance*, Proceedings of The Society for Psychical Research, June 1892

Holt, Henry, *On the Cosmic Relations*, Houghton Mifflin Co., Boston, 1914

Hyslop, James, *Science and a Future Life*, Herbert B. Turner & Co., Boston, 1905

Hyslop, James H., *Borderland of Psychical Research*, Colonial Press, Boston, 1906

Hyslop, James, *Psychical Research and The Resurrection*, Small, Maynard and Co., 1908

Hyslop, James, *A Record and Discussion of Mediumistic Experiements*, ASPR Proceedings, Volume 4, 1910

Hyslop, James, *President G. Stanley Hall's and Dr. Amy E. Tanner's Studies in Spiritism*, ASPR Proceedings, Journal of the American Society for Psychical Research, January 1911, Vol. V., No. 1, 93

Hyslop, James, *Some Secondary Evidences*, ASPR Journal, New York, May 1914

Hyslop, James, H., *Life After Death*, E. P. Dutton & Co., 1918

Hyslop, James H., *Contact with the Other World*, The Century Co., New York, 1919

Hyslop, James H. *The Doctrines of Professor James*, Journal of the American Society for Psychical Research, November 1919

Inglis, Brian, *Natural & Supernatural*, White Crow Books, UK, 2012

James, William, *Essays in Pragmatism*, Hafner Press, New York, 1948

James, William, *The Varieties of Religious Experience*, Collier Books, 1961

Johnson, Alice, *Cross-Correspondences*, Proceedings of the Society for Psychical Research, Vol. XXVII, January 1914

Kardec, Allan, *The Spirits' Book*, Amapse Society, Mexico, reprint from 1857

Lodge, Oliver, *The Survival of Man*, Moffat, Yard and Co., New York, 1909

Lodge, Sir Oliver, *Raymond or Life and Death*, George H. Doran Company, New York, NY, 1916

Lodge, Oliver, *Phantom Walls*, Hodder and Stroughton, Ltd., UK, 1929

Lodge, Oliver, *Past Years*, Charles Scribner's Sons, New York, 1932

Medhurst, R. G., *Crookes and the Spirit World*, Taplinger Publishing Co., 1972

Moore, W. Usborne, *Glimpses of the Next State*, Watts & Co., 1911

Moses, William Stainton, *Spirit Teachings*, Arno Press, New York, 1976, reprinted from 1924 edition published by London Spiritualist Alliance

Moses, William Stainton, *More Spirit Teachings*, Meilach.com

Mrozek, Donald J., *Sport and American Mentality 1880-1910*, The University of Tennessee Press, Knoxville, 1983

Murphy, Gardner & Ballou, Robert, *William James on Psychical Research*, The Viking Press, New York, 1960

Murphy, Gardner, *Challenge of Psychical Research*, Harper & Brothers, New York, 1961

Myers, F. W. H., *Human Personality and its Survival of Bodily Death*, University Books, Inc., New Hyde Park, NY, 1961 (reprint of 1903 book)

Piper, Alta L. *The Life and Work of Mrs Piper*, Kegan Paul, Trench, Trubner & Co., Ltd. London, 1929

Robbins, Anne Manning, *Both Sides of the Veil,* Sherman, French & Co., Boston, 1909

Rose, Eugene, *Nihilism*, Fr. Seraphim Rose Foundation, Forestville, CA, 1994

Sage, Michael, *Mrs. Piper & The Society for Psychical Research*, Bibliobazaar, NY, 1904/2007

Saltmarsh, H. F., *The Future and Beyond*, Hampton Roads, Charlottesville, VA, 2004

Savage, Minot J., *Can Telepathy Explain?* G.P. Putnam's Sons, New York, 1902

Tymn, Michael E. *The Articulate Dead*, Galde Press, Lakeville, MN, 2008

Wallace, Alfred Russel, *Miracles and Modern Spiritualism*, George Redway, London, 1896

Zammit, Victor, *A Lawyer Presents the Case for the Afterlife*, White Crow Books, UK, 2012

# Paperbacks also available from
# White Crow Books

Jesus of Nazareth with Simon Parke—*Conversations with Jesus of Nazareth*
ISBN 978-1-907661-41-9

Thomas à Kempis with Simon Parke—*The Imitation of Christ*
ISBN 978-1-907661-58-7

Julian of Norwich with Simon Parke—*Revelations of Divine Love*
ISBN 978-1-907661-88-4

Allan Kardec—*The Spirits Book*
ISBN 978-1-907355-98-1

Allan Kardec—*The Book on Mediums*
ISBN 978-1-907661-75-4

Emanuel Swedenborg—*Heaven and Hell*
ISBN 978-1-907661-55-6

P.D. Ouspensky—*Tertium Organum: The Third Canon of Thought*
ISBN 978-1-907661-47-1

Dwight Goddard—*A Buddhist Bible*
ISBN 978-1-907661-44-0

Michael Tymn—*The Afterlife Revealed*
ISBN 978-1-970661-90-7

Michael Tymn—*Transcending the Titanic: Beyond Death's Door*
ISBN 978-1-908733-02-3

Guy L. Playfair—*If This Be Magic*
ISBN 978-1-907661-84-6

Guy L. Playfair—*The Flying Cow*
ISBN 978-1-907661-94-5

Guy L. Playfair —*This House is Haunted*
ISBN 978-1-907661-78-5

Carl Wickland, M.D.—*Thirty Years Among the Dead*
ISBN 978-1-907661-72-3

John E. Mack—*Passport to the Cosmos*
ISBN 978-1-907661-81-5

Peter & Elizabeth Fenwick—*The Truth in the Light*
ISBN 978-1-908733-08-5

Erlendur Haraldsson—*Modern Miracles*
ISBN 978-1-908733-25-2

Erlendur Haraldsson—*At the Hour of Death*
ISBN 978-1-908733-27-6

Erlendur Haraldsson—*The Departed Among the Living*
ISBN 978-1-908733-29-0

Brian Inglis—*Science and Parascience*
ISBN 978-1-908733-18-4

Brian Inglis—*Natural and Supernatural: A History of the Paranormal*
ISBN 978-1-908733-20-7

Ernest Holmes—*The Science of Mind*
ISBN 978-1-908733-10-8

Victor Zammit—*Afterlife: A Lawyer Presents the Evidence.*
ISBN 978-1-908733-22-1

Casper S. Yost—*Patience Worth: A Psychic Mystery*
ISBN 978-1-908733-06-1

William Usborne Moore—*Glimpses of the Next State*
ISBN 978-1-907661-01-3

William Usborne Moore—*The Voices*
ISBN 978-1-908733-04-7

John W. White—*The Highest State of Consciousness*
ISBN 978-1-908733-31-3

Stafford Betty—*The Imprisoned Splendor*
ISBN 978-1-907661-98-3

Paul Pearsall, Ph.D. —*Super Joy*
ISBN 978-1-908733-16-0

**All titles available as eBooks, and selected titles available in Hardback and Audiobook formats from www.whitecrowbooks.com**

www.ingramcontent.com/pod-product-compliance
Lightning Source LLC
Chambersburg PA
CBHW030824090426

42737CB00009B/864